AMERICA'S
SACRED
CALLING

AMERICA'S SACRED CALLING

Building a New Spiritual Reality

By
John Fitzgerald Medina

Bahá'í
PUBLISHING
Wilmette, Illinois

Bahá'í Publishing
415 Linden Avenue, Wilmette, Illinois 60091-2844

13   12   11   10   4   3   2   1

Library of Congress Cataloging-in-Publication Data

Medina, John Fitzgerald.
 America's sacred calling : building a new spiritual reality / by John Fitzgerald
Medina.
    p. cm.
 Includes bibliographical references.
 ISBN 978-1-931847-79-7 (alk. paper)
 1. Bahai Faith—United States. 2. United States—Religion—Forecasting. 3.
Materialism—United States. 4. Materialism—Religious aspects—Bahai Faith. 5.
United States—Forecasting. I. Title.
 BP350.M435 2010
 297.9'3097301—dc22

                                                                2010027601

Cover design by Robert A. Reddy
Book design by Patrick Falso

For the Mystery of God,
'Abdu'l-Bahá:
"Blessed, doubly blessed, is the ground
which His footsteps have trodden"

For the beloved Shoghi Effendi,
the Priceless Pearl of the Bahá'í Revelation

For the Indians of the Americas, past, present, and future

And for my late brother in the Abhá Kingdom, Lou

CONTENTS

CONTENTS

PREFACE

We stand in desperate need of a second American Revolution, a revolution of the heart and soul. In my first book, *Faith, Physics, and Psychology: Rethinking Society and the Human Spirit*, I covered in extensive detail many of the grievous problems that continue to plague America and the world in general. In that book, I asserted that the economic, social, political, legal, educational, and environmental crises that we are currently facing are merely symptoms or manifestations of a still greater crisis—a crisis in worldview. Worldview is the set of values, beliefs, ideas, and assumptions through which one perceives reality. Worldview is inextricably linked to one's perception concerning the nature, the meaning, the purpose, and the goal of human life. The predominant worldview in America, and in the West, is commonly known as the Cartesian-Newtonian worldview. It is this worldview that I believe lies at the core of our problems and recurring crises. The Cartesian-Newtonian worldview has its origins in the Scientific Revolution, which started in Europe in the mid-1500s. It is a pervasively materialistic view of reality that emphasizes the truth of science, reason, logic, the natural, the material, and the secular, while at the same time dismissing or even denigrating the truth of religion, faith, intuition, the supernatural, the spiritual, and the sacred. A major theme of my first book and now also of this current book is that Western civilization itself has become unbalanced, disordered, and actually unhealthy to the spiritual, psychological, and physical development of human beings because of the destructive materialistic worldview that lies at its foundation. This second book expands upon the above

1

theme by arguing that, in the future, ironically, America (currently, the prime exporter of the Cartesian-Newtonian worldview) will actually play a crucial role in overthrowing this destructive materialistic view of reality. As will be shown in great detail in this book, the American nation is destined to play a critical role in the future development of a spiritually enlightened, peaceful, unified, and just global civilization. Indeed, this is America's true sacred calling.

As will be described later, in order to fulfill its exalted destiny America must first overcome various cultural obstacles that are preventing it from manifesting its true sacred calling. In this regard, it is very important that we understand that, as noted above, the primary problems that are plaguing America today are just symptoms of a far deadlier disease—a disease of the human soul that is rooted in materialism. Materialism is the belief that this physical world in which we live is true reality. Materialism is also the related belief that the material aspects of one's physical existence (clothing, cars, houses, etc.) are of primary importance. Contrary to this, the spiritual wisdom of the various religious traditions maintains that this physical world is not true reality. This physical world is just a manifestation or a projection from a deeper, truer spiritual reality. This is essentially what the religious mystics have been telling us for thousands of years. One of the main purposes of religion is to help us become awakened to this deeper spiritual reality. We can catch a glimpse of this spiritual reality through prayer, mystical experiences, good deeds, and self-sacrificing service to others. Of course, when our physical bodies die, our souls will wing their way to the deeper reality—to the spiritual kingdom of God.

Ultimately, one's perception of true reality determines the trajectory, the meaning, and the purpose of one's life. A person, for instance, who believes that this physical world is all that there is, is going to perceive his or her mission in life very differently in comparison to someone who believes that this false reality is just a training ground or classroom for the soul where one learns moral and spiritual lessons in preparation for the afterlife. A materialistic view of reality keeps people focused on the pleasures, desires, and concerns of this world and is thus the primary cause of many people's hedonism, self-centeredness, and inordinate focus on the pursuit of physical wealth, power, and status.

The most obvious manifestation of the materialistic view of reality is the rampant commercialism and consumerism that pervade Western culture. Distressingly, the deep level to which materialism has invaded the very heart of America is demonstrated by the fact that even many devoutly religious people are taking part in consumerism and commercialism with almost the same reckless abandon as the general population. Studies show that even Americans who claim to have a strong religious faith show no appreciable difference in their adherence to crass materialism—they spend their personal energy, time, money, and other resources in much the same fashion as all other Americans. Ironically, in spite of its ultimately destructive consequences, consumerism seems to be the one force that unites practically all Americans, regardless of race, ethnicity, and socioeconomic background. Indeed, countless numbers of Whites, Blacks, Latinos, Asians, Middle Easterners, Christians, and non-Christians have bought into the materialistic vision of the "good life" that has been sold to them by the ubiquitous forces of corporate commercialism that pervade American culture. Sadly, Americans have amassed high levels of debt in search of the "good life," and yet, studies consistently show a persistent unhappiness among Americans at all levels of society, including the upper middle class and the rich. Comprehensive research also shows that materialism is linked with a higher incidence of depression, anxiety, anger, headaches, stomachaches, and backaches. It is also linked with lower levels of self-esteem and community affiliation as well as depressed scores on "measures of self-actualization and vitality." In essence, Americans are futilely attempting to satisfy psychological and spiritual needs through physical consumption. Many people are also spending their energy and time on materialistic pursuits while neglecting and trampling upon the precious aspects of life that can truly fulfill their needs such as meaningful relationships with family, neighbors, friends, and religious communities. Indeed, studies show that considerable numbers of American parents are not spending

PREFACE

sufficient time and effort to appropriately bond with their children. Such a lack of bonding has been shown to have a detrimental effect on the neural development of young children, especially on the limbic system—a part of the brain that is associated with motivation and emotional development. This is troubling since research shows that many antisocial individuals, criminals, and troubled adults are people who did not properly bond with their caregivers early in life. Indeed, many American children are now spending more time "bonding" with mechanical substitutes (Internet, video games, and television) than with parents. In the end, such a banal despiritualized existence is devoid of any true meaning and purpose, and thus, it contributes to a mass poverty of the soul.[1]

It must be emphasized that the discussion above should not be taken to mean that America or Western civilization is inherently evil or that other cultures are better. To the contrary, in my view, no culture currently exists that can serve as a healthy alternative to Western culture. Our only hope lies in the creation of an entirely new cultural paradigm. Before we can resolve the major American and global problems that are facing us, we need to leave behind the false materialistic view of reality that lies at the core of Western civilization. We need to adopt a holistic view of reality that is capable of integrating mind, body, and spirit; of harmonizing science and religion; and of unifying reason and logic on the one hand with faith and intuition on the other.

We live in an exciting era that is pregnant with both challenges and opportunities. As covered in detail in my first book, we are currently witnessing the emergence of a new wave of spiritual energy that is transforming the consciousness of every person who is willing to tune into it. This spiritual wave of energy is sweeping the earth and is tearing down old defective institutions and old destructive ways of being. At the same time, it is slowly helping to raise up new enlightened institutions and new healthy ways of thinking and acting. Indeed, humanity is entering a new higher stage in its spiritual evolution. Things that seemed impossible in the past, such as the unification of the human race and the creation of a peaceful, just, and unified world order, now seem not only possible but inevitable.

The spiritual wave of energy has given birth to new complementary movements that are coalescing to form a broad front in the spiritual battle to transform the earth and its peoples. My first book explores three of these movements: the self-actualization (personal transformation) movement that was spearheaded by the late Abraham Maslow; the Bahá'í Faith, an independent world religion whose pivotal aim is the unification of humankind; and the modern holistic movement, which is based on research and theories from a diversity of disciplines such as quantum physics, psychology, economics, ecology, education, cosmology, medicine, and philosophy.

All three of the above movements challenge the prevailing Western cultural paradigm that is based on scientific materialism. All three promote the integration of science and religion. The Bahá'í Faith even asserts that religion itself, often due to "unintelligent dogmas" and unnecessary superstitious traditions, has often been the cause of conflict with science. Along these lines, the Bahá'í writings state,

> If religion were in harmony with science and they walked together, much of the hatred and bitterness now bringing misery to the human race would be at an end. . . . God made religion and science to be the measure, as it were, of our understanding. Take heed that you neglect not such a wonderful power. Weigh all things in this balance. . . . Put all your beliefs into harmony with science; there can be no opposition, for truth is one. When religion, shorn of its superstitions, traditions, and unintelligent dogmas, shows its conformity with science, then will there be a great unifying, cleansing force in the world which will sweep before it all wars, disagreements, discords and struggles—and then will mankind be united in the power of the Love of God.[2]

In this book, I will primarily center my attention on the principles, teachings, goals, plans, and activities of the Bahá'í Faith, especially as it pertains to Bahá'í prophecies concerning the destiny of America. This book is not intended to be an introduction to the Bahá'í Faith, but a few words should be said about this young religion so that the

concepts covered in this book can be properly understood. The Bahá'í
Faith is not a sect or denomination of another religion. It is an independent world religion that was founded in 1844 in what is now Iran.
Its Prophet-Founder, Bahá'u'lláh (1817–1892), enunciated three central principles: 1) the Oneness of God—the idea that irrespective of
what we call God, whether it's Yahweh, Allah, Brahman, or the Great
Spirit, we are still worshipping the same God; 2) the Oneness of Religion—the idea that, in actuality, there is only one evolving religion,
the Religion of God, and what we perceive to be "different religions"
are actually just different stages in the evolution of the one unfolding
Religion of God; This principle maintains that all the major world religions were divinely revealed by Messengers of God, and thus, they all
share the same universal virtues such as love, generosity, forgiveness,
humility, compassion, justice, truth, and so forth; and 3) the Oneness
of Humanity—the idea that, regardless of one's race, ethnicity, and
background, we are all children of God; we are all brothers and sisters
of one human family.

Bahá'u'lláh also enunciated several other principles, which, considering the time period, were truly revolutionary: the harmony of science
and religion, the elimination of all forms of prejudice, the equality of
women and men; the elimination of the extremes of wealth and poverty, and the adoption of a universal auxiliary language. The primary
aim of the Bahá'í Faith is the spiritual unification of humankind into
one global family and the creation of a divinely inspired global civilization. Bahá'u'lláh wrote over one hundred volumes of material that
Bahá'ís regard as divinely revealed sacred scripture. Before His passing,
Bahá'u'lláh drafted a will (a covenant) in which He appointed His
eldest son, 'Abdu'l-Bahá (1844–1921), as the authorized interpreter of
His writings. 'Abdu'l-Bahá, in his years as head of the Faith, wrote an
extensive body of material that Bahá'ís consider to be sacred and binding on all believers. Likewise, before his passing, 'Abdu'l-Bahá wrote
a Will and Testament in which he appointed his grandson Shoghi
Effendi as the head and Guardian of the Bahá'í Faith. The Guardian
wrote innumerable letters, epistles, and books that are also considered
authoritative and binding on all believers.

PREFACE

In His writings Bahá'u'lláh stipulated the eventual creation of a Universal House of Justice, which would act as the supreme governing body of the Bahá'í Faith. After the passing of Shoghi Effendi, the first Universal House of Justice was elected in 1963. This supreme body of nine members is elected every five years, and it is now charged with guiding the affairs of the worldwide Bahá'í community. The Universal House of Justice is seated at the Bahá'í World Center in Haifa, Israel. Its writings are considered authoritative and binding on all Bahá'í believers. Thus the canon of authoritative Bahá'í texts is made up of the writings of Bahá'u'lláh, 'Abdu'l-Bahá, Shoghi Effendi, and the Universal House of Justice.

According to the teachings of the Bahá'í Faith, humankind is presently in a transition period between adolescence and adulthood. Regarding this, Shoghi Effendi writes,

Humanity is now experiencing the commotions invariably associated with the most turbulent stage of its evolution, the stage of adolescence, when the impetuosity of youth and its vehemence reach their climax, and must gradually be superseded by . . . maturity. . . . Then will the human race . . . acquire all the powers and capacities upon which its ultimate development must depend.[3]

There is some evidence that we are indeed entering into a new epoch in human development. For instance, growing numbers of people, from a diversity of backgrounds throughout the world, are increasingly tapping into the spiritual powers unleashed by the dispensation of Bahá'u'lláh and are using His writings as a blueprint to help them build a better world. By internalizing the illuminating and life-affirming teachings of Bahá'u'lláh, such people (even some from antagonistic ethnic and religious backgrounds) have been able to work together in a spirit of self-sacrifice, service, and love even in circumstances that are still rife with hatred, disorder, and violence. In many cases, some people who have adopted the Bahá'í teachings have shown great courage by promoting progressive principles (such as the oneness of religion and the equality of men and women) that are at variance with the cultural and religious norms of the societies in which they live.

In the coming chapter, it will be shown that before we can reach the pinnacle of human evolution on this planet, we must first experience some level of suffering and discomfort. The earth is essentially giving birth to an entirely new world order and global civilization, and like any other birthing process, this will entail some labor and birth pains. Indeed, Bahá'u'lláh declared, "The whole earth is now in a state of pregnancy. The day is approaching when it will have yielded its noblest fruits . . ." In this case, old defective institutions will increasingly come crashing down while humanity will be forced by the fires of tribulation to abandon old harmful ways of acting and thinking. The Universal House of Justice explains that "the great Plan of God" is "working through mankind as a whole, tearing down barriers to world unity, and forging humankind into a unified body in the fires of suffering and experience." All of this is sure to elicit high levels of fear and anxiety. At the same time, we must remain aware that this is a divinely guided process. Indeed, we can take some solace in knowing that whatever tribulations humanity must yet undergo are for our own perfecting. We can also take comfort in knowing that this process will ultimately produce an unprecedented leap forward in the historic evolution of humankind. Referring to humanity, Shoghi Effendi writes, "Its present state, indeed, even its immediate future, is dark, distressingly dark. Its distant future, however, is radiant, gloriously radiant—so radiant that no eye can visualize it." He further states, "God's purpose, . . . is none other than to usher in, in ways He alone can bring about, . . . the Great, the Golden Age of a long-divided, a long-afflicted humanity." It is my hope that this book contributes, even in a small way, to this blessed divinely guided process.[4]

Chapter One

THE END OF THE WORLD
AS WE KNOW IT

Rome, at the height of its imperial glory, seemed like an invincible citadel of might, glory, and opulence. Indeed, for many centuries, the Roman Empire stood tall on the ruins of other once great civilizations. For the peoples of the ancient world, Rome represented the apex of military, economic, political, cultural, and technological achievement. The popular saying was that "all roads lead to Rome," and it is likely that many Roman citizens perceived their empire as being somehow timeless and beyond the reach of decay and disintegration. Then, like all other proud empires that came before it, Rome also fell. What had once seemed invincible and timeless was shown to be riddled with holes. When the Visigoths sacked Rome in 410 A.D., they found an empire that, for several generations, had already been crippled by moral bankruptcy; crass materialism; political corruption; stark poverty amidst incredible wealth; and civil strife involving mob violence, slave revolts, and peasant uprisings.

In his book, *A History of Knowledge*, historian Charles Van Doren makes an interesting comparison between the ancient Romans and modern Americans:

The later Roman empire had been dedicated to power, wealth, and worldly success . . . [The Romans lived] . . . enjoying all that the world could provide and paying little heed to the demands of Christianity even though it was the official religion of the state. . . . We live today in a world that is as deeply devoted to material things as was the late Roman world. [The Romans] spent more time in baths and health clubs than in churches, temples, libraries. . . . They were devoted to consumption. A man could make a reputation by spending more than his neighbor, even if he had to borrow the money to do it. . . . They were excited by travel, news, and entertainment. . . . Cultural productions of late Roman times, from books to extravaganzas in the theaters and circuses that occupied a central place in every Roman city . . . dealt with amusing fictions . . . with a fantasy peace and happiness that did not exist in their real lives. They were fascinated by fame and did not care how it was acquired. If you were famous enough, the fact that you might be a rascal or worse was ignored. . . . Romans cared most about success. . . . They were proud, greedy, and vain. In short, they were much like ourselves.[1]

When the Roman citizens finally witnessed the demise of their once vaunted civilization, one wonders how many ever realized that their prevailing decadent materialistic worldview had played a pivotal role in their own destruction. Indeed, the now famous St. Augustine (354–430 A.D.), a Roman citizen and bishop who lived to witness the impending fall of Rome, did come to this realization. In his book, *The City of God*, Augustine made a strong distinction between two different metaphorical "cities," the City of Man and the City of God. The City of Man was "human—material, fleshly, downward-turning," while the City of God was "divine—spiritual, turning upward toward the Creator of all things." Augustine argued that Pax Romana represented the City of Man and could never be the City of God because, even though Christianity was the state religion, the Roman state itself was incapable of being holy. Augustine maintained that the luminous City of God already existed in every person, whether a pauper or a king, and anyone could find this city by listening to the teachings of the "inward teacher"—the Word of God as revealed by Christ. Augustine asserted that the pomp and glitter of Rome obscured the true brilliance of the Christian message. According to Augustine, the fall of Rome, in a sense, was ordained by God and gave Christians the opportunity to set a new course toward the glory of the Heavenly City and away from the vain pursuit of earthly glory.[2]

By reinterpreting Roman history from a Christian spiritual standpoint, St. Augustine laid out a new plan for history that underscored the principle that worldly power, like that of Rome, ultimately ends in ruin whereas the triumph of the City of God is truly glorious and divinely ordained. Augustine emphasized that the historical struggle between the City of God and the City of Man would continue eternally. Indeed, as we now stand at the beginning of the twenty-first century, it is becoming increasingly apparent that the City of Man has gained domination over the hearts and minds of vast numbers of peoples. Disconcertingly, many of the omens of impending doom that were evident in the final twilight years of the Roman Empire are now similarly apparent within present-day Western civilization. Along these lines, it is significant to point out that Shoghi Effendi noted a clear connection between the declining fortunes of the modern West and the downfall of the Roman Empire. In a 1934 general letter to the Bahá'ís of the West, Shoghi Effendi refers to "the signs of an impending catastrophe, strangely reminiscent of the Fall of the Roman Empire in the West, which threatens to engulf the whole structure of present-day civilization." In this same letter to Western Bahá'ís, he further states, "How disquieting the lawlessness, the corruption, the unbelief that are eating into the vitals of a tottering civilization!" Similarly, in a 1948 communication to the American Bahá'ís, he characterizes modern society as being: "politically convulsed, economically disrupted, socially subverted, morally decadent and spiritually moribund."[3]

In addition to making a link between the decline of the modern West and the fall of Rome, it is possible to make a strong comparison between present-day Bahá'ís who live in the West and the early Christians who lived within the ancient Roman Empire. The early pious Christians did not fit in the Roman Empire, and in a similar way, Bahá'ís do not fit in today's Western culture. Like Christians whose values and beliefs were at variance with the prevailing Roman culture, many Bahá'ís are increasingly finding themselves under the influence of a Western globalized culture that is at variance with the Bahá'í worldview. Importantly, no other culture currently exists in the world that can serve as a healthy alternative to Western civilization. Indeed, in substantial ways, all known cultures fall short when compared to the luminous standards set by Bahá'u'lláh. The only choice is the creation of an entirely new divinely inspired global civilization, which Bahá'ís are laboring to establish.

Akin to the many Romans who probably never imagined an ignominious end to their mighty empire, many of today's people may find it inconceivable that the technologically advanced, militarily powerful, and materially prosperous West is a "tottering civilization." It is increasingly clear, however, that from whatever angle we view the modern world, it stands in grave peril both inwardly and outwardly. As mentioned in the preface, my earlier book, *Faith, Physics, and Psychology: Rethinking Society and the Human Spirit* (Bahá'í Publishing, 2006) provides a detailed analysis of the economic, social, political, spiritual, moral, and environmental crises that are increasingly plaguing the current Western-dominated world order. One of the major theses of that book is that Western civilization has become chaotic and destructive due to its underlying worldview.

The prevailing Western worldview (commonly referred to as the Cartesian-Newtonian worldview) is a pervasively materialistic view of reality. Within the context of this despiritualized worldview, one's perception of "reality" is defined solely by one's five senses and their extension via scientific instruments. This materialistic perspective is essentially based on the faulty "old science" understanding that the physical universe is true reality and also on the related belief that the material aspects of one's existence are of primary importance.

In contrast, the Bahá'í writings assert that true reality actually exists only in the unseen spiritual worlds of God and that the physical world around us is simply a projection from that true reality. Within this context, people are to be regarded as being primarily spiritual entities, souls, who happen to be living a physical human existence. Meanwhile, the material world should be regarded simply as a "classroom for the soul" where one should endeavor to learn spiritual lessons and to conform one's will to the will of God (as expressed in sacred texts). In order to reach our highest capacities as spiritual entities, we must struggle to acquire virtues (generosity, compassion, justice, patience, honesty, forgiveness, unity, love, and so forth) that will assist us both in this world and also when we physically die and pass into the spiritual worlds of God.

In relation to this, my earlier book (*Faith, Physics, and Psychology*) explains in detail my assertion that the latest findings in quantum physics are providing some validation for the Bahá'í view of reality—namely, that the physical universe is merely a manifestation of a more true, deeper spiritual reality. Quantum physics is also providing some validation for the Bahá'í understanding of the "oneness of the cosmos"—that we live in a holistic universe in which spirit, matter, consciousness, energy, forces, space, and time are interconnected and interrelated. This Bahá'í perspective harmonizes science and religion, and unites mind, body, and spirit. Unfortunately, in spite of growing evidence that supports the validity of the Bahá'í holistic worldview, many scientists still continue to subscribe to a materialistic view of reality that rejects any such talk of spiritual matters.

In essence, with the advent of the Scientific Revolution about 500 years ago, Western culture has developed an exaggerated sense of trust in science as the ultimate arbiter of truth to the exclusion of religion. Because of such blind faith in science, scholars have hopelessly attempted to formulate solutions to world problems based on the same mechanistic "old science" worldview that is ultimately the source of many of these problems. It would probably never occur to a considerable number of today's academic scholars that many current social, economic, and political problems are largely the result of humanity's wayward and unrepentant relationship with God.

It is my belief that the rising forces of irreligion and materialism that are repeatedly condemned in the Bahá'í writings are directly related to the consolidation of the despiritualized Cartesian-Newtonian worldview in the West and its rapid expansion to other countries throughout the world. Shoghi Effendi warns of the "prevailing spirit of modernism, with its emphasis on a purely materialistic philosophy, which, as it diffuses itself, tends increasingly to divorce religion from man's daily life." Similarly, keeping in mind that Western civilization was born in Europe, it is significant to note that Shoghi Effendi refers to Europe as the cradle of a "godless," a "highly-vaunted yet lamentably defective civilization." Likewise, in a publication aimed at the American Bahá'ís, he maintains that the United States lies in the tight grip of an "excessive and enervating materialism" and that the "lights of religion are fading out" and the "forces of irreligion are weakening the moral fibre."[4]

Such an irreligious and materialistic view of life has led to the creation of superficial consumerist societies that promote self-indulgence, instant gratification, and the hedonistic pursuit of physical wealth, power, and status. Corporate commercialism, for instance, encourages the multiplication of wants and desires and continually entices man's lower nature. In contrast, traditional spiritual wisdom maintains that true personal happiness, harmony, and peace are based upon the reduction of desires and the development of spiritual virtues such as contentment, humility, and self-sacrifice.

The Bahá'í Faith emphasizes that individuals who exclusively pursue the false physical reality and become attached to the pleasures, desires, and cares of the material world will ultimately find themselves in utter loss and lamentation. Indeed, as noted in the preface, in spite of incredible material prosperity, surveys and studies continue to show high and rising levels of general unhappiness and clinical depression among Americans and Europeans at all socioeconomic levels including the upper and middle classes. Most disturbing are studies that show that American children and adolescents are suffering from very high, and in many cases escalating, rates of suicide, homicide, depression, drug abuse, mental illness, sexually transmitted diseases, anxiety disorders, addictions, and various forms of violent behavior such as assaults, bullying, and even self-mutilation. Sadly, the United States has more boys and young men incarcerated in psychiatric hospitals, prison, and juvenile detention than any other country in the world. In fact, an

April 23, 2008 *New York Times* article reports that the "United States leads the world in producing prisoners"—it has more people in prison than any other nation on earth. Even if we account for differences in population among the various countries, the United States still has the world's highest incarceration rate per capita.[5]

Such entrenched maladies and corruptions among the most prosperous, technologically advanced generation in history should be interpreted as a cry for true meaning and purpose. We are witnessing a poverty of the soul on a mass level. Based on such findings, it is becoming increasingly evident that Western societies are materially rich, and yet, spiritually poor. The debauched unhappy lives of the countless Hollywood stars, famous sports figures, music icons, and financial moguls who spend much of their time and energy in pursuit of fame and fortune are a tragic testament to the ultimate emptiness of such a spiritually and morally bankrupt approach to life. Our societies stand in desperate need of adopting overarching spiritual values and guiding principles that can assist people to live fulfilling, courageous, meaningful lives—lives that honor the highest potentialities of human beings and transcend the existential fears, anxieties, and petty concerns of this temporal physical world.

It should be noted that Western ideas and practices have now spread widely due to many historical influences such as the Scientific Revolution, the Industrial Revolution, capitalism, socialism, communism, and colonialism—all of which emanated from Europe and the United States and then affected all areas of the globe. Other contemporary influences have also contributed to the rapid dissemination of Western culture such as the rise of powerful U.S.- and European-based multinational corporations, the advent of global communication and transportation, the ascendancy of U.S.-dominated global capitalism, the popularity of U.S. pop culture (such as American music and movies) in foreign nations, U.S. and European military interventions, immigration, and numerous other factors.

Consequently, Western culture now acts as an influential and appealing subculture in many nations—even in nations that claim to be non-Western. Along these lines, Azadeh Moaveni, a former *Time* Magazine and *Los Angeles Times* reporter who lived several years in Iran and the Middle East and who subsequently authored the book, *Lipstick Jihad: A Memoir of Growing Up Iranian in America and American in Iran*, reports that the Shiite theocracy of Iran officially bans many Western influences, and yet, American TV sitcoms (such as *Sex in the City*), cosmetic surgery, MTV, Hollywood movies, designer labels, weblogs, and sexually explicit Internet chat rooms are quite popular among young Iranians. She describes, for instance, teenage girls in Tehran, Iran who (in private) "worked fiercely to imitate music videos and Hollywood movies to every last detail" and who would show up at social occasions wearing tight, revealing, "wildly inappropriate clothes, called lebass-e mahvarayee, satellite dress, after the inspiring TV medium."[6]

The main point here is that the spread of Western culture and its embedded secular worldview acts as a barrier to the establishment of a peaceful global order based on the teachings of Bahá'u'lláh. The Bahá'í writings state,

> The Bahá'ís should realize that today's intensely materialistic civilization, alas, most perfectly exemplified by the United States, has far exceeded the bounds of moderation, and, as Bahá'u'lláh has pointed out in His Writings, civilization itself, when carried to extremes, leads to destruction. The Canadian friends should be on their guard against this deadly influence to which they are so constantly exposed, and which we can see is undermining the moral strength of not only America, but indeed of Europe and other parts of the world to which it is rapidly spreading.[7]

The Bahá'í writings describe Bahá'u'lláh as the "Divine Physician" Who has brought a remedy for the ills of society. As such, His teachings are intended to fulfill the needs and to address the problems of humankind at this current stage of human evolution on the planet. Sadly, the writings explain that the peoples of the world will experience increasing levels of travail because most have largely ignored, and in some cases, outright rejected Bahá'u'lláh's divine remedy. Indeed, various Bahá'í passages state that humanity will experience "chaos and confusion," "intolerable calamities," "unprecedented commotions," and "torment-ing trials" that "are essential instruments for the establishment of the immutable Will of God on earth." The writings maintain that it is only through such tribulations that humanity will finally realize that "religion is the impregnable stronghold and the manifest light of the world."[8]

Referring specifically to the United States, Shoghi Effendi explic-itly asserts that the "American nation" stands in "great peril" and that it will suffer "woes and tribulations," that are "mostly inevitable and God-sent." He explains that it is through these calamities that God is preparing the United States, its citizens, and the American Bahá'í com-munity for the special roles that they will play in helping to establish an entirely new divinely ordained world order and planetary civilization.[9]

In the chapters to come, we will examine the uniquely exalted na-ture and station of Bahá'u'lláh, the Promised One of all religions and the Inaugurator of a new, universal spiritual cycle. We will also explore the epic, God-given mission of the American Bahá'í community and the tumultuous, yet ultimately glorious, destiny of the United States in light of the prophecies contained in the Bahá'í writings. As will be discussed further in the next chapter, it is my intention to ground this study in the crucial understanding that the Messenger of God for this age, Bahá'u'lláh, has now appeared in the world, and He has generated "forces" and "creative energies" that are already guiding the special destiny of the United States and its peoples. The writings state,

> . . . the great republic of the West [U.S.], government and people alike, is . . . slowly, painfully, unwittingly and irresistibly advancing towards the goal destined for it by Bahá'u'lláh . . . if we would read aright the signs of the times, and appraise correctly the significances of contemporaneous events that are impelling forward both the American Bahá'í Community and the nation [U.S.] . . . to their ultimate destiny, we cannot fail to perceive the workings of two simultaneous processes . . . destined to culminate . . . in a single glorious consummation. One of these processes is associated with the mission of the American Bahá'í Community, the other with the destiny of the American nation.[10]

As described earlier, Bishop St. Augustine reinterpreted the fall of Rome from a Christian religious perspective. In similar fashion, this work is focused on an interpretation of historical and contemporary events from a distinctly Bahá'í scriptural worldview as opposed to the prevailing secular worldview. The Bahá'í worldview is comprehensive and holistic in the sense that it accounts for both the material and spiritual dimensions of phenomena as exemplified by the Bahá'í principle of the harmony of science and religion. In contrast, the works of most present-day academic scholars are still centered on mechanistic theories that vainly attempt to explain the world's problems and solutions in purely physical terms. By definition, such secular rationales are limited because they do not account for the God-ordained mystical processes that are tearing down old structures and simultaneously erecting new structures.

In essence, the world, as we know it, is coming to an end. This does not mean that the world is coming to a physical end. Rather, it means that the old outworn ideas, assumptions, values, practices, and institutions of the current world are destined to die out. Along these lines, Bahá'u'lláh urges us to "die to the world and all that is therein . . ." Death here is not referring to one's physical death but rather to a death of the old harmful ways and to one's rebirth into true reality, the new life of the spirit that arises from recognizing Bahá'u'lláh as the new Messenger of God for this Day and then adhering to His divine laws and principles. It is my hope that this book can serve as a springboard to inspire others, especially American Bahá'ís, to leave behind the unworkable shibboleths, impotent idols, and "vain imaginings" of American Western culture and to see the world with new eyes: "Close one eye and open the other. Close one to the world and all that is therein and open the other to the hallowed beauty of the Beloved."[11]

Chapter Two

BAHÁ'U'LLÁH, THE SUPREME MANIFESTATION OF GOD

The opening lines of Shoghi Effendi's book, *The Promised Day Is Come*, proclaim,

A tempest, unprecedented in its violence . . . catastrophic in its immediate effects, unimaginably glorious in its ultimate consequences, is at present sweeping the face of the earth. . . . Bewildered, agonized and helpless, it [humanity] watches this great and mighty wind of God invading the remotest and fairest regions of the earth, rocking its foundations, deranging its equilibrium, sundering its nations, . . . uprooting its institutions, dimming its light, and harrowing up the souls of its inhabitants. . . . The powerful operations of this titanic upheaval are comprehensible to none except such as have recognized the claims of both Bahá'u'lláh and the Báb [Messenger Who proclaimed the coming of Bahá'u'lláh]. . . . This judgment of God, as viewed by those who have recognized Bahá'u'lláh as His Mouthpiece and His greatest Messenger on earth, is both a retributory calamity and an act of holy and supreme discipline. It is at once a visitation from God and a cleansing process for all mankind. Its fires punish the perversity of the human race, and weld its component parts into one organic, indivisible, world-embracing community. . . . Mankind . . . [is]

being simultaneously called upon to give account of its past actions, and is being purged and prepared for its future mission. . . . God . . . [can] neither allow the sins of an unregenerate humanity to go unpunished, nor will He be willing to abandon His children to their fate, and refuse them that culminating and blissful stage in their long, their slow and painful evolution throughout the ages, which is at once their inalienable right and their true destiny."[1]

This prophetic passage makes it clear that the tormenting trials and tribulations that humanity is increasingly experiencing are intended to purge and prepare mankind for "its future mission." It is through these calamities that mankind will be prodded to evolve to its highest stage of material and spiritual development and to fulfill its glorious "true destiny."

It is important to emphasize that, according to the above passage, people who have "recognized the claims of both Bahá'u'lláh and the Báb," and likewise, those who have "recognized Bahá'u'lláh as His [God's] Mouthpiece and His greatest Messenger on earth" have been blessed with a special potential or capacity. They have been given the bounty to be able to truly comprehend the nature of God's "tempest." In other words, the Bahá'í writings contain the keys that can enable one to understand the origin, purpose, and outcome of the "titanic upheaval" and the "judgment of God" that the earth's peoples are destined to experience. The following statement of Shoghi Effendi clarifies this point even further:

The powerful operations of this titanic upheaval are comprehensible to none except such as have recognized the claims of both Bahá'u'lláh and the Báb. Their followers know full well whence it comes, and what it will ultimately lead to. Though ignorant of how far it will reach, they clearly recognize its genesis, are aware of its direction, acknowledge its necessity, observe confidently its mysterious processes, ardently pray for the mitigation of its severity . . .[2]

It must be made clear that, just like all other people, the Bahá'ís will have to suffer through the catastrophic upheavals of the world. However, even during times of intense distress, the power of knowledge and understanding will give the Bahá'ís the capacity to keep their composure and to maintain their faith and hope, especially since they know that God's "tempest" will be "unimaginably glorious in its ultimate consequences." In contrast, Shoghi Effendi states that the generality of people will only be able to watch in bewilderment and agony as the world becomes increasingly enmeshed in trials, tribulations, and catastrophes: "Humanity, gripped in the clutches of its [the tempest's] devastating power, is smitten by the evidences of its resistless fury. It can neither perceive its origin, nor probe its significance, nor discern its outcome. Bewildered, agonized and helpless, it watches this great and mighty wind of God invading . . ."[3]

Thus contrary to the efforts of many academics who attempt to predict the outcome of world events from a strictly secular standpoint, it is clear that any discussions pertaining to the destiny of the world, if they are to be complete, must include certain understandings regarding the divinely ordained dispensation of Bahá'u'lláh. Indeed, a straightforward exposition of the station and mission of Bahá'u'lláh should be a prerequisite to any such discussions concerning destiny. We must first look at the claims of Bahá'u'lláh because, as already mentioned, His dispensation contains the keys that can help us to comprehend the past, current, and future state of the world.

The Bahá'í Faith asserts that humanity's collective redemption is inextricably linked to the recognition that Bahá'u'lláh is the Messenger of God for this age. In short, without Him, there is no redemption for collective humanity, and therefore, all talk of destiny becomes a moot point. With this in mind, the sections that follow expound upon the uniquely exalted nature of Bahá'u'lláh's revelation. This chapter explores Bahá'u'lláh's glorious station as the Promised Redeemer of all religions, critiques the notion that mankind can save itself, examines the evolutionary nature of the religion of God, and discusses the "coming of age" of the human race.

Can Humanity Save Itself?

The Bahá'í writings make it clear that humanity has "strayed too far and suffered too great a decline to be redeemed" even through the devoted efforts and concerted actions of even its best rulers, statesmen, economists, and moralists. The writings also state that appeals for "mutual tolerance" as well as extensive manmade schemes promoting "organized international co-operation" will not "succeed in removing the root cause of the evil that has so rudely upset the equilibrium of present-day society." Furthermore, even if people could ingeniously devise "the machinery required for the political and economic unification of the world" this would still not resolve the deepening crises that are afflicting humanity. In short, all the manmade reforms of the system are to no avail. People who place their hopes upon such economic, political, legal, and technological reforms will be grievously disappointed when they continue to see the worldwide system crashing down under the weight of disunity, injustice, violence, and moral corruption.[4]

Shoghi Effendi asserts that what is needed now is "unreserved acceptance of the Divine programme," enunciated by Bahá'u'lláh, which embodies "God's divinely appointed scheme for the unification of mankind in this age."[5] In relation to this, another passage from the Bahá'í writings states:

> . . . the revivification of mankind and the curing of all its ills can be achieved only through the instrumentality of His [Bahá'u'lláh's] Faith. . . . "That which the Lord hath ordained as the sovereign remedy and mightiest instrument for the healing of all the world is the union of all its peoples in one universal Cause, one common Faith. This can in no wise be achieved except through the power of a skilled, an all-powerful and inspired Physician. This, verily, is the truth, and all else naught but error."[6]

The revelation of Bahá'u'lláh released mysterious spiritual forces throughout the planet and infused the entire creation with new potentialities, powers, and immense capacities. In one of His sacred tablets, Bahá'u'lláh declares, "We have . . . breathed a new life into every human frame and instilled into every word a fresh potency." This fresh infusion of spiritual energy, however, acts like a double-edged sword. On the one hand, it represents the sword of justice, unity, peace, and integration that is helping to create a divinely inspired new world order. On the other hand, it is the sword of tribulation, purgation, and disintegration that is rending asunder the defective social, economic, political, and cultural institutions and worldviews of the old order. The writings speak of a "God-born Force" that has "upset the equilibrium of the world and revolutionized its ordered life" and that acts "even as a two-edged sword," which sunders on the one hand "age-old ties" while "unloosing, on the other, the bonds that still fetter the infant and as yet unemancipated Faith of Bahá'u'lláh." Similarly, the writings refer to the "rumblings" of a "catastrophic upheaval" that is to simultaneously proclaim "the death-pangs of the old order and the birth-pangs of the new." In his book, *The Advent of Divine Justice*, Shoghi Effendi affirms that people can actually strengthen their faith if they make sure to observe the aforementioned "God-born Force" and its resultant tribulations within the glorious context of "the purposes, the prophecies, and promises of Bahá'u'lláh."[7] He states,

> A world, dimmed by the steadily dying-out light of religion, heaving with the explosive forces of a blind and triumphant nationalism; scorched with the fires of pitiless persecution, whether racial or religious; deluded by the false theories and doctrines that threaten to supplant the worship of God and the sanctification of His laws; enervated by a rampant and brutal materialism; disintegrating through the corrosive influence of moral and spiritual decadence; and enmeshed in the coils of economic anarchy and strife—such is the spectacle presented to men's eyes, as a result of the sweeping changes which this revolutionizing [God-born] Force, as yet in the initial stage of its operation, is now producing in the life of the entire planet. . . .

So sad and moving a spectacle, bewildering as it must be to every observer unaware of the purposes, the prophecies, and promises of Bahá'u'lláh, far from casting dismay into the hearts of His followers, or paralyzing their efforts, cannot but deepen their faith, and excite their enthusiastic eagerness to arise and display . . . their capacity to play their part in the work of universal redemption proclaimed by Bahá'u'lláh.[8]

Beholding the Face of God

The coming of Bahá'u'lláh ushered in the Day of God, the Day that all the previous Messengers of God had longed to witness: "Every Prophet hath announced the coming of this Day, and every Messenger hath groaned in His yearning for this Revelation . . ." The Scriptures of the various world religions have all prophesied the advent of the Promised One of All Ages, the sacred Being Who shall redeem the whole of mankind and establish the Kingdom of God on earth. Bahá'u'lláh claims to be none other than this World Redeemer. As a tribute to the superlative character of the Bahá'í dispensation, 'Abdu'l-Bahá, the son of Bahá'u'lláh, declares, "Centuries, nay ages, must pass away, ere the Daystar of Truth shineth again in its mid-summer splendor . . ." He furthermore states that the "mere contemplation" of the Bahá'í dispensation "would have sufficed to overwhelm the saints of bygone ages— saints who longed to partake for one moment of its great glory."[9]

The uniquely transcendent power and glory of the Bahá'í dispensation can be significantly attributed to an unprecedented spiritual event—for the first time in religious history, a supremely powerful spiritual entity known as the "Most Great Spirit" manifested itself here on Earth in the physical form of a Messenger or Manifestation of God (please note that the terms *Messenger, Manifestation,* and *Prophet* are used interchangeably throughout this book). This Most Great Spirit animated and acted through the physical person of Bahá'u'lláh. In contrast, all the Prophets prior to Bahá'u'lláh were animated by the power of the Holy Spirit. It is through the agency of the Holy Spirit that all the former Messengers were able to reveal the Will and the

Word of God from age to age. It is fascinating to note that the Most Great Spirit, an entity that is eternal, somehow created or brought into existence the Holy Spirit. In the following passage, Bahá'u'lláh confirms that the Holy Spirit was indeed begotten by the supreme power of the Most Great Spirit: "The Holy Spirit Itself hath been generated through the agency of a single letter revealed by this Most Great Spirit, if ye be of them that comprehend."[10]

When referring to the exalted nature of His own revelation, it is startling to note that Bahá'u'lláh proclaims, "None among the Manifestations [Messengers] of old, except to a prescribed degree, hath ever completely apprehended the nature of this Revelation." The writings also state, "But for Him [Bahá'u'lláh] no Divine Messenger would have been invested with the robe of prophethood, nor would any of the sacred scriptures have been revealed." Shoghi Effendi reinforces the idea that Bahá'u'lláh's revelation stands unparalleled in the annals of religion when he states, "Baha'u'llah has appeared in God's Greatest Name, in other words . . . He is the Supreme Manifestation of God. . . . There are no Prophets, so far, in the same category as Bahá'u'lláh, as He culminates a great cycle begun with Adam." Along similar lines, Shoghi Effendi explains, "Bahá'u'lláh is the greatest Manifestation to yet appear, the One Who consummates the Revelation of Moses. He was the One Moses conversed with in the Burning Bush. In other words Bahá'u'lláh identifies the Glory of God-Head on that occasion with Himself."[11]

The astonishing passage above confirms that it was Bahá'u'lláh (or the Most Great Spirit) Who spoke to Moses on Mount Sinai. It is this same Spirit that later manifested Itself in the divine Personage of Bahá'u'lláh. Adib Taherzadeh, a Bahá'í scholar and author, explains: "In past Dispensations God's Revelation had been indirect through the intermediary of the Holy Spirit. In this Dispensation, however, for the first time the Most Great Spirit of God has revealed Itself directly to Bahá'u'lláh and ushered in the Day of God."[12]

It must be emphasized that when we speak of the greatness of Bahá'u'lláh, we are not referring to the human being or to the physical person of Bahá'u'lláh; we are referring to the Most Great Spirit that animated Him. In the writings, when Bahá'u'lláh proclaims that He is the "Voice of God" or that He is the "Face of God," He is referring to the Most Great Spirit. Likewise, some passages declare that it is Bahá'u'lláh Who sent all the Messengers of the past; such passages are actually referring to the Most Great Spirit and not to the physical person of Bahá'u'lláh. This understanding is consistent with the following quote in which Bahá'u'lláh testifies that He Himself sent Jesus Christ to the world:

> We, in truth, have sent Him Whom We aided with the Holy Spirit (Jesus Christ) that He may announce unto you this Light . . . Arise, in My Name. . . . The voice of the Burning Bush [Bahá'u'lláh—the Most Great Spirit] is raised in the midmost heart of the world, and the Holy Spirit calleth aloud among the nations: "Lo, the Desired One is come with manifest dominion!" . . . This is, truly, that which the Spirit of God (Jesus Christ) hath announced, when He came with truth unto you . . ."[13]

The statements above, which emphasize the incomparable greatness of Bahá'u'lláh's revelation seem to contradict the Bahá'í principle that God's Messengers are all inherently one and that there is no basic difference between them. A careful reading of the writings, however, shows that no such contradiction exists. Statements that emphasize the supreme nature of Bahá'u'lláh's revelation can only be truly understood within the context of the concept of progressive revelation as explained below.

Why is Bahá'u'lláh the Supreme Manifestation of God?

The world's religions may often seem like completely different contending spiritual impulses, but according to the principle of progressive revelation, the various world religions should actually be seen as representing different stages in the evolution of the one religion of God. Similar to the way that a person evolves during his or her own lifetime, the religion of God also unfolds in a progressive manner. An individual goes through the developmental stages of infancy, childhood, adolescence, and then adulthood. During these various stages of growth, the physical, intellectual, and spiritual powers of the individual increase, but at each stage, the individual is still the same person (he or she retains the same identity). Likewise, the religion of God has also evolved through various stages of development. The coming of each successive Messenger has represented a step forward in the evolutionary progress of God's one religion. At each stage, a new Manifestation has arisen to reveal a broader and deeper measure of truth based on the ever increasing potentialities and receptivity of humanity. However, in reality, the single unfolding religion of God has always remained one and the same. Again, this is akin to an individual who evolves in stages and exhibits greater powers at each stage while retaining the same identity.

With the above in mind, it is fully consistent to state that Bahá'u'lláh's revelation represents an immeasurable increase in the powers and capacities that are latent in the unfolding religion of God, and yet, it is also true that His revelation remains as one, in reality, with all the former revelations. His religious dispensation includes and yet transcends the previous dispensations. Indeed, it would be accurate to say that the Bahá'í revelation fulfills or consummates all former revelations. Along these lines, Bahá'u'lláh announces,

> In this most mighty Revelation . . . all the Dispensations of the past have attained their highest, their final consummation. That which hath been made manifest in this preeminent, this most exalted Revelation, stands unparalleled in the annals of the past, nor will future ages witness its like."[14]

The Bahá'í writings make it clear that the evolutionary progress of the religion of God provides the impetus for the evolution of mankind itself. For millions of years, collective humanity has been slowly evolving under the guiding influence and direction of divine Messengers. These

Manifestations have appeared from time to time throughout the planet with unique teachings specifically suited to carry forward the civilizing process of mankind. In short, it is this progressive revelation of God's Word that serves as the driving force for the evolution of all creation.

In this new age, humanity has finally reached the stage of maturity where it is ready to acknowledge the oneness of the human race and to create a peaceful, just, spiritually enlightened world federation of nations. The Bahá'í writings emphasize that humanity's entrance into maturity corresponds perfectly with the advent of Bahá'u'lláh's revelation. In the following passage, Shoghi Effendi explains that the uniquely elevated nature of the Bahá'í dispensation is directly connected to the coming of age of mankind:

> . . . the Messengers of God are all inherently one; it is their Message that differs. Bahá'u'lláh appearing at a time when the world has attained maturity, His message must necessarily surpass the message of all previous prophets. . . . This is because the stage of maturity is the most momentous stage in the evolution of mankind . . .[15]

Thus the religion of God and collective humanity are coevolving. As humanity evolves toward higher levels of capacity, each successive Messenger also shows forth a commensurate increase in capacity and intensity in order to challenge the new potentialities and receptivity of the human race.

In order to truly appreciate the momentous character of the Bahá'í revelation, we must first understand that, within the framework of progressive revelation, the whole purpose of the religious dispensations of the past has been to instigate the evolutionary transformations necessary to prepare humanity for the coming of God's supreme Manifestation, Bahá'u'lláh. Shoghi Effendi states,

> The successive Founders of all past Religions Who, from time immemorial, have shed, with ever-increasing intensity, the splendor

of one common Revelation at the various stages which have marked the advance of mankind towards maturity may thus, in a sense, be regarded as preliminary Manifestations, anticipating and paving the way for the advent of that Day of Days when the whole earth will have fructified and the tree of humanity will have yielded its destined fruit.[16]

As we shall see, the coming of age of the human race corresponds not only with the advent of Bahá'u'lláh's revelation, but it corresponds also with the birth of an entirely new universal spiritual cycle.

Chapter Three

THE DAWNING OF
A NEW SPIRITUAL CYCLE

It is remarkable to note that Bahá'u'lláh's revelation represents the culmination of one spiritual cycle, the Prophetic Cycle, while at the same time, it also represents the inauguration of an entirely new spiritual cycle, the Cycle of Fulfillment. The Prophetic Cycle started with Adam (Book of Genesis), and it ended with Muḥammad. Some of the Messengers within the Prophetic Cycle, such as Abraham, Krishna, Moses, Zoroaster, Buddha, Christ, and Muḥammad, inspired major world religions or movements. We do not know the names of all the Messengers, but we do know that God sent His Messengers to diverse peoples throughout the planet. All of these Messengers of God prophesied the coming of a world Redeemer—Bahá'u'lláh, the Promised One of all ages. Hence Bahá'u'lláh's dispensation fulfills the prophecies that are contained in the holy books of all the previous Prophets. His dispensation will continue for at least 1,000 years before another Messenger appears with a new revelation. The overall Cycle of Fulfillment is destined to endure for 500,000 years, and it will include the appearance of many other Manifestations of God. The glorious dawning of this new cycle is a spiritual event that stands unparalleled in the history of this planet, and yet sadly, it appears that vast segments of humanity remain unaware of the incredible magnitude and stunning significance of this seismic shift in the one unfolding religion of God. This chapter examines the Bahá'í concept of spiritual cycles, explains some of the barriers that may prevent one from recognizing the dawning of this new spiritual cycle (including misconceptions regarding Muḥammad and erroneous notions concerning personal salvation), elucidates why the existing religions are essentially impotent to save humanity without the power of Bahá'u'lláh's revelation, and highlights a few of the unique features and early successes of the Bahá'í Faith.

Him Whom God Shall Make Manifest

The momentous transition out of the Prophetic Cycle occurred in 1844 and was signalized by the physical appearance in Iran of a unique Manifestation, the Báb. The Báb's distinctive Mission was to metaphorically "open the gate" into the Cycle of Fulfillment, to announce a break with the Islamic dispensation, and to proclaim the imminent coming of the Promised One, Bahá'u'lláh. The title "the Báb" means "the Gate," and it signifies that the Báb, an independent Messenger of God with His own divinely revealed Book and laws, stood like a gate between two distinct spiritual cycles.

In accordance with the principle of progressive revelation described earlier, the Báb stands elevated beyond all the previous Messengers of the Prophetic Cycle. Bahá'u'lláh states that the Báb is the "Point round Whom the realities of the Prophets and Messengers revolve," and Whose "rank excelleth that of all the Prophets." In spite of this unique rank, the Báb testifies, in numerous passages, that His own revelation pales in comparison to the revelation of Bahá'u'lláh. The Báb refers to Bahá'u'lláh as "Him Whom God shall make manifest" and declares, "I Myself am, verily, but a ring upon the hand of Him Whom God shall make manifest—glorified be His mention!" Likewise, the Báb states that "a thousand perusals of the Bayán [Holy Book revealed by the Báb] cannot equal the perusal of a single verse to be revealed by Him Whom God shall make manifest." And also, "The whole of the Bayán is only a leaf amongst the leaves of His [Bahá'u'lláh's] Paradise."[1] It is significant to note that although the Báb acknowledges His own exalted station and that of Bahá'u'lláh, He then also explains that one must exhibit reverence toward all previous Messengers:

This doth not mean, however, that one ought not to yield praise unto former Revelations. On no account is this acceptable, inasmuch as it behooveth man, upon reaching the age of nineteen, to render thanksgiving for the day of his conception as an embryo. For had the embryo not existed, how could he have reached his present state? Likewise had the religion taught by Adam [the first Messenger of the Prophetic Cycle] not existed, this Faith would not have attained its present stage. Thus consider thou the development of God's Faith until the end that hath no end.[2]

The Báb's Mission spanned only six years before He was martyred in 1850 by a firing squad at the insistence of religious clerics who felt threatened by His Message, which seemed to contradict some Islamic teachings. Even now, significant numbers of Muslims remain antagonistic to the Bahá'í Faith because they consider it to be an apostasy since both the Báb and Bahá'u'lláh proclaimed Themselves to be Manifestations of God with the sovereignty and authority to abrogate the laws and teachings of the Islamic dispensation. Regrettably, the general understanding among many Muslims has been that no other independent Messengers of God can come after Muḥammad because He has the title "Seal of the Prophets" from the Qur'án. This title has typically been interpreted to mean that Muḥammad is the last independent divine Prophet and that any other holy Messengers that come after Him will only supplement the Qur'án and not alter its major tenets. The Bahá'í writings, however, explain that Muḥammad is titled "the Seal of the Prophets" because He represents the last Manifestation of God within the Prophetic Cycle. Meanwhile, as explained earlier, the Bahá'í writings make the distinction that the Báb stands between spiritual cycles while Bahá'u'lláh's revelation inaugurates an entirely new cycle.

The concept of spiritual cycles reinforces the idea that every aspect of God's creation goes through various stages of evolutionary growth. Each spiritual cycle has a beginning and an end and then a rebirth or resurrection at a higher stage of development. This can be represented by a spiral staircase in which the completion of each circular movement or cycle up the staircase takes you to a higher elevation. When you travel 360 degrees (a full circle) on a spiral staircase you end up facing in the same direction, but this time you are higher up, which means that you have a broader, more far-reaching view. Along these lines, it can be said that the Prophetic Cycle has already gone full circle up the "staircase," and now, the Cycle of Fulfillment is beginning at a higher "spiritual elevation."

All Religions Have a Spring, Summer, Fall, and Winter

Interestingly, the large spiritual cycles described above are made up of smaller mini-cycles. Indeed, the dispensation or "religion" brought by each Manifestation represents a mini-cycle contained within the framework of God's larger spiritual cycles. For instance, the dispensation of Muḥammad (the religion of Islam) is a mini-cycle within the larger Prophetic Cycle.

Each mini-cycle (religion) goes through a process similar to the changing seasons of the year. The advent of a new Messenger represents the divine springtime or a time of spiritual regeneration and growth. The new Messenger comes to revivify the one unfolding religion of God and to bring teachings intended to awaken people from their spiritual stupor in the same way that plants and animals arise from the dormancy of winter. As large numbers of people respond and adhere to the new teachings and laws of that particular Messenger, the summer stage begins where that specific dispensation evinces its mightiest powers to transform the world and its peoples. Eventually, however, the religion enters its fall season where its creative powers begin to fade, and then, it enters the winter period where that particular religion essentially loses its effectiveness to transform people. During the winter period, the religion essentially dies, but it is then ready to be reborn or resurrected when another Messenger arises at the spiritual springtime to proclaim a new dispensation. 'Abdu'l-Bahá confirms this concept:

Furthermore, just as the solar cycle has its four seasons the cycle of the Sun of Reality [the Dispensation of the Messenger] has its distinct and successive periods. Each brings its . . . springtime. . . .

After the spring, summer comes with its fullness and fruitage spiritual; autumn follows with its withering winds which chill the soul . . . until at last the mantle of winter overspreads and only faint traces of the effulgence of that divine Sun [Messenger] remain. Just as the surface of the material world becomes dark and dreary . . . so the winter of the spiritual cycle witnesses the death and disappearance of divine growth and extinction of the light and love of God. But again the cycle begins and a new springtime appears. In it the former springtime has returned, the world is resuscitated, illumined and attains spirituality; religion is renewed and reorganized, hearts are turned to God, the summons of God is heard and life is again bestowed upon man.[3]

Within the Bahá'í analogy of spiritual seasons, it is fascinating to note that the appearance of a new Manifestation is, in essence, the resurrection or return of the former Messenger. For instance, Christ is the resurrection of Moses while Muḥammad is the resurrection of Christ. Along these same lines, the Báb affirms that He "is the Resurrection of the Apostle of God [Muḥammad]." The Báb testifies that His own revelation is "for the purpose of gathering the fruits of Islám from the Qur'ánic verses which [Muḥammad] hath sown in the hearts of men." Indeed, it must be emphasized that each new Messenger embodies the essential qualities and attributes of all the previous Messengers. Therefore, a rejection of Bahá'u'lláh, the Manifestation of God for this Day, is tantamount to a rejection of all the Messengers of the past. The writings state, ". . . verily, he who turns away from this Beauty [Bahá'u'lláh] hath also turned away from the Messengers of the past and showeth pride towards God from all eternity to all eternity."[4]

If This is the Day of God
Then Why is it Such a Secret?

One may validly ask: If this is indeed the Day of God, then why have the vast majority of people remained unaware of the coming of the Promised One and the dawning of this new Day? An analogy is useful here. The dawning of a new revelation is similar to the dawning of the physical sun. At the break of dawn, only a few people living in the upper mountaintops become aware of the dim rays of the rising sun while the people living in the depths of the valleys and canyons remain enshrouded in darkness. As the sun rises higher, however, its rays become more direct and powerful, and eventually, the rest of the earth becomes illumined. Similarly, at the dawning of a revelation of God, the rays of the new revelation are faint. Also, many people remain wrapped in the spiritual darkness of countless manmade obstructions (superstitions, traditions, and prejudices) that prevent them from seeing the divine light. Eventually, however, akin to the increasing power of a rising sun, the new revelation evinces a spiritual power that is born of almighty God, and it sweeps aside the dark veils of human ignorance that obscure the light of truth.

A sense of humility and well attuned spiritual eyes and ears are necessary in order to actually recognize the divine station of the new Manifestation and to hearken unto His words. Sadly, in the early stages of every dispensation, the vast majority of the people typically do not recognize the divine character of the new Manifestation. In the beginning, only a few people are able to acknowledge and accept the broader dimension of truth embodied in the latest revelation. Indeed, some fanatically attempt to disrupt and destroy the new Messenger and His believers. In time, however, the Cause of God ultimately prevails against incredible odds, and large numbers of people come to embrace the new Faith. This pattern has been typical of all past religious dispensations as epitomized by the Christian and Islamic revelations, which began with only a few persecuted believers and eventually grew into huge influential religions.

For many people, the misinterpretation of religious scriptures can be a serious hurdle that prevents them from recognizing the new Manifestation of God. As already mentioned, the sacred scriptures of each of the world's religions have messianic prophecies that foretell the coming of the Promised One of all ages. In similar form, they all expect the coming of a world Redeemer, Who shall establish the Kingdom of God on earth and unite all of mankind. The Hindus, for instance, expect the return or reincarnation of Lord Krishna—the

"Tenth Avatar," the "Immaculate Manifestation of Krishna," while the Buddhists wait for the appearance of a Supremely Enlightened One, the "Buddha of universal fellowship," "Maitrya-Amitabha" Who shall reveal "His boundless glory." The Jews await the "King of Glory," the "Lord of Hosts," Who "shall be established upon the throne of David" and Who "shall judge among the nations." The Christians anticipate the "Glory of God," the return of Christ, Who "shall come in the glory of His Father" and with "all nations" gathered before His throne. The Muslims, meanwhile, expect the "Great Announcement," the "Day" whereon "God" will "come down" and "the angels shall be ranged in order." Bahá'u'lláh, Whose name means the "Glory of God," claims to be the fulfillment of all of these messianic prophecies and others. Unfortunately, many religious people expect a literal, physical fulfillment of the prophecies contained in their sacred scriptures. For instance, many Christians believe that during the Second Coming, trumpets will be heard while Christ literally comes down from heaven on clouds surrounded by angels, and all people throughout the planet will be able to simultaneously see this grand entrance. The Bahá'í writings explain that many such prophecies should be understood symbolically. For instance, the clouds are symbols of the intellectual, emotional, cultural, scientific, and religious veils or obstructions that prevent people from recognizing the new Manifestation of God.[5]

The tendencies described above explain why the Day of God seems like a well kept secret. In short, we must remain cognizant of the fact that we are still experiencing only the dawning point of the Day of God. The Bahá'í dispensation is still in its infancy. In time, as the Sun of Truth rises higher, the Faith will evince ever greater powers, and the manmade obscurations that are hiding the matchless glory of Bahá'u'lláh will increasingly melt away.

Western Bias Against Islam as a Barrier to Recognizing Bahá'u'lláh

Various people who have investigated the teachings of the Bahá'í Faith seem surprised that the Bahá'ís accept Islam as a divinely revealed religion especially since many thousands of Bahá'ís have been killed at the hands of Muslims, and even now, the Bahá'ís continue to suffer religious persecution and imprisonment in Islamic Iran, the birthplace of the Bahá'í Faith. For a considerable number of Westerners, Islam does not seem like an evolutionary advancement nor does it seem like a step forward from Christianity. Indeed, many people harbor a view of Islam as a retrograde religion. This biased perspective casts doubt on the whole Bahá'í concept of progressive revelation, and it also calls into question the station of Bahá'u'lláh Himself since He seems to be validating a false prophet and a counterfeit religion. In spite of such biased Western views, and also notwithstanding the behavior of some extremist Muslims whose violent acts lend credence to such views, the Bahá'í writings maintain that Muhammad was indeed an exalted Manifestation of God. The writings state,

They [Bahá'ís] must strive to obtain, from sources that are authoritative and unbiased, a sound knowledge of the history and tenets of Islam—the source and background of their Faith—and approach reverently and with a mind purged from preconceived ideas the study of the Qur'án which, apart from the sacred scriptures of the Bábí and Bahá'í Revelations, constitutes the only Book which can be regarded as an absolutely authenticated Repository of the Word of God.[6]

Karen Armstrong, a highly respected religious historian and author of several bestselling books including *A History of God, Islam: A Short History, Buddha,* and *The Battle for God,* is a good example of an "authoritative and unbiased" source. In her groundbreaking book, *Muhammad: A Biography of the Prophet,* she states,

The barriers of . . . hostility and fear, which once kept the religions in separate watertight compartments, are beginning to fall. . . . But one major religion seems to be outside this circle of goodwill and, in the West at least, to have retained its negative image. In the West we have a long history of hostility towards Islam . . . which in recent years has seen a disturbing revival in

Europe. . . . the old hatred of Islam continues to flourish on both sides of the Atlantic and people have few scruples about attacking this religion, even if they know little about it.[7]

It is indeed disturbing that many people in the West have equated Islam with terrorism, fanaticism, and the mistreatment of women. To hold such hostility toward Islam, however, is to ignore sizable portions of history that show that the teachings of Muḥammad inspired the creation of an Islamic civilization that was significantly respectful of Jews and Christians and was centuries ahead of other civilizations in its treatment of women. In A.D. 622, among the incredibly barbaric tribes of Arabia, Muḥammad, as a Prophet of God, entered the city of Medina and began to build the world's first community of Muslims. Within sixty years of His revelation, the hostile Arabian tribes were transformed into a spiritually enlightened national unit. The Baháʼí writings specifically challenge the Western myth that Muḥammad was the "Great Pretender" who founded a blasphemous religion:

> Americans and Europeans have heard a number of stories about the Prophet which they have thought to be true, although the narrators were either ignorant or antagonistic: most of them were [Christian] clergy; others were ignorant Muslims who repeated unfounded traditions about Muḥammad which they ignorantly believed to be to His praise. . . . the traditions which the clergy quote, and the incidents with which they find fault, are all exaggerated, if not entirely without foundation.[8]

While Europe was still in its dark ages, the Muslims quickly built an incredibly advanced civilization known for its enormous contributions to literature, philosophy, mathematics, science, medicine, engineering, astronomy, arts, and architecture. For instance, in Spain (the Muslims ruled Spain for seven hundred years), the Muslims built impressive schools, universities (the first one founded in Europe), libraries, hospitals, cultural centers for the arts, medical schools, and magnificent mosques. The Muslims allowed Jews, Christians, and sometimes even the poor classes and women to use these institutions in a spirit of mutual respect and tolerance. European Christians were permitted to study the plentiful books of many of the great prolific Muslim scholars such as the philosopher Averroes (his writings were required reading at the University of Paris), the physician Avicenna (who wrote a medical textbook that was used in European universities for several centuries), the mathematician al-Khwarizmi (considered by many to be the father of Algebra), the surgeon Abulcasis (who wrote a thirty-volume encyclopedia of medical practices), as well as the engineer Alhacen, the astronomer Avempace, the early chemist Jabir, and the physician Rhazes. The Arabs were also gifted linguists and were able to translate Greek, Egyptian, Indian, and Jewish texts into Arabic. For instance, they translated the important writings of some of the ancient Greek thinkers such as Socrates, Plato, and Aristotle. These translated texts, which contained some of the philosophy and knowledge of ancient Greece, were also made available to Westerners.

Many of the famous Muslim scholars, including those mentioned above and many others, were polymaths—in other words they were very well versed in a wide range of subjects. Indeed, they can be regarded as being the original "Renaissance men." Along these lines, the Bahá'í writings state,

. . . the Renaissance [the "rebirth" of European culture] is . . . essentially Muslim in its origins and foundations. . . . the Arabs regenerated and transformed by the spirit released by the religion of Muḥammad were busily engaged in establishing a civilization the kind of which their contemporary Christians in Europe had never witnessed before. It was eventually through Arabs that civilization was introduced to the West. It was through them that . . . philosophy, science and culture . . . found their way to Europe. . . . It is wholly unfair to attribute the efflorescence of European culture during the Renaissance period to the influence of Christianity. It was mainly the product of the forces released by the Muḥammadan Dispensation.[9]

In similar fashion, Jared Diamond, UCLA professor and author of the book, *Guns, Germs, and Steel: The Fates of Human Societies*, states,

> Until . . . A.D. 900, Europe west or north of the Alps contributed nothing of significance to Old World technology or civilization; it was instead a recipient of developments from the eastern Mediterranean, Fertile Crescent (in the Middle East), and China. Even from A.D. 1000 to 1450 the flow of science and technology was predominantly into Europe from the Islamic societies stretching from India to North Africa, rather than vice versa.[10]

Throughout the Muslim world, religious tolerance was the rule rather than the exception. Indeed, Jews and Christians were allowed to worship freely and to keep synagogues and churches even though they had to pay a tax. Even during the Crusades, the historical records show that the Muslim fighters often conducted themselves with high levels of morality and nobility while battling against the Christian onslaught into the Middle East. In contrast, Christian Crusaders earned a notorious reputation for pillaging and indiscriminately murdering Muslims, Jews, and indeed, any non-Whites in the Holy Land.[11]

Ironically (in light of what was stated above), one of the most entrenched and unfair Western myths regarding Muḥammad is that He created a violent religion of the sword. The Bahá'í writings bluntly reject this notion:

> The military expeditions of Muḥammad, on the contrary, were always defensive actions . . . they [Arab tribes] united to exterminate Him and all His followers. It was under such circumstances that Muḥammad was forced to take up arms. . . . Look at it with justice. . . . Muḥammad never fought against the Christians; on the contrary, He treated them kindly and gave them perfect freedom. . . . Muḥammad said, "If anyone infringes their rights, I Myself will be his enemy, and in the presence of God I will bring a charge against him." In the edicts which He

promulgated it is clearly stated that the lives, properties and honor of the Christians and Jews are under the protection of God. . . . Should the Christians desire to build a church, Islam ought to help them. . . . Nevertheless, after a certain time, and through the transgression of both the Muḥammadans and the Christians, hatred and enmity arose between them. Beyond this fact, all the narrations of the Muslims, Christians and others are simply fabrications, which have their origin in fanaticism, or ignorance, or emanate from intense hostility.[12]

In her aforementioned biography of Muḥammad, historian Armstrong provides extensive detailed evidence showing that Muḥammad was very restrained, well-reasoned, and diplomatic in His approach to defending His community. Indeed, she asserts that the incredibly hostile circumstances of the time left Him no recourse but to use military means as a form of defense. She explains that Islam was born in an area that was largely devoid of social and political order. Not only was Arabia outside the civilized world, it was also going through a period of disintegration and religious confusion. Unlike this hopelessly chaotic environment of early Islam, Christianity was primarily born in the fairly organized Roman Empire. The Roman laws and institutions "imposed, however brutally, a certain peace and social security." Therefore, Christian missionaries, such as St. Paul, could travel extensively throughout the Roman Empire helping to spread the Gospel message—this would have been impossible for the early Muslims because "in Arabia an unprotected man could be killed with impunity on the road." Furthermore, the members of the most powerful tribe in Arabia, the Quraysh (from the city of Mecca) were determined to destroy the Muslims.[13] It is within this context that Muḥammad created a theology of the "just war" in which it is sometimes necessary to fight in order to protect the innocent and to preserve justice. Armstrong states,

Muḥammad had arrived in Medina in September 622 as a refugee [from Mecca] who had narrowly escaped death . . . the *umma* [community of believers] faced the possibility of extermination. In the West we often imagine Muḥammad as a warlord, brandishing his sword in order to impose Islam on a reluctant world by force of arms. The reality was quite different. Muḥammad and the first Muslims were fighting for their lives and they had also undertaken a project in which violence was inevitable.... The *umma* was able to put an end to the dangerous violence of Arabia only by means of a relentless effort.[14]

In developing a theology of just war, Muḥammad instituted one of the most misunderstood and misquoted concepts of Islam—the *jihad,* which Westerners typically translate as "holy war." Several Arabic words can be used to signify armed combat such as sira'a (combat), harb (war), qital (killing), or ma'araka (battle). However, Muḥammad used the word *jihad* which is "a vaguer, richer word with a wide range of connotations." This word connotes an intellectual, spiritual, moral, and physical struggle or effort "to conquer the forces of evil in oneself and in one's own society in all the details of daily life." It also signifies a struggle to create a just, equitable, and decent society based on honorable laws where the vulnerable and poor are protected. Within this paradigm, combat and warfare might sometimes be necessary, but it is only a small part of the overall *jihad.*[15] In the following passage, 'Abdu'l-Bahá affirms that Muḥammad used warfare properly and justly, and furthermore, he declares that Christ would have taken the same actions as Muḥammad:

If Christ Himself had been placed in such circumstances ... what would have been Christ's conduct ... If this oppression had fallen only upon Himself, He would have forgiven them ... but if He had seen that these cruel ... murderers wished to kill, to pillage and to injure all these oppressed ones, and to take captive the women and children, it is certain that He would have protected them and would have resisted the tyrants. What objection, then, can be taken to Muḥammad's action? ... To free these tribes from their bloodthirstiness was the greatest kindness, and to coerce and restrain them was a true mercy. They were like a man holding in his hand a cup of poison, which, when about to drink, a friend breaks and thus saves him. If Christ had been placed in similar circumstances, it is certain that with a conquering power He would have delivered the men, women and children from the claws of these . . . wolves.[16]

Another Western myth that continues to have the enduring power to denigrate Islam is that Muḥammad instituted a religion that is inherently anti-woman. Notwithstanding this myth, many historians now support the view that the teachings of Muḥammad actually uplifted the status of women. As will be described below, Muḥammad, in the seventh century, granted women some rights that were truly revolutionary at that time. Indeed, Charles Smith, a University of Arizona professor of Middle East history, points out that women "did not gain similar rights in Europe until the end of the nineteenth century." The revelation of Muḥammad gave women the right to keep some of their own earnings, granted women the right to a portion of the father's inheritance and the discretion to use it as they saw fit, allowed women to be witnesses in court with some limitations, abolished female infanticide, specified that the wife must receive a dowry from the husband upon marriage (the wife is allowed to use this dowry as she chooses and the husband cannot take it back in the event of a divorce), placed limits on polygamy, stipulated that orphan girls should not be forced to marry their guardians, specified ways to equitably resolve marital problems, and provided women the right to initiate divorce proceedings. It is also significant to note that if a Muslim married a Christian woman, he was not allowed to prevent her from going to church, and if she died, he was required to place her remains in the care of the Christian clergy. Furthermore, historian F. Roy Willis, the author of the book, *World Civilizations: From Ancient Times Through the Sixteenth Century*, explains that in the early years of Islam women were permitted to worship with the men in mosques; also, some women were allowed to study in religious institutions, and a few even became scholars in theology. Additionally, the wives of Muḥammad and the caliphs were permitted to participate in the political decision-making process.[17]

As it pertains to women, Muḥammad's Western critics often level charges of male chauvinism against Him because he condoned the practice of polygamy. A close look at this practice, however, shows that these charges are without merit. It is true that the Qur'án allows for four wives, but this decree must be placed within a proper historical context before it can be understood. In the seventh century, due to incessant warfare, there was very likely a shortage of men in Arabia. In the patriarchal society of that time, every man who died often left behind wives, daughters, sisters, and other relatives who had to be provided for and protected. Muḥammad was highly concerned about the abundance of unmarried women who could be easily exploited. He dealt with this issue by allowing for a limited and regulated form of polygamy. It must be emphasized that, in the pre-Islamic period, men could have as many wives as they desired, and as already mentioned, these women could be treated like slaves with no rights at all. Thus, within the above context, the Qur'ánic decree of four wives was actually a limitation rather than a license for new abuse. Muḥammad allowed this in order to give the surplus of widows and orphaned girls the opportunity to be married and to enjoy the legal rights of marriage.

Thus contrary to the Western stereotype of exotic harems created to fulfill the sexual appetites of Muḥammad and His male followers, polygamy actually served the critical, real needs of the Muslim community of that time. It must also be emphasized that Muḥammad added another regulation that protected the interests of women. He insisted that the husband must be scrupulously fair with all of his wives. If the husband is not confident that he can be strictly equitable with all of his wives, then he must maintain only one wife. According to historian Armstrong, Muslim law has extended this to mean that the husband must spend exactly "the same amount of time with each one of his wives," and must give each the exact same financial and legal status, as well as love all of them equally without the slightest preference for any one of them. This requirement, in actual practice, has had the effect of essentially ruling out polygamy in many (if not most) of the

Muslim communities of today. Armstrong explains that it "has been widely agreed in the Islamic world that mere human beings cannot" act with such impartiality, and thus, present-day Muslims should limit themselves to one wife. Indeed some Islamic countries have entirely forbidden polygamy based on Muḥammad's requirement.[18]

Sadly, even though Muḥammad inspired an impressive women's rights victory, the men began to introduce old gender prejudices into Islam, and over time, the advanced rights of women were eroded, especially through the use of ḥadíth (oral traditions that are attributed to Muḥammad and carry essentially the same authority as the actual writings contained in the Qur'án). Such oral traditions are open to interpretation and considerable numbers of them come from questionable origins and are of a dubious nature; yet they have been used in the Islamic world to reduce the status of women. Such corruptions of the true teachings, however, should not be allowed to cast a dark shadow on the exalted Prophet Muḥammad. Along these lines, Armstrong affirms that,

> . . . in fact the emancipation of women was dear to the Prophet's heart. . . . in the pre-Islamic period . . . women were treated as an inferior species, who had no legal existence. . . . What Muḥammad achieved for women was extraordinary. The very idea that a woman could be a witness or could inherit anything at all in her own right was astonishing. . . . In Christian Europe, women had to wait until the nineteenth century before they had anything similar: even then, the law remained heavily weighted towards men.[19]

Westerners often condemn Islam based on the current treatment of women in some fundamentalist Islamic countries. It is important to emphasize, however, that fundamentalist countries that impose very harsh measures against women—i.e. Saudi Arabia, where women are not permitted to even drive cars or vote, or Afghanistan, where women are routinely denied basic rights such as an education—are not representative of the overall Muslim world. Westerners typically assume that the Islam that is practiced in such rigidly extremist countries is the most authentic form of Islam. This is erroneous. Armstrong explains that the Wahhabism sect of Islam that controls Saudi Arabia is like the Christian Puritan sect that was once popular in England during the seventeenth century. In short, Puritanism and Wahhabism are not representative of their respective religions. Similarly, history professor Smith asserts that the harsh treatment of Saudi Arabian women is "the exception, not the norm" in the overall Muslim world. For example, even in the Shiite theocratic state of Iran, all women are allowed to vote, to be elected to parliament, to pursue professional careers such as law or medicine, and to drive cars even though they must remain veiled. The laws regarding the veil have recently been relaxed as reported by the book *Lipstick Jihad,* which states that it is now quite common to see women in Tehran with heavy makeup, wearing brightly colored skimpy veils and "scampering around in stiletto sandals and short tunics that [are] cinched at the waist."[20]

In relation to the above, it is truly ironic that Western Christians are often the first to point out the negative treatment of Muslim women as a way of showing the superiority of Christianity. Such a smug attitude is unwarranted considering the historical treatment of Christian women. It must be emphasized that the present-day rights of Western women were primarily won as a result of very recent secular movements and not as a result of Christian practices. Indeed, it would be fair to say that Western women won their rights in spite of the attitudes of many historical Christian leaders who believed that women were inferior and only fit for childbearing. Thomas Aquinas, for instance, a highly influential European Christian priest and future saint, stated that "woman is defective and misbegotten" and "woman is naturally subject to man, because in man the discretion of reason predominates." Based on such sentiments, Western women, for many centuries, were denied education and legal rights, were psychologically and physically abused by husbands who treated them as property, were not allowed to participate in religious leadership, and were suppressed from participation in the political process. French women, for instance, did not gain voting rights until 1945, and Swiss women were not permitted to vote until 1971.[21]

A considerable number of present-day Christians harbor a negative view of Islam. However, such a slanted view requires a very selective reading of history. Those who hold this view are very likely ignoring much of the information provided above, and often seem to consider the Christian historical record as somehow above reproach. In fact, the documented record shows a vast array of atrocities that were committed in the name of Christ such as the European Inquisitions, the Crusades, the burning of women as witches, and the genocide of American Indians. It is also significant to note that after the Christians took control of Spain in 1492, they required all Jews and Muslims to convert to Christianity or face imprisonment and expulsion. This is in striking contrast to the 700 year rule of the Spanish Muslims who, as mentioned above, allowed Jews and Christians to worship and study freely in a spirit of relative harmony. The tolerance of the Spanish Muslims also contrasts sharply with the intolerance of King Louis IX of France, a canonized saint of the Church and a vehement Muslim-hater who led two crusades against Islam. Louis is also known to have said that the best way to debate with a Jew was to slay him "with a good thrust in the belly as far as the sword will go."[22]

The long history of Western anti-Islamic hatred played a major role not only in the Crusades but also in the West's incursions into Muslim areas starting in the nineteenth century. During the 1800s and the early 1900s, the Europeans invaded and colonized the Islamic states of Algiers, Aden, Tunisia, Egypt, the Sudan, Libya, and Morocco; indeed, in 1920, "Britain and France carved up the Middle East between them" and took control of this region by setting up mandates and protectorates. Today's Muslim world views these more recent European imperialistic invasions as being a continuation of the Christian Crusades of the past. In many respects, the Muslims are not wrong in thinking this because, in actuality, Christian missionary work was an intrinsic part of these more recent incursions into Muslim lands. Missionaries typically showed a blatant contempt for Islam and supported the colonial invasions, no matter how bloody, as a means of bringing the Gospel to an inferior people. Significantly, in addition to anti-Islamic prejudice, the European conquerors began to develop a racial prejudice against the Arabs, who were viewed as being "irredeemably childish and the diametrical opposite" of the White European. Such contempt has been obvious in the historical efforts of American and European oil companies and Western intelligence agencies (such as the CIA) to destabilize Middle Eastern governments and to impose authoritarian regimes that do not serve the interests of the native Muslim peoples.[23] Armstrong makes a connection between the above history and the recent rise of radical Islamic fundamentalism:

. . . many Muslims are trying to discover a new identity and to return to their own roots. This has been a theme in the so-called fundamentalist movements in recent years. Not only have Muslims felt humiliated and degraded before the external power of the West, but they have felt disoriented and lost because their own traditions seem to be swamped by the dominant Western culture. The secularism which we have cultivated . . . has sprung from our own traditions, but in the Islamic countries it seems alien and foreign—of negative rather than positive import. A generation of people has grown up in the Islamic world at home neither in the East nor in the West, and the answer . . . radical Muslims have sought to root themselves more securely in their Islamic past. Another theme of the new fundamentalism has been an attempt to get Islamic history back on the right track and to make the *umma* [Muslim community] effective and strong once again.[24]

At this point, it must be made clear that my endeavor to set the record straight on Muḥammad and His teachings should not be misconstrued as an attempt to paint a rosy picture of modern-day Islam. Like all the other faiths that came before it, Islam, a great religion that once helped to elevate the human condition, has now become subject to manmade corruptions that have altered the original intention of its beloved Prophet-Founder. In short, Muḥammad preached a message of peace, justice, reconciliation, and fellowship. Sadly, over time, this message has been progressively altered and tainted by the actions of unwise believers. This is nothing new. As explained earlier, all religions must go through a cyclical process from spring to winter. Nonetheless, the main point here is that Western efforts (by Christians and secularists) to impugn the blessed character and noble teachings of this mighty Prophet are untenable. The Bahá'í Faith rejects such biased notions and unequivocally affirms that this exalted Prophet contributed a key part to the progressive evolution of the one Religion of God:

> . . . an illiterate Man produced a book [Qur'án] in which, in a perfect and eloquent style, He explained the divine attributes and perfections. . . . In short, many Oriental peoples have been reared for thirteen centuries under the shadow of the religion of Muḥammad. During the Middle Ages, while Europe was in the lowest depths of barbarism, the Arab peoples were superior to the other nations of the earth in learning, in the arts, mathematics, civilization, government and other sciences. The Enlightener and Educator of these Arab tribes, and the Founder of the civilization and perfections of humanity among these different races, was an illiterate Man, Muḥammad. Was this illustrious Man a thorough Educator or not? A just judgment is necessary.[25]

"Christian Salvation"
as a Barrier to Recognizing Bahá'u'lláh

A few words must be said regarding the concept of salvation especially since it is a conception that has become grievously enshrouded with misunderstandings. Often, the very idea of salvation itself is offensive to people. The misguided notions of some Christians have not been very helpful in this regard. Significant numbers of Christians, for instance, contend that only believers in Christ are saved and that the followers of all other religions are doomed to suffer eternal damnation in hell. This stems from misinterpretations of the Bible that lead such believers to argue that Christ is the only Lord and Savior and that all other religions are false. In support of such claims, Christians often quote Jesus' words "I am the way, the truth, and the life: no man cometh unto the Father [God], but by me." Clearly, such notions call to question the very idea of progressive revelation and also cast a pall over the proclaimed station and mission of Bahá'u'lláh.

Contrary to the superiority claims of such Christians, Bahá'ís, as stated earlier, accept the divinity of all the Manifestations of God, Who founded the world's major religions. In this respect, it is necessary to understand that the divinity of Christ does not lie in His physical human frame, but rather, in the power of the Holy Spirit that animated Him. It was this power of the Holy Spirit that Jesus was referring to when He said that He is "the way, the truth, and the life." Importantly, this same Holy Spirit also animated all the other Prophets Who came before and after Christ within the Prophetic Cycle such as Abraham, Krishna, Moses, Zoroaster, Buddha, Muḥammad, and the Báb. Therefore, all of these other Prophets can also be considered "the way, the truth, and the life." These Messengers shared the same primary mission—to prepare humanity for the coming of the Promised One (Bahá'u'lláh), Who, according to prophecies contained in Their holy books, will bring the Kingdom of God on earth and will proclaim the oneness of religion and the universal fellowship of mankind.

Christian superiority claims are also inconsistent with the attributes of God. If God is indeed omniscient, omnipotent, and all-merciful, then why would He not allow His teachings and guidance to reach all peoples throughout the planet from the very beginnings of human evolution and development? Are we to believe that, before the advent of Christ, all people were unsaved, and that, even after the advent of Christ, people living in remote areas away from the Middle East (such as the American Indians) with no access to the Bible were also unsaved? It makes intuitive and logical sense that all people would have an equal opportunity to access divine guidance as they otherwise could not be held accountable for their failure to do so. The Bahá'í writings support the idea that, throughout time, God has sent His Messengers throughout the globe to spread His divine laws, commandments, and teachings to all peoples.

Most Protestant Christians also believe that they are saved solely by professing their faith in Jesus Christ and not as a result of any of their works (deeds). For instance, the popular notion of "once saved always saved" stipulates that Christians who have professed their belief in Jesus as their "Lord and Savior" can never lose their salvation regardless of their subsequent actions. According to this perspective, at the moment of death, an individual is judged and then sent either to eternal damnation (hell) or to eternal life (heaven). Of course, within this paradigm, any professed believers in Christ, are assured instant admittance to heaven (salvation). Critics, however, argue that ministers who preach this doctrine of "salvation through grace alone" are essentially giving people a license to do as they please because this doctrine would allow even incorrigibly malicious people, such as habitual swindlers, the security of knowing that they have a place in heaven with all other Christians. In contrast to such misconceptions, the Bahá'í writings make it clear that personal salvation requires both consistent work (deeds) on the part of individuals as well as the grace of God: "No matter how strong the measure of Divine grace, unless supplemented by personal, sustained and intelligent effort, it cannot become fully effective and be of any real and abiding advantage." Similarly, Bahá'u'lláh declares, "Let deeds, not words, be your adorning." Furthermore, in contrast to the false sense of security that is promulgated by many evangelical preachers, Bahá'u'lláh says "none knoweth what his own end shall be." Thus individual Bahá'ís cannot claim that they are saved, much less claim that anyone else is unsaved.[26]

The Bahá'í writings paint a very different picture of heaven and hell as compared to popular Christian understandings. In the Bahá'í paradigm, heaven and hell are spiritual states of the soul and do not refer to one particular static location or place. One can experience heaven or hell while yet here on Earth depending upon one's spiritual attitude, beliefs, and actions. Also, the terms heaven and hell are relative because there are levels of heaven and hell. Heaven means closeness to God while hell means separation from God. After death, individuals will experience different levels of heaven or hell depending upon the degree to which they evince (through their faith, virtues, and deeds) a closeness or a separation from God. On the one hand, people who, in this physical world, develop their spiritual attributes, seek guidance from the teachings of the Messengers (especially the latest Messenger), and live lives full of virtue and good deeds will likely be at the highest levels in the next world. Shoghi Effendi states, "Such earnest souls, when they pass out of this life, enter a state of being far nobler and more beautiful than this one. . . . We should face death with joy especially if our life upon this plane of existence has been full of good deeds."[27]

On the other hand, people who, in this physical world, neglect to develop their spiritual attributes, reject the teachings of the divine Messengers, and live self-centered lives full of misdeeds will likely be at the lowest levels in the next world. It should be noted that justice, mercy, rewards, and punishments, must all be placed in an eternal perspective. This means that we will not experience all the rewards of our good deeds and all the punishments of our bad deeds in this physical world—many rewards and punishments will not be experienced until we enter the next world.

In essence, the next world is made up of various gradations of consciousness and spiritual development. This is similar to the physical world, where we find a variety of creatures that exist at different levels of consciousness and development such as rocks, plants, animals, and human beings. Within this context, individuals who live their lives intransigently committed to godlessness will, after death, very likely enter the spiritual world at the lowest level similar to the rocks that exist at the lowest level in this physical world. However, even in the next world, such people will have the opportunity, if they put forth the effort, to develop themselves spiritually and to progress into the higher levels of heaven although they will be starting from a lower station. The writings state that individuals can "progress indefinitely, as spiritual progress in the other world is limitless" and also that the "progress of the soul does not come to an end with death" but it "starts along a new line." Furthermore, God's mercy is always in operation; thus, "He can accept into His heaven, which is really nearness to Him, even the lowliest if He pleases." In other words, there is no such thing as "eternal damnation" as described by some Christians. The opportunity to get closer to God (to evolve into the higher levels of heaven) is always available, but we must earnestly put forth the effort.[28]

Ministers emphasize that every human being is "fallen" (evil) as the result of the original sin that was committed by Adam and Eve, and that we can only be saved by Christ's sacrifice on the cross and His physical resurrection to wash us clean of our sins (atonement). The doctrine holds that Jesus Christ paid for the original sin, and we are now free (provided that we make a simple proclamation inviting Jesus into our hearts as Lord and Savior). Most Evangelical sermons contain this message in some form or other. Regrettably, such notions actually confuse the true nature of salvation. As will be explained below, the Bahá'í Faith does not support these typical Christian understandings such as the concept of original sin.

The Bahá'í writings state that "creation is purely good" and that human beings were created "noble." These teachings assert that human beings have two natures: a physical animalistic lower nature (the body and ego) and a higher spiritual nature (the soul). Both of these natures are good; however, the lower nature can "develop into a monster of selfishness, brutality, lust, and so on" unless it is placed under the control of the higher nature. The higher nature, or soul, is created by God at the moment of conception, and it is endowed with innate divine qualities and noble virtues such as the power of reason, willpower, the ability for self-sacrificing love, generosity, forgiveness, truthfulness, humility, and compassion. However, these qualities and virtues lie latent or dormant in the soul. Thus, while yet on this earth, one must struggle to awaken and to develop these innate traits so that they can be properly and consistently expressed. Indeed, the purpose of the Messengers is to provide a spiritual education so that human beings may learn to develop the innate qualities and virtues that lie dormant within them. Along these lines, the Bahá'í writings maintain that an evil force, person, or entity such as Satan or the

Devil does not exist. Even though human beings are created good (no original sin), they become capable of committing "evil" or "sin" when they allow their lower natures to dominate. Indeed, within this context, Satan is viewed as the personification of man's lower nature, the animalistic ego, which can take control over the higher spiritual nature. For the purposes of our main discussion, the point here is that some Christian notions such as original sin, evil, physical resurrection, atonement, Satan, and so forth, obscure the true reality of salvation—people are left with the impression that "being saved" is as simple as asking Jesus to simply "wash away our sins" and to protect us from the external "Devil"—in other words, a salvation without effort and a victory without any self-sacrifice. In actuality, salvation requires a lifelong internal struggle against the incessant, egotistical "self" (Satan). It is not a one-time event.

In contrast to prevailing Christian doctrines that place an exceedingly high emphasis on individualistic, personal salvation, the Bahá'í Faith primarily emphasizes the importance of the collective salvation of mankind. Shoghi Effendi, for instance, states, "The whole object of our lives is bound up with the lives of all human beings; not a personal salvation we are seeking, but a universal one. . . . Our aim is to produce a world civilization which will in turn react on the character of the individual. It is, in a way, the inverse of Christianity, which started with the individual unit and through it reached out to the conglomerate life of man."[29]

Thus, to be of any abiding value, the concept of salvation must be linked with actual efforts to "produce a world civilization." At this point in human evolution, people must move beyond the limited discourse of "being saved" and of having a "personal Lord and Savior" and must begin to talk of practical ways that they are contributing to universal salvation and the creation of a world civilization. The idea that people can easily and freely (without self-sacrifice) be saved by Jesus is likely to create a passive, complacent attitude in believers. This attitude shows up when believers (or "receivers") shop around for a church that can best fulfill their personal wants and needs rather than looking for a church that expects its members to be active participants who willingly volunteer their time and energy to support the needs of others. For Bahá'ís, the road to universal salvation is clear—they must first draw their inspiration and strength from the mystical forces unleashed by Bahá'u'lláh, and then, actively channel their energies, resources, and self-sacrificing deeds, through the world-encompassing communities, services, and institutions of the Bahá'í Faith. In short, as expressed by the Báb in the following passage, the days of "idle worship" are over and in this, the Day of God, people must now "gird up the loins of endeavor":

> You are the bearers of the name of God in this Day. You have been chosen as the repositories of His mystery. It behooves each one of you to manifest the attributes of God, and to exemplify by your deeds and words the signs of His righteousness, His power and glory. . . . For verily I say, this is the Day spoken of by God in His Book: "On that day will We set a seal upon their mouths yet shall their hands speak unto Us, and their feet shall bear witness to that which they shall have done." . . . Verily I say, immensely exalted is this Day above the days of the Apostles of old. Nay, immeasurable is the difference! You are the witnesses of the Dawn of the promised Day of God. You are the partakers of the mystic chalice of His [Bahá'u'lláh's] Revelation. Gird up the loins of endeavor, and be mindful of the words of God as revealed in His Book: "Lo, the Lord thy God is come, and with Him is the company of His angels arrayed before Him!" Purge your hearts of worldly desires, and let angelic virtues be your adorning. Strive that by your deeds you may bear witness to the truth of these words of God. . . . The days when idle worship was deemed sufficient are ended. The time is come when naught but the purest motive, supported by deeds of stainless purity, can ascend to the throne of the Most High and be acceptable unto Him.[30]

Why Are the Prevailing Religions So Impotent?

Unfortunately, vast segments of humanity are still clinging on to religions that have already finished their development cycles from spring to winter. Largely due to family and ethnic traditions as well as the misguided pressure of religious leaders, the masses of humankind continue to cleave onto the "wintry" religions of the past rather than recognizing the new dispensation for this Day. It is likely that many are following the religious traditions of their parents and grandparents without having given it much thought. Every human soul has the capacity to independently investigate and recognize the signs and tokens of God's Messengers, and yet, based on historical evidence, very few people actually recognize a new Manifestation when He first appears. Akin to the religious believers who first rejected Moses, or those who rejected Christ, as well as the multitudes who rejected Muḥammad and the Báb, many are currently turning a deaf ear to the claims of Bahá'u'lláh. The historical records support the assertion that people are most likely to cling onto the religion of their forefathers rather than to sincerely investigate the claims of a new Messenger. As a result of this tendency, the progressive revelation of the will of God has been consistently thwarted throughout history, and this has dramatically reduced the overall effectiveness of religion.

It is significant to note that the major religions of the world currently have huge bodies of believers, and yet, these large bodies of religious people have proven themselves quite powerless to effect real substantive transformation in today's world. In many parts of the United States, for instance, Christian churches are abundant and ubiquitous throughout the cities; nonetheless, all of the following problems continue unabated: government and business corruption, socioeconomic injustice, racial separation and disunity, broken marriages, alienated youth, abandoned elders, violence, addictions, crime, and immoral vices of all kinds.

Ironically, it would be fair to say that the various religions, as they are currently practiced, actually represent major impediments to spiritual growth, unity, peace, and justice because of the problems resulting from rigid fundamentalism, sectarian conflicts between denominations, traditional superstitious thinking, and religious prejudice and hypocrisy. Unfortunately, each separate religion continues to falsely claim that it solely and distinctively represents the will of God here on earth rather than acknowledging that it represents just a stage in the evolution of the one unfolding religion of God. Each religion of the past should be respected as having contributed its fair share to the common religious heritage of the human race; however, collective humanity cannot progress any further unless considerable numbers of people seek and ultimately find the latest teachings of God for this day. In this regard, it is important to emphasize that the Bahá'í Faith does not represent itself as a separate spiritual impulse but rather as the latest spiritual scion or sovereign descendant of the previous religious dispensations. As prophesied by the former Messengers, this spiritual scion will inevitably unify the family of religions. In the following passage, Shoghi Effendi eloquently and succinctly describes the station of the Bahá'í Faith in relation to the religions of the past:

In conclusion of this theme, I feel, it should be stated that the Revelation identified with Bahá'u'lláh abrogates unconditionally all the Dispensations gone before it, upholds uncompromisingly the eternal verities they enshrine, recognizes firmly and absolutely the Divine origin of their Authors, preserves inviolate the sanctity of their authentic Scriptures, disclaims any intention of lowering the status of their Founders or of abating the spiritual ideals they inculcate, clarifies and correlates their functions, reaffirms their common, their unchangeable and fundamental purpose, reconciles their seemingly divergent claims and doctrines, readily and gratefully recognizes their respective contributions to the gradual unfoldment of one Divine Revelation, unhesitatingly acknowledges itself to be but one link in the chain of continually progressive Revelations, supplements their teachings with such laws and ordinances as conform to the imperative needs, and are dictated by the growing receptivity, of a fast evolving and constantly changing society, and proclaims its readiness and ability to fuse and incorporate the contending sects and factions into which they have fallen into a universal Fellowship, functioning within the framework, and in accordance with the precepts, of a divinely conceived, a world-unifying, a world-redeeming Order.[31]

Sadly, due to the conflicting claims of the separate religions, many people have become disillusioned and do not know where to turn for spiritual guidance and truth. Bahá'u'lláh explains that the greatest human oppression occurs when people are unable to find spiritual truth because they are hopelessly confused by the misleading conflicting doctrines of religious leaders who all claim to be accurately interpreting the Word of God:

> Such a condition as this is witnessed in this day when the reins of every community have fallen into the grasp of foolish leaders. . . . On their tongue the mention of God hath become an empty name; in their midst His holy Word a dead letter. . . . Though they recognize in their hearts the Law of God to be one and the same, yet from every direction they issue a new command, and in every season proclaim a fresh decree. No two are found to agree on one and the same law, for they seek no God but their own desire, and tread no path but the path of error. . . . What "oppression" is more grievous than that a soul seeking the truth, and wishing to attain unto the knowledge of God, should know not where to go for it and from whom to seek it? For opinions have sorely differed, and the ways unto the attainment of God have multiplied.[32]

A cursory look at the history of religion shows that religious leaders, a class of supposedly learned people who should be the first to recognize the advent of a new Messenger, have ironically been some of the first to condemn the new Messenger and to renounce His dispensation as an apostasy or heresy. Quintessential examples of this are the crucifixion of Christ instigated by the Jewish Pharisees, the unholy persecution of Muḥammad at the hands of idolater religious leaders, and the martyrdom of the Báb (by firing squad) instigated by Muslim mullahs. Unfortunately, many religious believers even today are still choosing to automatically follow the lead of their ministers, priests, rabbis, mullahs, ulamas, monks, gurus, or other religious clergy rather than to follow their own independent search for truth wherever it may be found.

Ecclesiastical leaders have historically used all forms of social and psychological pressure (for example, the threat of hell-fire), and in some cases, even physical intimidation to keep their flocks from freely investigating spiritual questions and openly exploring other religions. This is likely why Bahá'u'lláh expresses some of His strongest censure against the many egotistical religious clerics, who in pursuit of worldly power, have effectively kept their followers from recognizing the truth of the Bahá'í dispensation. Bahá'u'lláh suffered incredible persecution (torture, imprisonment, and banishment) for about forty years of His life due to the actions of Muslim clerics who did everything in their power to attempt to destroy the Bahá'í Faith. Bahá'u'lláh notes that religious leaders who reject the new revelation from God are like beasts that prey upon their followers:

In leadership they have recognized the ultimate object of their endeavor, and account pride and haughtiness as the highest attainments of their heart's desire. They have placed their sordid machinations above the divine decree, have renounced resignation unto the will of God, busied themselves with selfish calculation, and walked in the way of the hypocrite. With all their power and strength they strive to secure themselves in their petty pursuits, fearful lest the least discredit undermine their authority or blemish the display of their magnificence. Were the eye to be anointed and illumined with the collyrium of the knowledge of God, it would surely discover that a number of voracious beasts have gathered and preyed upon the carrion of the souls of men.[33]

Partly to purify the religion of God from the above corruption and to redistribute religious authority in the hands of the common people, Bahá'u'lláh completely abolished the station of clergy within the Bahá'í Faith. The Faith is organized around administrative decision-making bodies known as spiritual assemblies. Every city where nine or more Bahá'ís reside has a Local Spiritual Assembly that helps to guide the Bahá'í community at the local level. There are also National Spiritual Assemblies to help guide and organize Bahá'í communities at the national level. Then at the international level, the Universal House of Justice is the supreme governing body of the Bahá'í world community. As a decision-making body comprised of nine elected members, the Universal House of Justice has ultimate authority in any questions regarding the Faith. It must be emphasized, however, that the individual members of the House of Justice have no special standing. Unlike the leaders of other religions, the members (*as individuals*) have no power to authoritatively interpret scripture or to determine official policies on matters pertaining to the Faith. The members of the House of Justice are democratically elected every five years while members of Local and National Spiritual Assemblies are elected every year. Spiritual Assembly members, just like members of the House of Justice, have no special standing or authority as individuals.

Professional clerical members typically pride themselves on their theological learning and their professed special ability to interpret abstruse scriptural passages and prophecies; thus, many such clerics reject the idea that the laypeople (the flock) have the ability to independently discover divine truth. However, the Báb makes it clear that pride in one's acquired knowledge can be a mighty barrier to recognizing a new Messenger of God: "such as are conceited will not suffer themselves to be guided. They will be debarred from the Truth, some by reason of their learning, others on account of their glory and power."[34]

Highly respected religious leaders, as well as any other learned people, who do not show forth a spirit of humility and self-effacement will be unlikely to recognize the transcendent powers of the Bahá'í revelation. Along these lines, the Bahá'í writings point out that in Isfahan, a Persian city known for its religious seminaries and its vast numbers of respected Muslim clerics, "only its sifter of wheat" recognized the Báb as a Manifestation of God.[35] Noting that many seemingly pious people will dismiss or reject the advent of the Promised One (Bahá'u'lláh), the Báb states,

This is the mystery . . . concerning this Revelation . . . the abased shall be exalted and the exalted shall be abased. Among those to whom it will never occur that they might merit the displeasure of

God, and whose pious deeds will be exemplary unto everyone, there will be many who will become the personification of the nethermost fire itself, when they fail to embrace His [Bahá'u'lláh's] Cause; while among the lowly servants whom no one would imagine to be of any merit, how great the number who will be honored with true faith and on whom the Fountainhead of generosity will bestow the robe of authority.[36]

Thus in the face of confusion among prominent religious leaders, as well as widespread disillusionment and despair in the general ranks of people, the revelation of Bahá'u'lláh represents the dawning of a new divine springtime, a luminous message of peace and hope that contains within it the God-given power to truly transform the hearts and minds of a weary humanity. In contrast, the religions of old are akin to a body without the spirit. These religions may even have many earnest believers who are sincerely trying to apply religious disciplines and teachings; however, they are attempting to create a new world with outmoded tools that are no longer effective in this new spiritual cycle. Many such believers yearn to be transported into new domains of the spirit, but are unfortunately attempting to travel to the new spiritual realms on a dated religious "vessel" whose powers and capacities are greatly diminished. Along these lines, Bahá'u'lláh describes Himself as the "Divine Physician" Who knows the ailments of today's peoples and is able to prescribe the necessary remedies. He laments, however, that other "ignorant physicians" (some religious leaders and government officials) are attempting to do the work that only He can do. Bahá'u'lláh explains that every age has special divine remedies, and the religious prescriptions of the past will not cure the problems of today:

> The Prophets of God should be regarded as physicians whose task is to foster the well-being of the world and its peoples. . . . Little wonder, then, if the treatment prescribed by the physician in this day should not be found to be identical with that which he prescribed before. How could it be otherwise when the ills

affecting the sufferer necessitate at every stage of his sickness a special remedy? In like manner, every time the Prophets of God have illumined the world . . . they have invariably summoned its peoples to embrace the light of God through such means as best befitted the exigencies of the age in which they appeared.[37]

Great Strides in a Short Period of Time

In spite of its young age, the Bahá'í Faith has already made tremendous strides that are unparalleled in religious history. For instance, it is now the second most widespread religion on earth, second only to Christianity in terms of geographic distribution. By way of comparison, it is significant to note that Christianity was a tiny obscure religion for about the first three hundred years of its existence until Constantine, a Roman emperor, became a Christian convert. It then took several centuries more for Christianity to spread to diverse parts of the world beyond the Mediterranean region. In contrast, the Bahá'í Faith has been in existence for only a little over a century and a half, and yet, it is now probably the most diverse organized body of people on earth including individuals from more than 2,100 ethnic, racial, and tribal groups from throughout the planet.

Another impressive aspect of this relatively young Faith is that its unity, as a single distinct religion, is still intact. In contrast, a perusal of religious history reveals that each of the major world religions quickly splintered apart into a variety of contending sects after the passing of its particular Prophet-Founder. This was clearly the case with Christianity. It broke into a multiplicity of competing groups within a short period after the crucifixion of Christ. It is important to understand that, prior to the Bahá'í dispensation, the Messengers of God did not leave written covenants or clearly written instructions regarding the naming of a successor. As a result of this, schism occurred, and each of the great religions of the past tragically fractured apart. Quite simply, in each case, infighting became a major problem because the believers lacked a clear successor who could make binding decisions and who could deliver authoritative interpretations of the religion's holy scriptures.

Bahá'u'lláh, unlike all the previous Messengers, left explicit written guidance as to who would be His immediate successor. This covenant with His believers is known as the "Lesser Covenant," and it is unprecedented in the history of religion. Before His ascension, He wrote the "Book of the Covenant" as well as other documents in which He named His eldest son, 'Abdu'l-Bahá, as His successor. This Covenant stipulated that all Bahá'ís were to turn to 'Abdu'l-Bahá as the exemplar and head of the Faith as well as the authoritative interpreter of the Bahá'í sacred scriptures. In the passage below, 'Abdu'l-Bahá explains the importance of the Covenant, and in the process, he quotes an excerpt from the writings of Bahá'u'lláh:

> Inasmuch as great differences and divergences of denominational belief had arisen throughout the past, every man with a new idea attributing it to God, Bahá'u'lláh desired that there should not be any ground or reason for disagreement among the Bahá'ís. Therefore, with His own pen He wrote the Book of His Covenant, addressing His relations and all people of the world, saying, "Verily, I have appointed One ['Abdu'l-Bahá] Who is the Center of My Covenant. All must obey Him; all must turn to Him; He is the Expounder of My Book, and He is informed of My purpose. . . . Whatsoever He says is correct, for, verily, He knoweth the texts of My Book. Other than He, no one doth know My Book."[38]

As noted in the quote above, Bahá'u'lláh gave 'Abdu'l-Bahá the title "Center of the Covenant"—a Covenant, which was to preserve the unity of the believers and protect the faith from schism. In 1908, 'Abdu'l-Bahá (as authorized by the Covenant of Bahá'u'lláh) wrote a will formally known as the Will and Testament of 'Abdu'l-Bahá. In this official document, he named his grandson Shoghi Effendi as his successor who likewise was to maintain the unity of the believers. Shoghi Effendi passed away in 1957 without naming a successor, and thus, he was the last individual who acted as head of the Bahá'í Faith.

Fortunately, as a part of His Covenant, Bahá'u'lláh not only appointed His immediate successor, but He also left written instructions for the eventual creation of the Universal House of Justice, the democratically elected institution that all present-day Bahá'ís turn to as the supreme governing body of the Bahá'í Faith. The House of Justice now maintains the unity of the believers by providing authoritative guidance on various spiritual and administrative matters. Importantly, as Bahá'u'lláh conferred the power of infallibility upon this institution in His writings, its decisions are considered to be infallible. It is also significant to note that the House of Justice, as the primary legislative authority of the Bahá'í Faith, is empowered to create new laws (as well as repeal its own laws) as necessary in order to meet the needs of an evolving humanity. Bahá'u'lláh, Himself, endowed the House of Justice with this legislative authority. Any new laws, however, must not contravene any of the writings of Bahá'u'lláh, 'Abdu'l-Bahá, and Shoghi Effendi. The writings of these three figures as well as the writings of the Universal House of Justice are considered authoritative, infallible, and binding by all Bahá'ís throughout the world.

At various times in Bahá'í history, some egotistical personalities have attempted to split off to form their own sects. Such splinter groups, however, have attracted only a handful of people and have quickly died for lack of membership. These attempts to break the unity of the Faith have failed miserably due to the enduring power of the Covenant of Bahá'u'lláh.

Thus, in a relatively short period of time, the Bahá'í Faith has successfully established itself as a unified body of diverse believers, who all turn to the same authoritative writings and to the same supreme governing institution for direction and guidance. This is important because a religion cannot unify the people of the planet unless it itself is unified. In many places throughout the globe, diverse groups of Bahá'í believers (including some people who were previously hostile to each other) now worship together in Bahá'í gatherings and peacefully work together in service projects to uplift their communities.

In one of His sacred tablets, Bahá'u'lláh declares, "We, verily, have come for your sakes, and have borne the misfortunes of the world for your salvation."[39] The early successes of the Bahá'í Faith in fostering peace and unity speak volumes regarding the supreme power of His revelation to bring salvation to the world. It is within this context and with the other understandings developed in this chapter that we can now turn our attention to describing more specifically the destiny of the United States and the mission of the American Bahá'í community.

Chapter Four

THE NATION THAT "WILL LEAD ALL NATIONS SPIRITUALLY"

After the September 11 attacks on the World Trade Center's Twin Towers and during the war that followed, countless Americans proudly displayed bumper stickers, posters, t-shirts, and even coffee mugs that proclaimed "God bless America." In the aftermath of the terrorist attack, many Americans expressed their solidarity by gathering together to pray and to sing patriotic songs such as "God Bless America" and "America the Beautiful," which states in part, "America! America! God shed His grace on thee . . ." Such mixing of religious symbolism and nationalism is not a new phenomenon. Indeed, for many generations, Americans have been raised on a steady diet of nationalism that utilizes religious symbolism to express the assumption that the Americans are somehow God's new chosen people. This can be traced back to the Puritans of the early 1600s, who believed that they were preordained to build a pure Christian utopia in America or God's "City Upon a Hill." These colonists identified America as the New Canaan and viewed the American Indians as satanic forces who had to be thrown out or destroyed like the ancient Canaanites of the Bible. Likewise, during the revolutionary war, many colonists intentionally adopted Biblical imagery to portray themselves as the new Israelites who had the divine right to rule the American Promised Land with the help of the American Joshua or Moses (George Washington) while the British were portrayed as the Egyptian soldiers. The book *God's New Israel: Religious Interpretations of American Destiny* provides a detailed look at how Promised Land imagery played an important role in shaping English colonial thought.

Starting in the 1840s, Americans routinely cited the popular doctrine of manifest destiny to justify the conquest of vast segments of the North American continent. Based on this doctrine, many Americans believed that it was their God-given destiny to conquer the land from "sea to shining sea" and to claim territories in other parts of the world even if it meant attacking and dispossessing American Indians, Mexicans, and other peoples. Along these lines, as a part of what became known as the "White man's burden," many Americans also developed the belief that it was the inevitable duty of the "superior" White race to dominate, to Christianize, and to eventually civilize the "inferior" non-White races. To this day, considerable numbers of Americans subscribe to a political ideology that is a mixture of Christian Evangelism and a form of militant nationalism that is rabidly pro-America often at the expense of other nations and peoples.

Despite such erroneous and unjustified use of the Bible in support of U.S. nationalism, it is important to emphasize here what should already be obvious—the Bible (written nearly 2,000 years before the American Revolution) does not mention in any shape or form the United States of America or its destiny. In essence, the early colonists and then subsequently the American citizens developed a Christian-based nationalistic mythology from thin air, a mythology that does not find any justification in the Bible.

Having said the above, it is fascinating to note that, unlike the Bible, the Bahá'í writings do have a treasure trove of information regarding the United States. In fact, a plethora of passages from the Bahá'í writings explain that the United States and its peoples do indeed have a special divine destiny. However, this special destiny has nothing to do with the faulty manmade notions described above. In fact, as will be shown in this chapter, America will be able to attain its true destiny only if it discards its false nationalistic doctrines. As will also be explained, the destiny of the United States is inextricably linked with the God-given mission of the American Bahá'ís. The writings make it clear that the nationwide community of American Bahá'ís who are resolutely building their institutions across the United States will play a crucial role in helping the United States to fulfill its ultimate destiny.

The Exalted Distinctions of the United States and the American Bahá'í Community

The Bahá'í writings acclaim the United States as the place where the "splendors of His light shall be revealed, where the mysteries of His Faith shall be unveiled," and as the nation that "will lead all nations spiritually." These scriptures also state that America will "evolve into a center from which waves of spiritual power will emanate, and the throne of the Kingdom of God will, in the plenitude of its majesty and glory, be firmly established." In a similarly prophetic passage, 'Abdu'l-Bahá states, "The American nation is equipped and empowered to accomplish that which will adorn the pages of history, to become the envy of the world, and be blest in both the East and the West for the triumph of its people." Furthermore, he affirms that the Americans are "indeed worthy of being the first to build the Tabernacle of the Great Peace and proclaim the oneness of mankind." He also declares that "heavenly illumination" will "stream" from America "to all the peoples of the world."[1]

Meanwhile, various Bahá'í passages refer to the special mission of the American Bahá'ís, who are acclaimed as "the champion-builders of the mightiest institutions of the Faith of Bahá'u'lláh," as "the torchbearers of a world-girdling civilization," and as "the spiritual descendants of the dawn-breakers [first believers] of the Heroic Age of our Faith." Shoghi Effendi acknowledges the "American Bahá'í Community" as being "exalted, singled out among sister communities of East and West." The writings further proclaim that this community "will 'find itself securely established upon the throne of an everlasting dominion,' when 'the whole earth' will be stirred and shaken by the results of its 'achievements' . . ." Similarly, referring to the American Bahá'ís, 'Abdu'l-Bahá declares, "Consider how exalted and lofty is the station you are destined to attain; how unique the favors with which you have been endowed." He adds, "Be not concerned with the smallness of your numbers, neither be oppressed by the multitude of an unbelieving world. . . . Exert yourselves; your mission is unspeakably glorious."[2]

Why were the United States and
Its Peoples Granted Special Distinctions?

At this point, one may wonder why the United States and the American Bahá'í community were singled out for such exalted distinctions. Were they singled out because of their inherent superiority? Interestingly, the writings make it clear that this was most definitely not the case. To the contrary, Shoghi Effendi emphasizes that these distinctions were granted not "by any reason of inherent excellence" of the United States and its peoples, but instead, "precisely by reason of the patent evils" that are pervasive within the American nation. He explains that, in this way, Bahá'u'lláh can best demonstrate to an unbelieving world that His revelation has the redemptive power to transform evil and vice into enlightenment and virtue. In other words, under such perverse and decadent circumstances, the Bahá'í Faith can display its immense capacity to develop and inspire a community of fervent American believers whose essential principles and virtues will stand in striking contrast to the "political corruption and the moral license increasingly staining the society to which they belong."[3] Shoghi Effendi states,

> It is by such means as this that Bahá'u'lláh can best demonstrate to a heedless generation His almighty power to raise up from the very midst of a people [Americans], immersed in a sea of materialism, a prey to one of the most virulent and long-standing forms of racial prejudice, and notorious for its political corruption, lawlessness and laxity in moral standards, men and women [Bahá'ís] who, as time goes by, will increasingly exemplify those essential virtues of self-renunciation, of moral rectitude, of chastity, of indiscriminating

fellowship, of holy discipline, and of spiritual insight that will fit them for the preponderating share they will have in calling into being that World Order and that World Civilization of which their country, no less than the entire human race, stands in desperate need.[4]

At the beginning of this chapter, I pointed out that much of our nation's nationalistic fervor is steeped in religious symbolism and Christian-inspired myths that find no justification in the Bible. Imbued with such erroneous nationalistic notions, some Americans, especially Christian Evangelicals, still seem to believe that God granted the United States and its people uniquely special blessings because of their moral, spiritual, and/or racial superiority. As already stated emphatically above, the Bahá'í Faith unequivocally rejects such notions of inherent American superiority. Furthermore, it must also be made clear that this nation's special destiny did not begin with the arrival of the Puritans to America in the early 1600s as claimed by many Evangelicals. Rather, as stated by Shoghi Effendi, this process started with "the outbreak of the first World War [1914] that threw the great republic of the West [the United States] into the vortex of the first stage of a world upheaval." In short, the special destiny of the United States is not directly linked with Christianity and the American Christian denominations but rather with the mystical processes that were set in motion by the Bahá'í dispensation and the American Bahá'í community.[5]

Some politicians often speak about the need to go back to "our roots as a Christian nation." For instance, the U.S. president during the 1980s delivered a speech calling on Americans to return to the values of "that old Pilgrim, John Winthrop" (John Winthrop is the Puritan leader who in 1630 stated that he and his followers were specially ordained by God to build a "City Upon a Hill" in America). Likewise, in the 1990s, another U.S. president stated, "let us [Americans] renew the solemn commitment that John Winthrop and his fellow Pilgrims made." Many conservative Christians, such as the presidents mentioned above, subscribe (sometimes unconsciously) to a philosophy known as "American Exceptionalism," which asserts that the United States is somehow special, almost holy, an exception, and set apart in relation to all other countries. Recent advocates of this philosophy argue that the United States, because of its "exceptionalism," should sometimes stand above (be an exception to) the international laws of nations. This philosophy, of course, stands in direct opposition to the idea of building a strong, binding code of international laws and treaties. Along similar lines, many Christian fundamentalists believe that the United States, as a powerful "Christian nation," has the God-given duty to battle Islam (which they view as evil) and also to resist any form of world government as exemplified by their often derisive attitude against the United Nations. Such notions and attitudes are readily apparent in Evangelical and American conservative radio, television, internet, and print media. The disdain for world government stems from the belief that such efforts undermine the sovereignty of the United States and thus limit its ability to act unilaterally in defense of its unique Christian worldview and traditions.

Interestingly, the term "new world order" has been used with different connotations in American discourse. In one context, it is used to mean an international order that is peaceful, but largely under the direction and control of the United States. The term was used in this context by a U.S. president during the First Persian Gulf War (1991) between the U.S. and Iraq. In other venues, this term has a completely negative connotation—archly conservative Americans are typically contemptuous of any movement or philosophy that, in their view, seems to be imposing what they commonly call a "new world order." As used in such a context, the term, "new world order" is a reference to a future world government that will limit the absolute sovereignty of the United States. This is highly ironic because, as will be explained in detail in the next section, the Bahá'í writings also use the term "New World Order" but with an entirely different connotation. The Bahá'í use of this term predates, by about a century, the derogatory use of the term that is typical among highly conservative Americans. Thus Bahá'í terminology is likely to set off all types of alarms in the minds of certain Americans.

Furthermore, in the view of many fundamentalist Christians, efforts to establish a world government or to impose a "new world order" are associated with the work of the Antichrist, who will supposedly attempt to establish his reign across the world (a misinterpretation of the Bible). Related to this is the belief that Jesus Christ will return again to establish the Kingdom of God on earth. Within this context, Christians differ as to who will actually be "saved" as a result of the "second coming" and who will be condemned to eternal damnation. Some fundamentalist Christians, for instance, believe that Catholics will not be saved, and some even believe that only members within their denomination will be saved. The "purity" of one's beliefs is the question here, which goes to show that the Puritan streak still runs strong within the American psyche. The Puritans left the supposedly impure Christianity of Europe in order to create a pure form of Christianity in America. For some present-day Christians, the idea of forming a world government is antithetical to the idea of maintaining the purity and separation of Christian America in preparation for the second coming of Christ. As mentioned above, even American presidents still exhort Americans to return to the values of their "Puritan roots." Ultimately, this Puritan streak manifests itself as a form of nationalism. Furthermore, many traditional Christians are generally raised with the expectation that the Kingdom of God on earth will appear supernaturally, magically, and instantly with the return of Christ. Within this Christian context, humankind will essentially play a passive role—the Kingdom will be established solely as an act of God. Thus the belief here is that there is no need for human beings to waste their time attempting to create a so-called new world order.

Sadly, from a Bahá'í standpoint, all the faulty attitudes and philosophies described above continue to serve as impediments that hinder the progress of America toward its true role in the world. Contrary to such views that portray the United States as being almost holy in relation to other countries, the Bahá'í writings explicitly state that, at the onset of WWI (1914), this nation was endowed with a special divinely inspired destiny expressly due to its moral, spiritual, political, and social deficiencies. Along these lines, the following Bahá'í passage mentions the false doctrine of absolute national sovereignty as well as some other deficiencies that the nation must successfully address before it can fulfill its true destiny—a destiny that will increasingly be forged in the crucible of trials and tribulations:

The American nation . . . stands . . . in grave peril. The woes and tribulations which threaten it are partly avoidable, but mostly inevitable and God-sent, for by reason of them a government and people clinging tenaciously to the obsolescent doctrine of absolute sovereignty and upholding a political system, manifestly at variance with the needs of a world already contracted into a neighborhood and crying out for unity, will find itself purged of its anachronistic conceptions, and prepared to play a preponderating role . . . in the unification of mankind, and in the establishment of a world federal government on this planet. These same fiery tribulations will not only firmly weld the American nation to its sister nations in both hemispheres, but will through their cleansing effect, purge it thoroughly of the accumulated dross which ingrained racial prejudice, rampant materialism, widespread ungodliness and moral laxity have combined, in the course of successive generations, to produce, and which have prevented her thus far from assuming the role of world spiritual leadership forecast by 'Abdu'l-Bahá's unerring pen—a role which she is bound to fulfill through travail and sorrow.[6]

The World Order of Bahá'u'lláh

At the beginning of this book, it was emphasized that any discussions pertaining to the destiny of the world, if they are to be complete, must be considered in light of the station and claims of Bahá'u'lláh. Indeed, a crucial understanding that was covered in earlier chapters is that the collective redemption of humankind is inextricably linked to the recognition that Bahá'u'lláh is the Messenger of God for this age, the awaited Promised Redeemer of all religions. In short, without Bahá'u'lláh, there is no redemption (and therefore no destiny) for collective humanity. Another fundamental understanding that was discussed earlier is that the revelation of Bahá'u'lláh has released mystical "forces" and "creative energies" throughout the planet and has infused the entire creation with new powers and immense capacities. In fact, it is these forces and creative energies that are already guiding the special destiny of the United States and its peoples. Furthermore, another key understanding is that Bahá'u'lláh, as the Mouthpiece of God on earth, has proclaimed that the will of God for this age is the establishment of world unity—the unification of humanity into one global family. This is why all the teachings of the Bahá'í Faith revolve around the pivotal concept of the "oneness of humanity." This is also why, as will be covered in this section, Bahá'u'lláh, unlike any other Messenger of the past, conceived of an entire system of universal laws and institutions that will ultimately lead to the establishment of a world government, a permanent peace between nations, and a united, divinely inspired global civilization.

The Bahá'í writings have an abundance of prophetic passages that explain that the United States and the American Bahá'í community will both play fundamental and vital roles in the creation of the "World Order of Bahá'u'lláh"—an entirely new, unified, and just global federation of nations based on the teachings of Bahá'u'lláh (also known as the "New World Order"). However, before we can speak more specifically about the special roles of the United States and the American Bahá'ís, it is important that we first cover, in some detail, the unique nature and features of the World Order that is described in the writings of Bahá'u'lláh, 'Abdu'l-Bahá, Shoghi Effendi, and the Universal House of Justice.

The vast and incomparable New World Order is envisaged as a unified, just, and peaceful global federation of nations based on the principles and teachings of Bahá'u'lláh. In one of his letters, Shoghi Effendi provided a summary of the essential aspects of the future World Order. The quote below includes only a part of Shoghi Effendi's important summary:

The unity of the human race, as envisaged by Bahá'u'lláh, implies the establishment of a world commonwealth in which all nations, races, creeds and classes are closely and permanently united, and in which the autonomy of its state members and the personal freedom and initiative of the individuals that compose them are definitely and completely safeguarded. This commonwealth must, as far as we can visualize it, consist of a world legislature, whose members will, as the trustees of the whole of mankind, ultimately control the entire resources of all the component nations, and will enact such laws as shall be required to regulate the life, satisfy the needs and adjust the relationships of all races and peoples. A world executive, backed by an international Force, will carry out the decisions arrived at, and apply the laws enacted by, this world legislature, and will safeguard the organic unity of the whole commonwealth. A world tribunal will adjudicate and deliver its compulsory and final verdict in all and any disputes that may arise between the various elements constituting this universal system. . . . A world script, a world literature, a uniform and universal system of currency, of weights and measures, will simplify and facilitate intercourse and understanding among the nations and races of mankind. In such a world society, science and religion, the two most potent forces in human life, will be reconciled, will cooperate, and will harmoniously develop. . . . The economic resources of the world will be organized, its sources of raw materials will be tapped and fully utilized, its markets will be coordinated and developed, and the distribution of its products will be equitably regulated. . . .

A world federal system, ruling the whole earth and exercising unchallengeable authority over its unimaginably vast resources, blending and embodying the ideals of both the East and the West, liberated from the curse of war and its miseries, and bent on the exploitation of all the available sources of energy on the surface of the planet, a system in which Force is made the servant of Justice, whose life is sustained by its universal recognition of one God and by its allegiance to one common Revelation—such is the goal towards which humanity, impelled by the unifying forces of life, is moving.[7]

The New World Order, as envisaged by Bahá'u'lláh, is described as unfolding in three successive stages extending over a fairly large period of time into the future. Bahá'ís believe that the first stage is already occurring. It is a period of widespread suffering and social breakdown that will progressively increase in intensity and scope. It is understood that all peoples and nations will be dramatically and pervasively affected by the increasing turmoil. According to Bahá'í prophecy, at some point in the undisclosed future an unprecedented worldwide cataclysmic crisis will occur that will signal the end of this first stage.

It is prophesied that, as a result of the unprecedented global convulsion, all the countries of the world will agree to pursue and enforce a political peace, which they will impose upon themselves through the establishment of international structures designed to safeguard the security of all nations. Based on a formal arrangement of "collective security," it is believed that all nations will agree to collectively arise against any aggressor nation in order to prevent the recurrence of war. Regarding this, Bahá'u'lláh states, "Should any one among you take up arms against another, rise ye all against him, for this is naught but manifest justice."[8]

According to current Bahá'í understandings, the second stage in humanity's development toward the New World Order is actually a multi-step process with no clear beginning point. This multi-step process may possibly even overlap somewhat with the first stage (the period of intense turmoil). However, the establishment of the worldwide political peace described in the paragraph above is regarded as a defining milestone in the development of the second stage. The second stage is commonly known among Bahá'ís as the Lesser Peace, and it primarily refers to the permanent cessation of all warfare as opposed to an all-encompassing, universal peace of complete (material and spiritual) proportions. It is believed that the nations of the world will eventually create a political peace of expediency that can be compared to the body without the soul. It is significant to note that, according to Bahá'í prophecy, the Lesser Peace will occur even though most of the world's people will be unaware of the Bahá'í dispensation. Shoghi Effendi explains that the nations of the earth will be "unconscious" of Bahá'u'lláh's revelation, "and yet unwittingly enforcing the general principles which He has enunciated." We must keep in mind that the mysterious spiritual forces unleashed by His revelation are constantly at work—relentlessly shaping human destiny and moving all nations and peoples (no matter how unwitting) closer to world unity. According to Bahá'í understandings, humankind will remain in the second stage of development for a long period of time before it enters into the third and final stage known as the "Most Great Peace."[9]

It is believed that, after an extended period of evolutionary development during the second stage, the peoples of the earth will become increasingly spiritualized and will eventually come to acknowledge the claims of the Bahá'í Faith. According to Bahá'í prophecy, this "spiritualization of the masses" will culminate in humanity's recognition of Bahá'u'lláh as the Promised One of all ages. It is prophesied that the generality of humanity will accept the Bahá'í dispensation and will internalize and begin to consciously implement Bahá'u'lláh's divine teachings for the unification of humankind. This milestone in human evolution is known as the Most Great Peace. The writings make it clear that this all-encompassing universal peace can come to pass only "consequent to the recognition of the character, and the acknowledgment of the claims, of the Faith of Bahá'u'lláh." Bahá'ís believe that the advent of the Most Great Peace will signal the official beginning or emergence of the World Order of Bahá'u'lláh along with its Bahá'í World Commonwealth (a world federation of nations based on the teachings of Bahá'u'lláh). Bahá'ís speak of the "unfurling of the banner of the Most Great Peace," which will proclaim to all of humankind that the glorious World Order is finally emerging.[10]

One of the most important features of the World Order of Bahá'u'lláh is that it will ultimately lead to the establishment of a world civilization that will "signalize the advent of the Kingdom of God on this earth." Along these lines, Shoghi Effendi explains that the promised World Order is "the shell ordained to enshrine that priceless jewel, the [divine] world civilization."[11] He further states,

Then will the coming of age of the entire human race be proclaimed and celebrated by all the peoples and nations of the earth. Then will the banner of the Most Great Peace be hoisted.

... Then will a world civilization be born, flourish, and perpetuate itself, a civilization with a fullness of life such as the world has never seen nor can as yet conceive. Then will the Everlasting Covenant be fulfilled in its completeness. Then will the promise enshrined in all the Books of God be redeemed, and all the prophecies uttered by the Prophets of old come to pass . . .[12]

Contributions to the World Order by the United States

The World Order of Bahá'u'lláh will become a glorious reality in the distant future. As mentioned above, the World Order will be created by the actions of both Bahá'ís and non-Bahá'ís. In this regard, we must keep in mind that the will of God is all powerful and all pervasive. In this Day, all things, in some shape or form, are ultimately contributing to God's will, which is to unify humanity. Thus some humanitarian philosophies and causes, while not completely in accord with the Bahá'í teachings, are nevertheless contributing toward the creation of the World Order of Bahá'u'lláh. For instance, some of the positive actions of the United Nations contribute to world unity and therefore contribute (no matter how unwittingly) toward the establishment of Bahá'u'lláh's Order. Along these lines, the Bahá'í writings explain that the American nation will play a vital role in the creation of the New World Order even though its "government and people alike" will largely remain unaware that they are "slowly, painfully, unwittingly, and irresistibly advancing towards the goal destined for it by both Bahá'u'lláh and 'Abdu'l-Bahá." Shoghi Effendi notes that America will promote "indirectly the institutions that are to be associated with the establishment of His World Order." He explains that this nation will play an essential role in helping to bring about the "political unification of the Eastern and Western Hemispheres." He further adds that it is also destined to play a vital role in "the emergence of a world government and the establishment of the Lesser Peace, as foretold by Bahá'u'lláh."[13]

Fittingly, Shoghi Effendi points out that 'Abdu'l-Bahá offered the following advice to a highly placed official of the U.S. federal government: "You can best serve your country if you strive, in your capacity as a citizen of the world, to assist in the eventual application of the principle of federalism, underlying the government of your own country, to the relationships now existing between the peoples and nations of the world."[14]

In *Citadel of Faith*, Shoghi Effendi enumerates some of the ways that the United States has already contributed toward the future establishment of the New World Order. For instance, he states,

This nation so signally blest, occupying so eminent and responsible a position in a continent so wonderfully endowed, was the first among the nations of the West to be warmed and illuminated by the rays of the Revelation of Bahá'u'lláh. . . . This nation, moreover, may well claim to have, as a result of its effective participation in both the first and second world wars, redressed the balance, saved mankind the horrors of devastation and bloodshed involved in the prolongation of hostilities, and decisively contributed, in the course of the latter conflict, to the overthrow of the exponents of ideologies [Nazism and Fascism] fundamentally at variance with the universal tenets of our Faith."[15]

Shoghi Effendi particularly recognizes the efforts of the "immortal Woodrow Wilson" to establish a League of Nations after World War I as an attempt to prevent future wars. Indeed, he asserts that the spiritual process associated with America's destiny "received its initial impetus through the formulation of President Wilson's Fourteen Points," and then "suffered its first setback" when the U.S. Congress refused to join the League. Nonetheless, he adds that Wilson "must be ascribed the unique honor, among statesmen of any nation" of having "voiced sentiments so akin to the principles animating the Cause of Bahá'u'lláh." Shoghi Effendi also commends Franklin D. Roosevelt's lead in helping to draft the 1941 Atlantic Charter, a joint declaration between the United States and Britain that laid down several principles for all nations including access to raw materials, the renunciation of all aggression, freedom from want and fear, disarmament of aggressor nations, and so forth. He furthermore speaks positively of the U.S. support for Greece and Turkey after World War II (the United States provided financial assistance to the war-torn nations of Europe through the Marshall Plan). He especially praises America's efforts to establish the United Nations during the San Francisco Conference. In 1947, he refers to the "splendid initiative taken, in recent years by the American government" to establish the United Nation's "permanent seat in the city of New York." He says that this effort "acquired added significance through the choice of the City of the Covenant [title given to New York City by 'Abdu'l-Bahá] itself as the seat of the newly born organization."[16]

As described in the paragraphs above, the mysterious spiritual forces released by Bahá'u'lláh have been guiding and will continue to guide the American government and the generality of Americans to "unwittingly" (without knowing) and "irresistibly" play a key role in the creation of the New World Order. In essence, the American citizens and their government are largely unaware of the divine hand that is shaping their actions in service to Bahá'u'lláh's vision. In contrast to this, the American Bahá'ís have been and will continue to be very conscious of the role that they must play (as laid out in the Bahá'í writings) in helping to bring about the World Order. In other words, the American Bahá'ís are very aware of how their goals and actions fit within the divine plan of God for this age. Regarding this, Shoghi Effendi describes "the workings of two simultaneous processes." One process directly serves the interests, goals, and administrative system of the Bahá'í Faith and is associated with the "mission of the American Bahá'í Community." The other process promotes indirectly the institutions and structures that will help establish the World Order and is associated with the "destiny of the American nation."[17] In *The Advent of Divine Justice*, he similarly states,

For no matter how ignorant of the Source from which those directing energies proceed, and however slow and laborious the process, it is becoming increasingly evident that the [American] nation as a whole, whether through the agency of its government or otherwise, is gravitating, under the influence of forces that it can neither comprehend nor control, towards such associations and policies, wherein, as indicated by 'Abdu'l-Bahá, her true destiny must lie. Both the community of the American believers, who are aware of that Source, and the great mass of their countrymen, who have not as yet recognized the Hand that directs their destiny, are contributing, each in its own way, to the realization of the hopes, and the fulfillment of the [prophetic] promises . . . of 'Abdu'l-Bahá."[18]

It would help here to differentiate between "a destiny" on the one hand and "a mission" on the other. It is possible to have a destiny (or to be destined to achieve something), and yet be completely unaware of it. However, a mission is something that one consciously accepts and executes. For instance, an individual who takes on a mission to reduce illiteracy in his/her community will consciously make goals and plans in order to successfully achieve this mission. It is within this context that we need to understand the destiny of the United States and the mission of the American Bahá'í community. In the case of the United States, it is destined to take part in actions that will indirectly and unwittingly promote the institutions (national and international) that will help to establish the World Order of Bahá'u'lláh. The American Bahá'í community, however, is fully aware of its God-given mission, and thus it will create goals and launch plans in order to achieve this mission. In the section that follows, we will discuss this unique mission and the vital contributions that the American Bahá'ís will make toward the creation of the World Order. Indeed, as will be explained in detail, the glorious World Order already exists in "embryonic form" within the administrative framework of the Bahá'í Faith.

Contributions of the American Bahá'í Community to the World Order of Bahá'u'lláh

Before we can discuss the contributions that the American Bahá'ís will make toward the establishment of the World Order, we must first cover some details regarding the Bahá'í system of governance, known as the "Administrative Order." It is important to clearly differentiate between the Administrative Order and the World Order. As explained earlier, the glorious World Order of Bahá'u'lláh will emerge in the distant future after humankind progresses through three distinct stages of development (tribulation, the Lesser Peace, and then the Most Great Peace). Furthermore, the World Order will emerge as a result of the actions of Bahá'ís and non-Bahá'ís. In contrast, the Administrative Order is already in operation even though it still needs to mature. Also, by definition, the Administrative Order has been created exclusively by Bahá'ís—it consists of Bahá'í institutions and laws.

The Administrative Order is essentially a divinely inspired governance system designed to manage the local, national, and international affairs of the worldwide Bahá'í community. It is made up of the institutions and laws that were specified by Bahá'u'lláh as a means to govern the community of His followers into the future. The writings state the following regarding the unique character of the Bahá'í Administrative Order:

This Administrative Order is fundamentally different from anything that any Prophet has previously established, inasmuch as Bahá'u'lláh has Himself revealed its principles, established its institutions, appointed the person to interpret His Word and conferred the necessary authority on the body [Universal House of Justice] designed to supplement and apply His legislative ordinances. Therein lies the secret of its strength, its fundamental distinction, and the guarantee against disintegration and schism. Nowhere in the sacred scriptures of any of the world's religious systems, nor even in the writings of the Inaugurator of the Bábí Dispensation [the Báb], do we find any provisions establishing a covenant or providing for an administrative order that can compare in scope and authority with those that lie at the very basis of the Bahá'í Dispensation.[19]

The Administrative Order was conceived by Bahá'u'lláh, and then actually designed and put into action by 'Abdu'l-Bahá and Shoghi Effendi under the terms and authorities granted by the Lesser Covenant. As explained earlier, this Covenant allowed for the orderly passing of authority from Bahá'u'lláh to 'Abdu'l-Bahá and then from 'Abdu'l-Bahá to Shoghi Effendi (refer to chapter three). The Covenant of Bahá'u'lláh also called for the future establishment of the present-day Universal House of Justice. All of these covenantal relationships were outlined in the writings of Bahá'u'lláh prior to His passing. Indeed, such clearly established written guidelines allowed for the creation of the Administrative Order, a worldwide system of religious governance that is unparalleled in history. Regarding this, some would say that the institutions of the Papacy of Christianity and the Caliphate of Islam with all of their respective ecclesiastical orders are equivalent to the Administrative Order of the Bahá'í Faith. This is grievously incorrect. Neither the Papacy nor the Caliphate is based on the written, binding, and conclusive instructions of Christ or Muḥammad respectively. The supposed authority and authenticity of these Christian and Muslim institutions along with their sacraments, rites, ceremonies, hierarchical clerical orders, and so forth are not based on the explicit, written guidance contained in the Bible or the Qur'án. Such lack of scriptural-based authority has resulted in the splintering of Christianity and Islam into a multiplicity of denominations and sects.

The two "pillars" of the Administrative Order are the Guardianship and the Universal House of Justice, both of which were conceived by Bahá'u'lláh. The Guardianship refers to the official office that was held by Shoghi Effendi as an authoritative interpreter of the sacred Bahá'í texts. Even though he is no longer living, his writings, as the Guardian of the Bahá'í Faith, are considered "living texts" in the sense that they are still authoritative and binding. As mentioned earlier, the democratically elected Universal House of Justice has the authority, as granted by Bahá'u'lláh, to legislate new laws and to repeal its own old laws in order to respond to the needs of the evolving worldwide Bahá'í community. Its laws, however, must not contravene the writings of Bahá'u'lláh, 'Abdu'l-Bahá, and Shoghi Effendi. The other major democratically elected, decision-making bodies of the Faith are the Local and National Spiritual Assemblies, which administer affairs at the local (city or village) and national levels respectively. Among other things, the Administrative Order is intended to protect the unity of the Faith, to propagate the teachings of Bahá'u'lláh, to organize and mobilize manpower and resources, to help provide children's education, to establish a pattern to Bahá'í community life such as the observation of holy days, feasts, and elections; to publish literature; to oversee finances, properties, and endowments; as well as to help establish the goals and help coordinate the overall actions of diverse local and national Bahá'í communities throughout the planet.

It is fascinating to note that, within the Bahá'í writings, the Administrative Order is viewed as the "embryonic form" of the future World Order. Indeed, Shoghi Effendi refers to the Administrative Order as "the embryonic World Order of Bahá'u'lláh" and also as the "Divine embryonic Order." Other Bahá'í passages describe the Administrative Order as being "the nucleus," "the precursor," and "the very pattern" of the future New World Order. Shoghi Effendi asserts that the laws and institutions of the Administrative Order "are destined to be a pattern for future society, a supreme instrument for the establishment of the Most Great Peace, and the one agency for the unification of the world, and the proclamation of the reign of righteousness and justice upon the earth." Thus the Administrative Order will play an absolutely key role in the development of the glorious World Order.[20]

In *The Advent of Divine Justice*, Shoghi Effendi noted that "the embryonic World Order of Bahá'u'lláh" (the Administrative Order) had already manifested its "first stirrings" within the United States. At that time (1939), the American Bahá'ís were already aware of the God-given mission and the sacred tasks that lay before them. In addition to *The Advent of Divine Justice*, which is primarily addressed to the American Bahá'ís, Shoghi Effendi wrote a vast series of letters aimed at the American believers. Many of these letters are contained in *Citadel of Faith* and some are contained in *The World Order of Bahá'u'lláh*. In all of these communications to the American believers, he covers a diversity of topics related to the Bahá'í Faith, but he particularly expounds upon the unique mission, tasks, goals, obstacles, and victories of the American Bahá'í community as well as the special destiny of the United States and its citizens. Largely as a result of Shoghi Effendi's letters (he started sending letters in 1922), the American Bahá'ís have been stunningly successful at developing and improving their own administrative system and then propagating this system within other countries throughout the globe. Using their community's administrative framework as essentially a model, they have traveled throughout the world and have spearheaded the effort to build the worldwide administrative structures and institutions of the Faith—the Administrative Order of the Bahá'í Faith.[21]

During the course of World War I, 'Abdu'l-Bahá wrote a series of letters to the believers of North America. These messages are collectively titled "The Divine Plan" for the promulgation of the teachings of Bahá'u'lláh throughout the globe. Commenting on the special significance of this, Shoghi Effendi states that the "American Bahá'í community" is "exalted, singled out among sister communities of East and West through revelation of the Tablets of the Divine Plan." 'Abdu'l-Bahá bestowed many other honors upon the American Bahá'ís, especially when he traversed the continental United States during 1912. At this time, he titled New York City the "City of the Covenant," and he also laid the cornerstone of the Bahá'í House of Worship on the outskirts of Chicago. Additionally, as highlighted at the beginning of this chapter, 'Abdu'l-Bahá made several prophetic pronouncements regarding the glorious destiny of the United States, and he indicated that it would become the "cradle" of the Administrative Order.[22]

In his various letters, Shoghi Effendi emphasizes that the American Bahá'ís do indeed have the God-given mission to spearhead efforts to build and consolidate the Administrative Order, and then, to use this worldwide administrative system to propagate Bahá'u'lláh's teachings throughout the globe as instructed by 'Abdu'l-Bahá's Divine Plan. Shoghi Effendi refers to the American Bahá'í community as "the cradle and stronghold of the Administrative Order of the Faith of Bahá'u'lláh." He also acclaims the American Bahá'ís as "the champion-builders of Bahá'u'lláh's embryonic Order." In other words, the American Bahá'í community is the cradle, the stronghold, and the champion-builder of the Administrative Order. This is a tremendously exalted station because, as mentioned earlier, the Administrative Order will serve as "the nucleus" and "the very pattern" of the future, glorious World Order. Not surprisingly then, Shoghi Effendi further acclaims the American Bahá'í community as the "chief creator and champion of the World Order of Bahá'u'lláh." Similarly, other Bahá'í passages affirm that the American believers will play a "preponderating role" in the development of the future World Order of Bahá'u'lláh.[23]

In *Citadel of Faith*, Shoghi Effendi enumerates some of the praiseworthy contributions that the American Bahá'ís have already made toward the creation of the future World Order. As we consider these contributions, it is imperative that we keep in mind here that all Bahá'í efforts to improve the Administrative Order (the "embryo") are sure to propel humankind ever closer to the actual establishment of the future World Order. In essence, a prime goal of the American Bahá'í community is to improve and consolidate the existing worldwide Bahá'í Administrative Order as much as possible.

Shoghi Effendi asserts that the vital mission of the American Bahá'í community "dates back to the revelation of those stupendous Tablets constituting the Charter of 'Abdu'l-Bahá's Divine Plan." He states that, after the passing of 'Abdu'l-Bahá, this community was "the first among all other Bahá'í communities in East and West to arise and champion" the Administrative Order, to "initiate its endowments" and to "establish and consolidate its subsidiary institutions." It built "the first Mashriqu'l-Adhkár [House of Worship] of the West, the holiest edifice ever to be reared by the hands of the followers of Bahá'u'lláh." He also declares that the American Bahá'ís have "the imperishable glory of having launched and successfully concluded" a campaign to establish the "structural basis of the Administrative Order of the Faith in all the republics of Central and South America." He praises this community for having "won the immortal honor of being the first to introduce the Faith in the British Isles, in France, and in Germany" and also for sending forth its teachers and pioneers to Latin America, India, China, Japan, New Zealand, Australia, the islands of the Pacific, South Africa, the Balkan Peninsula, Scandinavia, and the Baltic States. He furthermore lauds the efforts of American Bahá'ís to "champion the cause of the downtrodden and persecuted" Bahá'ís who live in Persia, Egypt, and Russia" and to defend their cases before ecclesiastical and political enemies of the Faith. He additionally praises the American believers for their exceptional Bahá'í national constitution and by-laws, for their swift development of material resources, for their wise, self-abnegating expenditure of funds, for their enhancement of Bahá'í literature, and for their generosity in assisting the needy among sister communities in other nations. He also extols the American Bahá'í community as the "dynamic agent responsible for the opening of the vast majority of the over two hundred sovereign states and chief dependencies of the globe to the Faith of Bahá'u'lláh."[24]

The work of the American Bahá'ís was broken into three separate campaigns. Starting in 1937, Shoghi Effendi directed the American believers to spearhead three separate plans to expand the Bahá'í Faith: a seven-year plan from 1937 to 1944 aimed primarily at Latin America, another seven-year plan from 1946 to 1953 to expand into Europe, and then a "Ten Year World Crusade" from 1953 to 1963 to massively expand the Faith into an additional 132 new countries and territories as well as to establish National Spiritual Assemblies in most of the countries of Latin America and Europe. All of the aforementioned plans were enormously successful, and exceeded the goals that had been established by Shoghi Effendi.

When Shoghi Effendi launched his campaigns, he encouraged the American Bahá'ís to travel to foreign lands to teach the Faith. Many stellar intrepid souls arose to answer the call of Shoghi Effendi. William Sears (1911–1992), for instance, left a successful career as a professional writer, editor, sports announcer, and actor to pioneer to Africa in order to teach the Bahá'í Faith. Sears was born in Duluth, Minnesota, but had lived in different parts of the United States before moving to Africa. In 1953, he and his family arrived in South Africa. From there, he traveled to almost every corner of the African continent. Sears proved to be a devoted and indefatigable teacher of the Faith. He was also a lover of humanity and wished to serve and help people wherever he traveled. In 1957, Shoghi Effendi appointed Sears a "Hand of the Cause of God." This is the highest distinction that a Bahá'í can get. As a Hand of the Cause, Sears expanded his travels to many different parts of the world. Despite getting Asian flu, hepatitis, malaria, tick fever, and almost being killed by cobras, he never stopped his travels in the service of his beloved Faith (he traveled the equivalent of twenty times around the world). In his final years, Sears' body was broken (he suffered from several infirmities), but his spirit remained as strong as ever. He is buried in Tucson, Arizona.

Dorothy Baker is yet another stellar American Bahá'í, among many, that also arose to answer the call of Shoghi Effendi to spread the teachings of Bahá'u'lláh far and wide. Baker (1898–1954) was born in Newark, New Jersey. After becoming a Bahá'í, she was soon recognized as an accomplished speaker, and she traveled across the United States delivering talks on the Faith, particularly at college and university campuses. She also served on various national Bahá'í committees such as the National Race Unity Committee and the Inter-America Committee (to spread the teachings to the Southern Hemisphere). In 1937, she was elected to the National Spiritual Assembly of the United States and Canada (at that time they were one entity). In the mid-1940s Dorothy began traveling to countries throughout Central and South America. She taught herself Spanish and was beloved by the Latin American people. She also traveled throughout Europe helping to bolster Local and National Spiritual Assemblies. In 1951, Shoghi Effendi appointed Baker a Hand of the Cause of God, which, as mentioned earlier, is an exalted rank. Sadly, on a return trip from India, Baker was flying on an airplane that inexplicably exploded in midair. Shoghi Effendi wrote, "[she] leaves a sad gap . . . She was exemplary in so many ways . . ."[25]

It is interesting to note that Shoghi Effendi was especially heartened by efforts to win the allegiance of American Indian peoples to the teachings of Bahá'u'lláh. In a letter to the American Bahá'ís, he reminds them of 'Abdu'l-Bahá's prophecy regarding the native peoples of the Americas. 'Abdu'l-Bahá prophesied that if the Indians become "educated and guided" in the teachings of Bahá'u'lláh, "there can be no doubt that they will become so illumined as to enlighten the whole world." In *Citadel of Faith*, Shoghi Effendi notes that by 1947 promising contacts had already been made with "the Cherokee and Oneida Indians in North Carolina and Wisconsin, with the Patagonian, the Mexican and the Inca Indians, and the Mayans in Argentina, Mexico, Peru and Yucatan, respectively."[26] In a separate communication, he states,

> In the Tablets of the Divine Plan, the Master pays the utmost attention to this most important matter [teaching the Bahá'í Faith to the Indians of the Americas]. He states that if the Power of the Holy Spirit today properly enters into the minds and hearts of the natives of the great American continents that they will become great standard bearers of the Faith, similar to the Nomads (Arabians) who became the most cultured and enlightened people under the Muḥammadan civilization.[27]

The early American Bahá'í community furthermore distinguished itself by promoting the cause of race unity even when crudely overt and violent forms of racism were still commonplace in the United States. As early as 1912, for instance, at a time when interracial marriage was illegal in many states within the United States, 'Abdu'l-Bahá encouraged the marriage of Louis Gregory, an illustrious African American Bahá'í, and Louisa Mathew, a White Bahá'í from England. 'Abdu'l-Bahá made it clear that interracial marriage is a praiseworthy means of advancing the unity of the races.

A few words should be said about Louis Gregory, one of the preeminent Bahá'ís involved in race unity work in the early American Bahá'í community. Gregory (1874–1951) was born in Charleston, South Carolina only eleven years after Lincoln's Emancipation Proclamation that abolished slavery. Gregory's parents had been slaves. He grew up amidst incredibly oppressive circumstances where African Americans were denied basic human rights. Whites also used all forms of violence to terrorize Blacks into submission (Gregory's grandfather was shot dead by the Ku Klux Klan). Gregory became one of the few Blacks of his era to get an education—he ultimately got a law degree from Howard University. He was highly attuned to the sufferings of his fellow Blacks, and was a social activist early in his career.

In 1909, Gregory became a Bahá'í, and calling himself a "racial amity worker," he lectured widely and wrote literature to support the cause of race unity. He wrote and spoke about the accomplishments of educated Blacks, the achievements of earlier Black civilizations, the intelligence of the dark-skinned races, and the application of Bahá'í teachings to racial problems. For the next forty years, he traveled extensively within the United States (especially in the South) spreading the Bahá'í message of the oneness of humanity and the elimination of all prejudice. He lectured in colleges, churches, clubs, public halls, and any venues that would receive his message. Indeed, the famous George Washington Carver developed a respect for the Bahá'í Faith due to the work of Gregory.

When 'Abdu'l-Bahá made his stupendous visit to America in 1912, he met Louis Gregory and even had him sit at the place of honor during a luncheon that was attended by several prominent members of the Washington D.C. community (at that time, Blacks were not allowed to eat with the Whites). During this time, 'Abdu'l-Bahá suggested that Gregory marry Louisa Mathew, an English Bahá'í. Sadly, the two suffered many indignities during an era in which racial prejudice was blatant and ingrained. During his travels in the South, for instance, she could not join him. He also once spent a night in jail for refusing to move to a segregated train. In the Bahá'í community, however, he was held in high esteem and was elected to the National Spiritual Assembly three separate times. Also, after his death in 1951, Shoghi Effendi posthumously appointed him as a Hand of the Cause of God. Shoghi Effendi wrote a telegram in which he stated, "Profoundly deplore grievous loss dearly beloved, noble-minded, golden-hearted Louis Gregory . . ."[28]

In 1940, the National Spiritual Assembly of the United States endeavored to promote race unity by holding a series of racially integrated meetings for the general public in Atlanta, Georgia. At that time, any interracial meetings, particularly in the deep South, were typically met with intense animosity by angry Whites and sometimes with outbursts of violence. For instance, in 1947, the Ku Klux Klan broke up a Bahá'í interracial meeting that was being held in Atlanta. Additionally, Olga Finke, a White Bahá'í living in Atlanta, was threatened to leave the city by the KKK after she allowed Louis Gregory to visit her home. The courage and steadfastness of many of the early White and African American Bahá'ís served as a living example of the transformative power of Bahá'u'lláh's teachings and thus helped the Bahá'í Faith to spread further within the United States.

At the conclusion of the aforementioned Ten Year World Crusade in 1963, members from fifty-six different National Spiritual Assemblies from throughout the world elected the first Universal House of Justice, the crowning achievement of the Administrative Order. Since then, the House of Justice, as authorized by the Covenant of Bahá'u'lláh, has added its own subsidiary institutions such as the "Boards of Counselors." These are groups of distinguished Bahá'ís who are appointed to five year terms and are empowered to advise assemblies and individuals as well as to protect and propagate the Bahá'í Faith. Furthermore, to the very present, the House of Justice (in the absence of Shoghi Effendi, who passed away in 1957) has also launched its own series of international plans to contribute to the "spiritual conquest of the planet." Most importantly, by acting as the unchallenged authority in all the affairs of the Faith, it has prevented schism and has maintained the unity of the Bahá'í Faith as one undivided body of believers.

The successes mentioned above must be placed in their proper historical perspective. When Shoghi Effendi was appointed as Guardian in 1921, the Bahá'í Faith was still very obscure, having only a small body of believers (about 100,000), who primarily resided in Persia. Outside of Persia, there were only a few groups of believers, primarily in India and North America (the United States and Canada). Bahá'í literature and organization were negligible and financial resources were meager. Now, however, largely due to the work of the American Bahá'ís (under the direction and guidance of Shoghi Effendi), the situation has changed dramatically. The Bahá'í Faith is presently the second most widespread religion on Earth in terms of geographic distribution, and it has rapidly expanded its population (about 6 million adherents). It is a highly organized, incredibly diverse body of believers including individuals from more than 2,100 ethnic, racial, and tribal groups from over two hundred countries and territories throughout the globe. The publication of Bahá'í-related literature has also tremendously expanded, and in fact, some of the writings of Bahá'u'lláh and 'Abdu'l-Bahá have been translated into over 700 languages. The Faith's growing influence can be shown by the fact that one of its bodies, the Bahá'í International Community, has been accorded the status of being a Nongovernmental Organization within the United Nations. Furthermore, the permanent seat of the Faith's international headquarters, the Bahá'í World Center (including its majestic monumental buildings), has now been completed in Haifa, Israel.

In short, the efforts of the American Bahá'í community toward fulfilling their mission have been splendidly successful. This will have great ramifications for the entire world because the Administrative Order is, as stated by Shoghi Effendi, "a supreme instrument for the establishment of the Most Great Peace, and the one agency for the unification of the world." Herein lies the supreme contribution that the American Bahá'ís have already made toward the establishment of the future World Order of Bahá'u'lláh. However, it must be emphasized that the mission of the American Bahá'ís is still very far from being accomplished. As will be further discussed later, some of this community's greatest exploits may still lie in the future.[29]

The Bahá'í House of Worship that stands in Wilmette, Illinois, the first Bahá'í Temple to be constructed in the Western World, is a strikingly beautiful edifice that serves as a symbol of the perseverance and devotion of the early American Bahá'ís. In the future, many Bahá'í Temples will be built throughout the world. They will play a central role in the community life of the Bahá'ís. Around each temple will be built homes for the elderly, colleges, schools, hostels, and administrative agencies. The cornerstone for the American Bahá'í Temple (also known as the "Mother Temple of the West") was laid down on May 1, 1912, by the hands of 'Abdu'l-Bahá himself. However, due to World War I, the Great Depression, and World

War II, the temple was not completed until 1953. Bahá'ís from cities throughout America and from a diversity of races and nationalities contributed time, energy, and funds toward the construction of the stunning structure. At times it appeared that the Temple would never be completed due to a lack of human resources and funds. However, the American Bahá'ís, notwithstanding their small numbers, persisted and sacrificed until the beautiful structure was built. This serves as a powerful metaphor. The American Bahá'ís, through their devoted efforts over time, were eventually able to witness the fruits of their labors when the majestic Temple was finally dedicated in 1953. In this same way, the early American Bahá'ís persisted in their efforts and sacrificed until they eventually witnessed the establishment of the nascent structures of the Administrative Order throughout the globe as well as the worldwide expansion of the Faith of Bahá'u'lláh. Quite possibly as a symbol of his love and admiration for the steadfast efforts of the American Bahá'ís, Shoghi Effendi called the American Bahá'í Temple "the holiest edifice ever to be reared by the hands of the followers of Bahá'u'lláh."[30]

In the next section, we will take a closer look at the impressive efforts and victories of the women of the early American Bahá'í community. It is significant to note that Shoghi Effendi gave special recognition to the general body of American Bahá'í women for the preponderating role that they played in the spread of the Faith both within the United States and throughout the globe.

The Indomitable Spirit of the American Bahá'í Women

It is inspiring to note that American Bahá'í women played a major and praiseworthy role in the promulgation of Bahá'u'lláh's teachings within the United States as well as throughout the world. Regarding this, Shoghi Effendi states,

I am moved, at this juncture, as I am reminded of the share which, ever since the inception of the Faith in the West, the handmaidens of Bahá'u'lláh, as distinguished from the men,

have had in opening up, single-handed, so many, such diver-
sified, and widely scattered countries over the whole surface of
the globe . . . to stress the significance of such a preponderating
share which the women of the West have had and are having
in the establishment of His Faith throughout the whole world.
"Among the miracles," 'Abdu'l-Bahá Himself has testified,
"which distinguish this sacred Dispensation is this, that women
have evinced a greater boldness than men when enlisted in the
ranks of the Faith." So great and splendid a testimony applies
in particular to the West, and though it has received thus far
abundant and convincing confirmation must, as the years roll
away, be further reinforced, as the American believers usher in
the most glorious phase of their teaching activities . . .[31]

One woman who stands out in this regard is Martha Root, referred
to by Shoghi Effendi as "that star-servant of Bahá'u'lláh . . . indomitable and immortal," "the archetype of Bahá'í itinerant teachers"
and the "foremost Hand [of the Cause of God]." Martha Root was
born in 1872 in Ohio and grew up mostly in Pennsylvania in a rural
setting. Her father, with whom she was very close, was a successful
businessman and a deacon in the Baptist Church. Although unusual
for women of her era, Root ventured out to attend Oberlin College
in 1889 before transferring eventually to the University of Chicago.
She later landed jobs as a journalist for several Pittsburgh newspapers.
Root was somewhat of an adventure woman, and in the course of her
burgeoning career as a journalist and editor, she traveled widely in
and out of the United States covering the latest fads and fashions such
as "automobilism," social happenings of the rich, Parisian cooking,
women's literary interests, and other feature stories (as opposed to hard
news). In 1908, Root met a Bahá'í named Roy Wilhelm, who hap-
pened to sit at a table near hers in a restaurant outside an interdenomi-
national missionary convention that she was covering for her paper.
After this chance meeting in which he introduced the Bahá'í teachings
to her, she began a correspondence with him that led her eventually to
investigate the Bahá'í Faith in earnest. Once she committed herself to

the new Faith, there was no looking back. She abandoned her career and directed her dauntless spirit and considerable writing and speaking capacities to furthering the Bahá'í Faith throughout the world.[32]

After meeting 'Abdu'l-Bahá in 1912 when he traveled to America to assist in efforts to expand the community and consolidate the early believers, Root became absolutely galvanized and was the first to set off, in 1919, in response to 'Abdu'l-Bahá's appeal for believers to arise and teach the new Message throughout all lands. She was 47 years old at the time and did not enjoy good health. Shoghi Effendi writes at length about her accomplishments, noting that she embarked

> with unswerving resolve and a spirit of sublime detachment, on her world journeys, covering an almost uninterrupted period of twenty years and carrying her four times around the globe, in the course of which she traveled four times to China and Japan and three times to India, visited every important city in South America, transmitted the message of the New Day to kings, queens, princes and princesses, presidents of republics, ministers and statesmen, publicists, professors, clergymen and poets, as well as a vast number of people in various walks of life, and contacted, both officially and informally, religious congresses, peace societies, Esperanto associations, socialist congresses, Theosophical societies, women's clubs and other kindred organizations . . .[33]

In addition to these feats, Root delivered lectures on the Bahá'í Faith at over 400 colleges and universities, published hundreds of articles in newspapers and magazines wherever she went, and gave numerous broadcast interviews. She placed Bahá'í books in libraries around the world, as well as assisted fledgling Bahá'í institutions in countries where these had been established or were about to become established. Among all of these accomplishments, Shoghi Effendi singled out one particular service as the "most superb and by far the most momentous" of all her services rendered to the Faith, namely, the response she "evoked" in Queen Marie of Romania, over the course of eight separate audiences with the Queen between 1926 and 1936 during which Root delivered the Message of Bahá'u'lláh. Queen Marie, a grand-daughter of Queen Victoria, who, nearly 60 years prior had received a tablet from Bahá'u'lláh, Himself, was the first sovereign to openly declare support for the new Faith. Queen Marie acknowledged her belief in Bahá'u'lláh, and commended the Bahá'í teachings to all men and women, in three encomiums, as well as other writings and letters, before her passing in 1938. Perhaps reflecting her own fearlessness, not unlike that of her Bahá'í teacher, the Queen wrote the following in a personal letter referring to her open support of the Bahá'í Faith:

> Some of those in my caste wonder at and disapprove my courage to step forward pronouncing words not habitual for crowned heads to pronounce, but I advance by an inner urge I cannot resist. With bowed head I recognize that I too am but an instrument in greater Hands, and I rejoice in the knowledge.[34]

Amazingly, all of these accomplishments of Martha Root were achieved despite a number of hardships. She endured nagging ill health throughout her journeys. This later turned out to be breast cancer, and it eventually took her life. Additionally, there was little available in the way of Bahá'í literature to assist in her efforts to disseminate information, and she subsisted on meager financial resources to support her journeys, which were partially funded by her Bahá'í friend Roy Wilhelm. Shoghi Effendi writes, ". . . neither the extremities of the climates to which she was exposed, nor the political disturbances which she encountered in the course of her journeys, could damp the zeal and deflect the purpose of this spiritu-ally dynamic and saintly woman." On her way home from her fourth trip around the world, she arrived in Honolulu, Hawaii in great pain from the advanced stages of the cancer. She eventually passed away at the age of sixty-seven.[35]

Shoghi Effendi describes the significance of her resting place (in Hawaii) and her station thus: "There in that symbolic spot between the Eastern and Western Hemispheres, in both of which she had labored so mightily, she died, on September 28, 1939, and brought to its close a life which may well be regarded as the fairest fruit as yet yielded by the Formative Age of the Dispensation of Bahá'u'lláh."[36]

In addition to Martha Root, five other American women were designated Hands of the Cause of God and made stellar contributions at the inception of the Faith in the West. The achievements of these famous women have been documented in various pieces of literature, recorded stories, and archival materials. Numerous other lesser known American women also boldly arose to advance the Bahá'í Faith both within and outside of America from the time of its appearance in the West in the late 1800s. A collection of literature from Bahá'í historians is emerging that documents the fascinating life histories and unique contributions of these lesser known women. No doubt, future historians will glean even more insight into the contributions of these women. I turn briefly to two more inspiring examples of American women, who, from very different life circumstances, chose to dedicate their lives to "the promotion of the Word of God" and in doing so, lived lives of detachment, courage, and dedication. These Bahá'í heroines helped to raise up the Administrative Order of the Faith in America at the local level.

The first is Ella Bailey. Born in 1864 in Houston, Texas, Bailey suffered an attack of polio during her childhood that left her permanently paralyzed in one leg. Her family had moved to San Diego County when she was still a baby, and she grew up in southern California before becoming a teacher and taking a position at a school in Berkeley. Having decided to remain unmarried so she could totally dedicate herself to her students and the greater community, Bailey established herself in the Berkeley area and set about a life of quiet service. Shortly after the turn of the century, when Bailey was approximately forty years old, she learned of the Bahá'í Faith from another indomitable Bahá'í teacher, Lua Getsinger. In 1912, Bailey traveled together with two other early women believers to Washington, D.C. to meet 'Abdu'l-Bahá. They then followed him to Chicago. She wrote records of her memories and impressions of those days with him. She particularly noted 'Abdu'l-Bahá's love for children and his emphasis on the importance of raising them spiritually, clearly a subject that was close to her heart. She wrote,

> 'Abdu'l-Bahá then stood and spoke [to the children] . . . "according to the words of Bahá'u'lláh you are the very lamps or candles of the world of humanity, for your hearts are exceedingly pure and your spirits are most delicate. . . . My hope for you is that your parents may educate you spiritually, giving you the utmost ethical training. May your education be most perfect so that each one of you may be embued with all the virtues of the human world. . . . I pray for all of you, asking God's aid and confirmation in your behalf."[37]

Following these confirming experiences with 'Abdu'l-Bahá, Bailey returned to California where she very humbly labored to serve the Bahá'í Faith in whatever way was needed in her local community while also continuing to work as a teacher until she retired due to illness in 1924. Known for her humility, patience, extreme gentleness, and tact, she was loved by all. One of her fellow believers later wrote about her quiet, exemplary deeds:

> Many were her secret sacrifices. She would give sumptuous dinners with friends who were oblivious to the fact that their hostess very often contented herself with tea, toast, and perhaps a little soup. Her whole day passed in cheering the brokenhearted, in helping the needy, in visiting the sick, and in refreshing the spirits of the unending stream of guests that came to see her.[38]

In 1925, Bailey was elected to the first Spiritual Assembly of Berkeley, California, and she was continuously elected each year for a total of twenty years of service on that body until the age of eighty-one. During that time, she worked to host monthly "amity" meetings to foster interracial harmony, to organize various meetings through her connections at the Berkeley Women's City Club, and to promote the training and teaching of children. She felt strongly that the spiritual education of children was vital to helping them shoulder the "responsibilities of a new social order" and to develop their ability to contribute to new modes of thought with their teachers and fellow students.[39]

When in 1953, Shoghi Effendi launched global plans to establish and consolidate the Bahá'í Faith in countries all over the globe, Bailey longed to join two of her friends who planned to move to Tripoli, Libya, to help with the efforts there. At her advanced age, she was worried that she might end up being a burden for her friends. When her friends contacted Shoghi Effendi to see if it would be alright to bring Ella Bailey, he cabled back immediately, "Approve Bailey accompany you." Already having suffered pneumonia that had caused her to move to a rest home, some friends had warned her that the move could shorten her life. In an endearing spirit of detachment and humor, she is reported to have responded, "I do not find it such a great sacrifice to give up living in a rest home." A little over a month in her new home in Tripoli, Ella Bailey passed away at the age of eighty-eight. Shoghi Effendi wrote the following tribute to her in a cablegram sent to an international Bahá'í conference in India: "Irresistibly unfolding crusade sanctified death heroic eighty eight year old Ella Bailey elevating her rank martyrs Faith shedding further lustre American Bahá'í community consecrating soil fast awakening African continent."[40]

A statement written by Shoghi Effendi at the time of the passing of Marion Jack, another intrepid woman, listed Ella Bailey among other illustrious souls who furthered the Cause. The statement also sheds light on the momentous accomplishments of these North American women:

This triumphant soul [Marion Jack] is now gathered to the distinguished band of her co-workers in the Abhá Kingdom; Martha Root, Lua Getsinger, May Maxwell, Hyde Dunn, Susan Moody, Keith Ransom-Kehler, Ella Bailey and Dorothy Baker, whose remains, lying in such widely scattered areas of the globe as Honolulu, Cairo, Buenos Aires, Sydney, Ṭihrán, Iṣfáhán, Tripoli and the depths of the Mediterranean Sea attest the magnificence of the pioneer services rendered by the North American Bahá'í Community in the Apostolic and Formative Ages of the Bahá'í Dispensation.[41]

Martha Root and Ella Bailey, both American women of European descent, had as their sisters in Faith, many African American women who also distinguished themselves as champions of the new Faith in a myriad of arenas, both in America and abroad. This is even more remarkable when one considers the overt and often violent forms of racism that were rampant throughout America. Furthermore, ingrained social attitudes in nineteenth and twentieth century America also clouded the ability of many White Bahá'ís to fully comprehend, much less practice, the implications of a Faith that has as its foundational principle the abandonment of all forms of prejudice. One such woman who persevered despite these odds and who made valuable contributions to the Cause is Zylpha Odysell Mapp (formerly Zylpha Johnson).

Born in Boston in 1890, Mapp spent most of her childhood years in Plymouth, Massachusetts. As a child she attended Sunday schools from four different Christian denominations, and thought deeply about the nature of God and the universe as she was growing up. The first African American woman to graduate from Plymouth High School in 1908 (interestingly, her father had been the first African American male to graduate from that same high school in the 1880s), Mapp's desire was to study nursing, which was not permitted until the age of 21 at that time. In the meantime, she met and married Alexander Mapp, a West Indian architect and builder from Barbados, and the couple moved to Cambridge, Massachusetts. After the birth of her fourth child, Mapp engaged in religious conversation with her dentist, also a West Indian, and he invited her to attend a Bahá'í informational meeting that evening. The year was 1916—four years after 'Abdu'l-Bahá's historical visit to America. Mapp continued to attend meetings and read as much as possible about the new Faith, eventually becoming a devoted believer. Thereafter, she opened her home to many visitors and activities related to spreading the Faith and became a beacon of "warmth, wisdom, and knowledge about the Bahá'í Faith."[42]

Using her own spheres of influence, Mapp labored unceasingly to teach the Faith directly. She held informal discussion groups called "firesides" at her home, and welcomed and embraced all who entered, delighting in researching answers to questions from seeking souls and pointing them to the Bahá'í writings. She participated in the administrative affairs of her local community, serving as the secretary of the Boston Spiritual Assembly from 1928 to 1934, even walking through winter snow drifts to commute back and forth to meetings. No less remarkable is her engagement of her entire family and her children in the life of the Bahá'í community. She raised all five of her children as Bahá'ís, and admonished them to excel in their education. Always thinking beyond the boundaries of her own home and city, Mapp opened up her Cambridge home to many foreign students and scholars in order to impart to them information about the Bahá'í Faith that they would then bring back to their home countries—perhaps her own way of contributing to international teaching goals. Clearly the lessons of these early years were not lost on her namesake, a daughter named Zylpha who was born in 1914 and, as an adult, moved to Uganda, Burkina Faso, India, and Botswana, respectively, in order to establish the Faith in those countries. This daughter also traveled to a host of other countries in Africa, Europe, and the Caribbean and earned the acknowledgement of Shoghi Effendi in her efforts.

A deeply "mystic" person who was very intuitive, Mapp sometimes had premonitions or feelings that helped her cope in times of difficulty. Most notably, she sensed the passing of 'Abdu'l-Bahá in 1921 before actually receiving the news, and as a result felt prepared for the shock and grief over his passing. She also drew on the power of prayer and the reassurance and guidance of the writings to withstand, unflinchingly, her commitment to the pivotal teaching of the Faith—the oneness of mankind. And again, the reality of being an African American believer also presented her with additional challenges to putting her faith into action in her own life. One incident, described by her daughter in a presentation about her mother's life is particularly telling. In 1922, the Mapp family moved to Avon, a small town of 2,000 White people outside the city of Boston. Her daughter writes, "We integrated the town." Sometime after the family took up residence, the home caught fire while the family was out. There is no indication in her daughter's notes as to the cause of the fire, but she states that her twelve-year-old brother ran to the burning home from the school and attempted to salvage items, finding a Bahá'í book entitled the Hidden Words amazingly open to the page which read: "O Son of Being, busy not thyself with this world, for with fire We test the gold, and with gold We test Our servants." Mapp's daughter notes that her mother's explanation of the event was thus: "The message from the Hidden Words tells us that the fire was God's way of bringing about a better understanding amongst the races in Avon." In another passage, Mapp's daughter writes that the tragedy "opened up the hearts of some townspeople and three families offered and provided shelter for us." Mapp and her husband rebuilt the house and remained in Avon for twenty-three years.[43]

After the passing of 'Abdu'l-Bahá, Mapp began to correspond regularly with Shoghi Effendi, who encouraged her "to devote her life to the unity and harmony of the black and white races in America." From this guidance, she immediately aligned her efforts with those of well-known African American Bahá'í Louis Gregory, who labored alongside several White Bahá'ís. As mentioned earlier, Gregory had also been encouraged by Shoghi Effendi to pursue "race amity" work. When Shoghi Effendi called for Bahá'ís in America to develop Local Assemblies according to city jurisdictions, Mapp wholeheartedly set about this work too, earnestly working to establish a Bahá'í Assembly in Avon, which had no other Bahá'ís living in it except the Mapp family.

Adding to these acts of courage and faith, Mapp also put her faith in action in another way by engaging in social action in every city or town where she lived. Described as a "Renaissance Woman in every sense of the word" she established a camp for underprivileged children from the Boston area that was sponsored by the Boston Urban League. She encouraged her sons and some friends who were musical and of diverse ethnic backgrounds to set up an orchestra and "give thanks to the people of Avon" by performing at charitable organizations, church functions, hospitals, and the like. At the same time, Mapp decided to further her own education so she would be in a better position to help people. She enrolled in and completed two and a half years of study at Portia Law School before having to leave due to the passing of her father as well as difficulties during the Great Depression.[44]

When her husband died in 1944, Mapp moved to New York where she affiliated herself with an orphanage and served as housemother for many children, both girls and boys. She later remarried only to lose her second husband in 1959 and moved back to Massachusetts, this time in Springfield.

Ever outwardly oriented, Mapp always involved herself in clubs and civic groups that enabled her to serve the general community while bringing a Bahá'í perspective to this service. While serving as an assistant treasurer with a Golden Ages club in Springfield, she read Bahá'í writings and was often called upon to speak about the oneness of humanity. In 1967, she was honored by a local newspaper as a "friend to children" after having served four years as the first Black president of the Springfield Federation of Women's Clubs, which took on projects for children throughout the city. She served as a Bahá'í member of an ecumenical group in Springfield, and while there initiated a project to hand-sew fifty to sixty dresses a year to be donated to young Indian girls residing on a reservation.

These are only a sampling of the activities she maintained while laboring to build up local Bahá'í administrative communities and teaching directly the message of Bahá'u'lláh to all those interested in learning more. In 1968, at the age of seventy-seven, Mapp traveled to Barbados, West Indies, in order to share the message of Bahá'u'lláh. She died peacefully in December, 1970 at the age of eighty, an illustrious devotee of Bahá'u'lláh whose lifetime spanned the last two years of Bahá'u'lláh's earthly presence, and the entire ministries of 'Abdu'l-Bahá and Shoghi Effendi, as well as the establishment of the Universal House of Justice in 1963.[45]

Recognizing Bahá'u'lláh as the Promised One is Not Sufficient

It must be made clear here that there is an important distinction between, on the one hand, humankind's universal recognition of Bahá'u'lláh as the Promised One (the advent of the Most Great Peace), and on the other, humankind's mass entrance into the Bahá'í Faith's Administrative Order (the advent of the World Order of Bahá'u'lláh). Bahá'u'lláh makes it clear that a simple declaration of belief in Him is not sufficient. Indeed, he states that it is necessary not only to accept His claim as the Promised One but also to abide by His ordinances, laws, commandments, and their associated institutions (His Administrative Order). In the Kitáb-i-Aqdas, the "Mother Book" of the Bahá'í dispensation, Bahá'u'lláh declares,

> The first duty prescribed by God for His servants is the recognition of Him [Bahá'u'lláh] Who is . . . the Fountain of . . . [God's] . . . laws, Who representeth the Godhead in both the Kingdom of His Cause and the world of creation. Whoso achieveth this duty hath attained unto all good; and whoso is deprived thereof, hath gone astray, though he be the author of every righteous deed. It behooveth every one who reacheth this most sublime station, this summit of transcendent glory, to observe every ordinance of Him [Bahá'u'lláh] Who is the Desire of the world. These twin duties are inseparable. Neither is acceptable without the other. . . .
>
> O ye peoples of the world! Know assuredly that My commandments are the lamps of My loving providence among My servants, and the keys of My mercy for My creatures. Thus hath it been sent down from the heaven of the Will of your Lord, the Lord of Revelation.[46]

When an individual recognizes and accepts the claims of Bahá'u'lláh as the Promised One, he or she enters (perhaps more consciously) into the work of world civilization-building, and is most effective in doing so by taking an active part in the Administrative Order of the Bahá'í

Faith. For some new believers, such active participation is a process of gradual education and realization, and for others, it is immediate. In either case it is a matter of love and obedience to Bahá'u'lláh, rather than a participation imposed by other Bahá'ís.

It is important to note that the foundation stone of this love for and obedience to Bahá'u'lláh is manifested in the individual believer's "firmness" in the Covenant. As described earlier, Bahá'u'lláh established a Covenant with the believers that delineates a clear line of authoritative and infallible successorship. This Covenant has prevented schism in the Bahá'í Faith. When an individual becomes a Bahá'í, he or she enters under the protecting wing of this Covenant and can turn with confidence to the authoritative writings of 'Abdu'l-Bahá, Shoghi Effendi, and the Universal House of Justice. He or she can also look to the Universal House of Justice to create new laws (or to repeal its own laws) in order to meet the needs of an ever-evolving humanity. The Local and National Spiritual Assemblies, though not infallible, are also sources of guidance for the individual.

Thus when an individual formally declares himself or herself as a Bahá'í, he or she is declaring a willingness to observe the authority of the covenantal relationships described above and also a willingness to strive to uphold the laws and ordinances of the Faith. This then enables the individual to participate fully at the grassroots level of the Administrative Order. Bahá'í individuals attend the Nineteen Day Feast, which is a basic building block of community life where the devotional, administrative, and social aspects of the local community come together. Individuals also participate in annual Bahá'í elections to select the membership of Local and National Spiritual Assemblies. Moreover, individual Bahá'ís make donations to Bahá'í Funds that sustain the material means necessary for the institutions to carry out their multiplicity of functions. Hence, the individual is inextricably linked with the overall Bahá'í community and also with the guiding institutions of the Faith.

It is these three categories—the individual, the community, and the institutions—that the Universal House of Justice has identified as the participants in the work of unifying the human race and of raising up a world civilization firmly established upon spiritual foundations. Each of these categories of participants has a role in this process that is distinct, yet complementary to that of the others. The paragraphs that follow will elucidate this point further.

As noted earlier, individual Bahá'ís strive to align their lives with the teachings of the Faith on a daily, moment-by-moment basis. This is done through daily prayer, daily reading of the writings, and personal daily reflection on the victories or challenges that are a part of one's own spiritual growth and development. Gathering together with other individuals to study or to "deepen" on the writings is also a way that the individual participates in his or her own spiritual growth as well as the spiritual growth of other individuals. This enhances community life. Translating this study into action through service to humanity is another critical aspect of the role of the individual. It is important to recognize, however, that proper coordination, guidance, and direction are needed in order to effectively harness the spiritual potential inherent in individuals and communities. This is where the role of the Bahá'í institutions and the power of Bahá'u'lláh's Covenant become very apparent. For instance, the Universal House of Justice has continued the work begun by 'Abdu'l-Bahá and Shoghi Effendi in formulating successive plans that guide, channel, and direct the energies of the believers. The ultimate goal of these plans is to contribute to the establishment of a divine civilization on Earth over a long period of time.

Currently, the plan of the Universal House of Justice entails the worldwide establishment of what are known as "training institutes." The goal of these institutes is to raise up large numbers of people throughout the world who are committed to transforming their societies and to establishing a divinely based world civilization. In these institutes, participants go through a sequence of study courses that are intended to help them develop practical skills that will, in turn, help them to spiritually and materially transform their societies at large. Based on the continuing guidance and direction of the Universal House of Justice, Bahá'í individuals, communities, and institutions are all currently focused on this worldwide endeavor. At this writing, the key line of action of these training institutes is to raise up more and more human resources (Bahá'í and non-Bahá'í) who wish to join in the work of community-building through the establishment and multiplication of four main core activities: devotional gatherings, children's classes, junior youth groups, and study circles. In an April 2010 letter to the Bahá'ís of the World, the Universal House of Justice described these core activities as:

> . . . meetings that strengthen the devotional character of the community; classes that nurture the tender hearts and minds of children; groups that channel the surging energies of junior youth; circles of study, open to all, that enable people of varied backgrounds to advance on equal footing and explore the application of the teachings to their individual and collective lives . . .[47]

Elsewhere in that same letter, the Universal House of Justice underscores the importance of developing "a culture which promotes a way of thinking, studying, and acting, in which all consider themselves treading a common path of service—supporting one another and advancing together, respectful of the knowledge that each one possesses at any given moment." The House of Justice further affirms that this constitutes the "dynamics of an irrepressible movement." Again, the entire purpose of such a movement is to advance all of humanity along a path toward divine civilization, the Kingdom of God on earth.

In short, the Kingdom of God on earth cannot be built solely by humanity's mass recognition of Bahá'u'lláh as the Promised One. It is essential that all such individuals also actively take part in the Administrative Order, which is intended to serve as "the precursor" to the World Order and its world commonwealth. This is not some onerous duty. On the contrary, it is a blessing that bestows happiness and joy. In its recent message to the Bahá'ís of the world, the Universal House of Justice notes that: "All are welcome to enter the community's warm embrace and receive sustenance from Bahá'u'lláh's life-giving message.

No greater joy is there, to be sure, than for a soul, yearning for the Truth, to find shelter in the stronghold of the Cause and draw strength from the unifying power of the Covenant."[48]

Shoghi Effendi likewise expounds upon the crucial need to participate in the Bahá'í Faith's Administrative Order. He notes that Bahá'u'lláh proclaimed Himself as the Promised One to a vast assortment of people through "books, Epistles, and Tablets." Unlike any other Messenger of the past, Bahá'u'lláh wrote and sent messages to kings, queens, emperors, ministers, ambassadors, elected representatives, "the chief magistrates of the Republics of the American continent," priests, monks, philosophers, wise men, mystics, poets, tradesmen, and the recognized ecclesiastical leaders of Judaism, Zoroastrianism, Islam, and Christianity (including the institutions of the Papacy as well as the Sultanate and Caliphate).[49]

In my view, had the generality of the world's peoples accepted His divine revelation at that time, humankind would have been spared from the horrors of the tribulation period and would have entered the Most Great Peace in a straightforward manner. However, this was not the case, and thus, Bahá'u'lláh prescribed that humankind must now go through the long evolutionary process of the Lesser Peace and so forth before it can achieve the Most Great Peace. However, it should be understood that, even if all of the world's peoples had immediately recognized the divine station of Bahá'u'lláh when He first proclaimed Himself, it still would have taken some time for humankind to build the Bahá'í administrative system along with the Bahá'í world federation of nations—the glorious World Order of Bahá'u'lláh. This again goes to show that humanity's recognition of Bahá'u'lláh as the Messenger of God for this day is only one part of the process of human redemption.

Shoghi Effendi also explains that there is a distinction between, on the one hand, Bahá'u'lláh's sacred passages in which He exhorts humanity to recognize His proclamation, and on the other, the sacred passages in which He is expounding upon the laws and institutions of the Administrative Order and the World Order. Interestingly,

Shoghi Effendi asserts that the latter passages are a "mightier" class of revelation as compared to the former, which are mainly devoted to proclaiming Bahá'u'lláh's station. For instance, he emphasizes that the Kitáb-i-Aqdas, a book that is chiefly dedicated to revealing Bahá'u'lláh's administrative laws and institutions, is "mightier" than the aforementioned proclamation letters that Bahá'u'lláh sent to kings, queens, ecclesiastical leaders, elected representatives, and so forth to proclaim His revelation. Accordingly, it is significant to note that the Kitáb-i-Aqdas is also known as "The Most Holy Book." Along these lines, Shoghi Effendi declares,

> Unique and stupendous as was this Proclamation [letters to kings, etc.], it proved to be but a prelude to a still mightier revelation of the creative power of its Author, and to what may well rank as the most signal act of His ministry—the promulgation of the Kitáb-i-Aqdas. . . . [This Book] may well be regarded as the brightest emanation of the mind of Bahá'u'lláh, as the Mother Book of His Dispensation, and the Charter of His New World Order. . . . [T]his Book . . . stands out . . . unique and incomparable among the world's sacred Scriptures. For, unlike the Old Testament and the Holy Books which preceded it . . . unlike the Gospels . . . unlike even the Qur'án which, though explicit in the laws and ordinances formulated by the Apostle of God, is silent on the all-important subject of the succession, the Kitáb-i-Aqdas, revealed from first to last by the Author of the Dispensation Himself, not only preserves for posterity the basic laws and ordinances on which the fabric of His future World Order must rest, but ordains, in addition to the function of interpretation which it confers upon His Successor ['Abdu'l-Bahá], the necessary institutions [such as the Guardianship and the Universal House of Justice] through which the integrity and unity of His Faith can alone be safeguarded.[50]

In short, the recognition of Bahá'u'lláh's station alone is not good enough for this, the Day of God. The pivotal concept of Bahá'u'lláh's entire revelation, and indeed the will of God for this Day, is the establishment of the "oneness of humankind." All the other teachings and principles of the Bahá'í dispensation revolve around this concept. This is why, Bahá'u'lláh conceived of His glorious World Order as the God-given instrument to accomplish this goal—the "ultimate fusion of all races, creeds, classes, and nations." By definition then, the best way that today's peoples can consciously contribute toward the establishment of the World Order is to give their all to perfecting the Administrative Order—"the one agency for the unification of the world, and the proclamation of the reign of righteousness and justice upon the earth."[51]

Two Processes—One Single Glorious Consummation

As described earlier, the American nation is destined to take part in actions that will indirectly and unwittingly promote the national and international institutions that will, in turn, help to establish the World Order of Bahá'u'lláh. This does not mean that all of the actions of this nation in the ensuing years will be positive or even moral. However, Shoghi Effendi explains that, as a result of the spiritual forces unleashed by the Bahá'í dispensation, the United States "is gravitating" toward "associations and policies" wherein its "true destiny must lie." Meanwhile, the American Bahá'ís have the mission to champion efforts to build and consolidate the Administrative Order, and then, to use this global administrative system to propagate Bahá'u'lláh's teachings throughout the planet. In essence, as will be shown in this section, the mission of the American Bahá'í community and the destiny of the United States are highly intertwined and eventually merge together. Both processes started at about the same time—during the course of the first World War when 'Abdu'l-Bahá penned his Divine Plan and the United States joined the war effort. Both processes will also end at the same time when the glorious World Order of Bahá'u'lláh finally emerges in the distant future. Regarding this, Shoghi Effendi notes that the "two simultaneous processes" (mission and destiny) are "distinctly separate, yet closely related and destined to culminate" in a "single glorious consummation." This unequivocally tells us that the mission of the American Bahá'ís and the destiny of the United States are far from being accomplished. In fact, they have barely started.[52]

At this point, it would be a good idea to review some of the milestones that will lead humanity to the New World Order, as outlined in the Bahá'í writings. As described in detail earlier, humanity still needs to go through several evolutionary stages of development that will include the following: a continuation of today's tribulation but in ever increasing bursts of intensity and scope; an unprecedented, catastrophic world crisis of monumental proportions; the permanent cessation of all warfare through a political peace known as the Lesser Peace, which all the nations will impose upon themselves through a formal agreement of collective security; then a long period of human evolution that will eventually lead to the "spiritualization of the masses," the full recognition of Bahá'u'lláh's claims by the world's peoples, and the widespread, conscious implementation of His teachings for the unification of humanity. This mass recognition and implementation of Bahá'u'lláh's message will result in the entrance of humanity into the Most Great Peace—a complete, all-encompassing peace based on the Bahá'í teachings. Humankind's entrance into the Most Great Peace will signalize the emergence of the World Order of Bahá'u'lláh. As stated by Shoghi Effendi, the emergence of the World Order "implies the establishment" of a Bahá'í World Commonwealth, a world federation of nations that will be based on "the very pattern" set by the Administrative Order. Please keep in mind that the Administrative Order is currently called the "embryonic World Order." However, by the time that humankind evolves to the Most Great Peace, the "embryo" will have progressively matured to become widely acknowledged as being the full-grown World Order. This will then allow for the creation of an entirely new, divinely inspired world civilization, the Kingdom of God on earth.

Regarding this chronology of milestones, it is significant to note that, according to Shoghi Effendi, the destiny of the American nation will "culminate in the unfurling of the banner of the Most Great Peace, in the Golden Age of the Dispensation of Bahá'u'lláh." He likewise states that the mission of the American Bahá'í community "will be consummated through the emergence of the Bahá'í World Commonwealth in the Golden Age of the Bahá'í Dispensation." These statements reinforce the understanding that the Most Great Peace (related to the United States' ultimate destiny) and the emergence of the Bahá'í World Commonwealth (related to the ultimate mission of the American Bahá'ís) will occur simultaneously. This, in turn, underscores the idea that the destiny of the United States and the mission of the American Bahá'ís are closely coordinated processes that are "distinctly separate, yet closely related." The U.S. government and its citizens are destined to somehow (without knowing it) lead the world's governments and its peoples to the Most Great Peace. Simultaneously, the American Bahá'ís, based on their unique mission, will consciously and deliberately lead the international Bahá'í effort to expand, consolidate, and eventually perfect the Administrative Order to the point that all of humankind will eventually recognize the Bahá'í Administrative Order as their true refuge and will join it in masses at the advent of the Most Great Peace. This will essentially signal the emergence of the World Order of Bahá'u'lláh, which, in turn, implies the birth of the Bahá'í World Commonwealth, the global federation of countries. As stated by Shoghi Effendi, this world commonwealth will be "sustained by its universal recognition of one God and by its allegiance to one common Revelation [the Bahá'í Faith]."[53]

The two distinct processes (the mission and the destiny) have a mysterious symbiotic relationship in which they mutually reinforce each other. It is fascinating to note, for instance, that Shoghi Effendi acclaims the United States as "that great republic—the shell that enshrines" the "precious" American Bahá'í community. Similarly, he declares that America is destined to serve as the "cradle and champion" of the "embryonic World Order of Bahá'u'lláh." Thus, on the one hand, the United States will unknowingly play the essential role of enshrining (protecting) the American Bahá'í community and of championing and cradling the Administrative Order of the Bahá'í Faith. On the other hand, Shoghi Effendi explains that the "creative energies" released by the Bahá'í Administrative Order (chiefly built by the American Bahá'ís) have permeated the United States with special powers that will enable it to fulfill its destiny. He states,

> The creative energies, mysteriously generated by the first stirrings of the embryonic World Order of Bahá'u'lláh [Administrative Order], have, as soon as released within a nation destined to become its cradle and champion, endowed that nation with the worthiness, and invested it with the powers and capacities, and equipped it spiritually, to play the part foreshadowed in [the writings of 'Abdu'l-Bahá].[54]

This passage underscores the symbiotic relationship between, on the one hand, the Administrative Order that released the creative energies (as a result of the work of the American Bahá'ís), and on the other, the American nation "destined to become its cradle and champion." The passage also alludes to several prophetic statements that were made by 'Abdu'l-Bahá in which he declares that the United States "will lead all nations spiritually" and that the Americans are "indeed worthy of being the first to build the Tabernacle of the Great Peace and proclaim the oneness of mankind." Indeed, Shoghi Effendi affirms that Bahá'u'lláh and 'Abdu'l-Bahá have "singled" out this nation "to become the standard-bearer of the New World Order envisaged in their writings."

Earlier, we discussed the specific contributions that the United States has already made toward the establishment of the New World Order. Shoghi Effendi enumerates these contributions in *Citadel of Faith*, and he additionally mentions some of the unique physical, economic, and social characteristics and qualities that will enable America to fulfill its sacred tasks. He notes the preponderating influence that America wields in the councils of the world as well as the material wealth and prestige that it enjoys. He mentions the tremendous political and economic power that it is capable of exerting on the world stage, and how its unparalleled productive capacity allows it to make major contributions to the alleviation of human suffering and the rehabilitation of nations and peoples. He furthermore touts the "idealism that animates its people." In *The Advent of Divine Justice*, Shoghi Effendi similarly points out the "qualities of high intelligence, of youthfulness, of unbounded initiative, and enterprise" that will help America to play its "future role in ushering in the Golden Age of the Cause of Bahá'u'lláh."[55]

Shoghi Effendi emphasizes, however, that America's "admittedly great characteristics and achievements" will ultimately not win the day. Sadly, this nation's "patent evils" and its moral, spiritual, and social deficiencies are too great. This means that, as stated by Shoghi Effendi, the "road leading to its destiny is long, thorny and torturous." At this point, it would be helpful to remember the symbiotic and mutually reinforcing relationship that exists between the destiny of the United States and the mission of the American Bahá'ís. As will be discussed in the next chapter, the American Bahá'í community, as a part of its mission, will play a key role in helping to purge the United States of the accumulated corruptions and deficiencies that, so far, have prevented it from fulfilling its true, noble role in the work of God.[56]

Chapter Five

THE STAGGERING RESPONSIBILITY OF THE AMERICAN BAHÁ'ÍS

As discussed in the previous chapter, the American Bahá'í community and the United States are both granted special God-given roles in the establishment of the World Order of Bahá'u'lláh. For instance, the American Bahá'ís were endowed by God with the mission to build, improve, and consolidate this Administrative Order, which will ultimately serve as "the very pattern" of the future New World Order. Meanwhile, the United States will serve the crucial roles of being, among other things, "the shell that enshrines" the American Bahá'í community and will also serve as the champion and cradle of the Administrative Order of the Bahá'í Faith. However, unlike the American Bahá'í community, which will be fully conscious of its mission, the United States is destined to unknowingly take part in actions that will promote institutions and circumstances that will be favorable to the establishment of the New World Order. In this chapter, we will take a closer look at the relationship between the mission of the American Bahá'í community and the destiny of the United States. As will be explained, the United States cannot fulfill its divinely inspired destiny until the American Bahá'ís, as demanded by their mission, help this nation to overcome its moral, spiritual, social, economic, and political maladies and corruptions.

Faults, Habits, and Tendencies
Inherited From Their Own Nation

'Abdu'l-Bahá made the following prophetic statement: "Should success crown your enterprise [the mission of the American Bahá'ís], America will assuredly evolve into a center from which waves of spiritual power will emanate, and the throne of the Kingdom of God, will, in the plenitude of its majesty and glory, be firmly established." This passage seems to be underscoring the idea that the American Bahá'ís have the responsibility of initiating or catalyzing the processes that will jumpstart America on its course toward fulfilling its own destiny.[1] Along similar lines, Shoghi Effendi wrote the following regarding the "staggering responsibility" of the American Bahá'ís to help erect the new World Order:

> How great, therefore, how staggering the responsibility that must weigh upon the . . . American believers, at this early stage in their spiritual and administrative evolution, to weed out, by every means in their power, those faults, habits, and tendencies which they have inherited from their own nation, and to cultivate, patiently and prayerfully, those distinctive qualities and characteristics that are so indispensable to their effective participation in the great redemptive work of their Faith. . . . [L]et them focus their attention, for the present, on their own selves, their own individual needs, their own personal deficiencies and weaknesses, ever mindful that every intensification of effort on their part will better equip them for the time when they will be called upon to eradicate in their turn such evil tendencies from the lives and the hearts of the entire body of their fellow-citizens. Nor must they overlook the fact that the World Order, whose basis they . . . are now laboring to establish, can never be reared unless and until the generality of the people to which they belong has been already purged from the divers ills, whether social or political, that now so severely afflict it.[2]

To truly apprehend the unique destiny of the United States and the special mission of the American Bahá'í community, it is critical to deeply meditate on the import of the following words of the above passage: ". . . the World Order . . . can *never be reared unless and until* ..." This fascinating passage serves as both a prescription and a prophecy. It makes it clear that, before the World Order of Bahá'u'lláh can ever be established, the American Bahá'ís must first eliminate certain "faults, habits, and tendencies" from their own lives, and then, they must play a critical role in helping to eradicate "such evil tendencies" from the lives of their fellow American citizens.[3]

A critical task, then, of the American believers is to determine the actual nature of the "faults, habits, and tendencies which they have inherited from their own nation." Fortunately, the Bahá'í writings provide some very strong, insightful guidance as to the nature of these deficiencies. At this point it would be helpful to quickly review some of the key points that were made in chapter one. Significantly, Shoghi Effendi made a strong comparison between the fall of the Roman Empire, and what appears to be the impending collapse of the modern West (including, of course, the declining fortunes of the United States). For instance, in a letter to Western Bahá'ís, he refers to "the signs of an impending catastrophe, strongly reminiscent of the Fall of the Roman Empire in the West, which threatens to engulf the whole structure of present-day civilization." In this same letter, he further states, "How disquieting the lawlessness, the corruption, the unbelief that are eating into the vitals of a tottering civilization!" For the purpose of advancing our current discussion in this section, it should be noted here that when the Roman Empire finally did collapse, it was a civilization that for several generations had already been riddled with crass materialism; moral bankruptcy; stark poverty amidst incredible wealth; political corruption; and civil strife including mob violence, slave revolts, and peasant uprisings. In the same way that the Christians of that day did not fit in to such a perverse and corrupt Roman society, the Bahá'ís of today do not fit into the current "tottering civilization." Indeed, in a letter to the American Bahá'ís, Shoghi Effendi describes modern society as being: "politically convulsed, economically disrupted, socially subverted, morally decadent and spiritually moribund." In essence, the values, beliefs, and goals of the American Bahá'ís are largely at variance with the prevailing culture of the United States.[4]

After reading the paragraphs above, some may get the impression that Bahá'ís are involved in a fringe religious group, a small band of insular zealots who are at odds with all the non-Bahá'í cultural elements around them. This is not the case. In actuality, Bahá'ís are encouraged to maintain a world-embracing outward looking orientation and to be actively engaged in the communities in which they live. Moreover, Bahá'ís are exhorted to have loving and close relations with family members, friends, and coworkers irrespective of their religious beliefs and affiliations. Furthermore, people who recognize the station of Bahá'u'lláh and wish to enroll in the Faith may easily do so; however, individuals are free to participate in most Bahá'í activities and projects without having to enroll as official members of the Faith.

Significantly, the broad-minded, universalistic principles and teachings of the Bahá'í Faith help to prevent the formation of rigid exclusionary, fundamentalist tendencies within it. These moderating principles and teachings include: the oneness of religion (an acceptance of the divine origins of all other major religions); the oneness of humanity; the emphatic rejection of any kind of race, class, and religious prejudice and fanaticism; the encouragement of independent investigation of truth; and the prohibition against proselytization or the use of any form of coercion or manipulation to convert others. Bahá'ís recognize that the universal teachings and principles described above are intended for the benefit of all of humanity and for the advancement of world civilization. As such, Bahá'ís in America and throughout the world are actively involved with non-Bahá'ís in service projects that are intended to uplift communities and to raise the fortunes of mankind. It is also important to note that, according to the Bahá'í teachings, the salvation of the individual is tied to the salvation of humanity. Indeed, major emphasis is placed on "collective salvation" rather than "personal salvation." Thus Bahá'í individuals do not have license to assert that they are saved or somehow spiritually superior, much less to claim that non-Bahá'ís are unsaved.

All of the factors mentioned above have likely helped to fuel the growth and apparent universal appeal of the Bahá'í Faith. This young religion, which emerged from the Middle East only 166 years ago, continues to spread and grow at a good pace both within the United States and in the world in general. It is now the second most widespread religion on the planet, second only to Christianity in terms of geographic distribution. Also, the Bahá'í International Community (BIC), an official body of the Baha'i Faith, has enjoyed recognition as a nongovernmental organization at the United Nations since 1948. The BIC collaborates with many other nongovernmental organizations, and it also holds consultative status with the United Nations Economic and Social Council and with the United Nations Children's Fund. Representatives of the BIC have offices in over eight locations throughout the globe and work to address issues involving human rights, health, environmental conservation, education, peace-building, women's equality, and sustainable development. Thus, far from being an insular small band of zealots who isolate themselves from society, Bahá'ís are an integral part of communities throughout the United States as well as worldwide.

Despite the fact that Bahá'ís are directly involved in society, the Bahá'í writings admonish them not to conform themselves to the prevailing corrupt paradigm, but instead to strive to transcend and transform it. Hence, Bahá'ís must remain cognizant of the fact that their worldview is not in accord with the prevailing cultural worldview of the United States and the West in general.

Dominated by a Mechanistic Despiritualized Worldview

The term *worldview* refers to the set of assumptions, values, beliefs, and ideas through which one perceives reality. It is possible for individuals to alter their perception of reality if they change their worldview. This means that different cultural groups may actually be perceiving different versions of reality, especially if these groups have radically different worldviews (such as the clash in perspectives that occurred between the European settlers and the American Indians during the colonial period). Worldview is inextricably linked to one's perception concerning the nature, the meaning, the purpose, and the goal of human life. Thus, due to their unique religious worldview, American Bahá'ís are increasingly finding themselves split between, on the one hand, their Bahá'í identity (based on Bahá'u'lláh's teachings), which they are aspiring to cultivate, and on the other, their American cultural identity (based on manmade, defective theories, values, beliefs, and ideas), which they have developed as a part of the acculturation and assimilation process within the United States. In short, if American Bahá'ís want to determine the "faults, habits, and tendencies which they have inherited from their own nation" as directed by Shoghi Effendi, then they must essentially look at the cultural worldview (the values, beliefs, assumptions, and ideas) that they have inherited from the dominant United States culture.

It is my belief that the "enervating materialism," "patent evils," "irreligion," and "godlessness," as well as the American "faults, habits, and tendencies" that are condemned in the Bahá'í writings are directly related to the domination of a Western view of reality commonly called the Cartesian-Newtonian worldview. As explained in the preface, this prevailing Western perspective is a pervasively materialistic view of reality that emphasizes the truth of science, reason, logic, the natural, the material, and the secular while ignoring or even denigrating the truth of religion, faith, intuition, the supernatural, the spiritual, and the sacred. Obviously, such a mechanistic perspective is antithetical to the Bahá'í worldview, and it acts as a barrier to the establishment of the World Order of Bahá'u'lláh. It is significant to note that the Cartesian-Newtonian worldview emerged in Europe and became consolidated in the United States, but it has now rapidly spread throughout the world even into nations that claim to be non-Western. It is this worldview that spawned the Scientific Revolution, the Industrial Revolution, laissez-faire capitalism, socialism, communism, imperialism (colonialism), as well as today's Western-dominated globalized capitalism with its powerful multinational corporations.

In light of the above, it is not surprising that Shoghi Effendi refers to Europe as the cradle of a "godless," a "highly-vaunted yet lamentably defective civilization."[5] Indeed, it is along these same lines that Shoghi Effendi, in a letter to the American Bahá'ís, issues one of his strongest condemnations of a cultural influence that is pervasive within the United States—the "evil" of materialism. While reading the following message from Shoghi Effendi, it is important to keep in mind that materialism is the most significant defining characteristic of the Cartesian-Newtonian, Western worldview. He states,

> pervading all departments of life—an evil which the [American] nation, and indeed all those within the capitalist system . . . share with [the Soviet Union] . . . is the crass materialism, which lays excessive and ever-increasing emphasis on material well-being, forgetful of those things of the spirit on which alone a sure and stable foundation can be laid for human society. It is this same cancerous materialism, born originally in Europe, carried to excess in the North American continent, contaminating the Asiatic peoples and nations, spreading its ominous tentacles to the borders of Africa, and now invading its very heart, which Bahá'u'lláh in unequivocal and emphatic language denounced in His Writings, comparing it to a devouring flame and regarding it as the chief factor in precipitating the dire ordeals and world-shaking crises that must necessarily involve the burning of cities and the spread of terror and consternation in the hearts of men. Indeed a foretaste of the devastation which this consuming fire will wreak upon the world, and with which it will lay waste the cities of the nations participating in this tragic world-engulfing contest, has been afforded by the last World War [WWII], marking the second stage in the global havoc which humanity, forgetful of its God and heedless of the clear warnings uttered by His appointed Messenger for this day, must, alas, inevitably experience. It is this same all-pervasive, pernicious materialism against which the voice of . . . ['Abdu'l-Bahá] was raised, with pathetic persistence, from platform and pulpit, in His addresses to the heedless multitudes . . . on the morrow of His fateful visit to both Europe and America . . ."[6]

It is indeed fascinating that, as noted above, Bahá'u'lláh Himself denounced materialism as being the "chief factor in precipitating" the "world-shaking crises" that are increasingly plaguing humanity. This alone shows the importance of this topic. The passage also reinforces the understanding that materialism, as a way of life, first emerged in Europe, was then amplified in the United States, and then spread to other parts of the world. This is all very consistent with the historical development of the secular, despiritualized Cartesian-Newtonian worldview.

Some people mistakenly equate materialism solely with consumerism (the inordinate buying of products and services) or commercialism (the selling of such things). It must be emphasized that consumerism and commercialism are merely symptoms of the "disease" called materialism. Indeed, it is possible for an individual to be against consumerism and commercialism (free of the symptoms), and yet still have the disease of materialism—this is true if the individual ignores or outright rejects religion as a force in his or her daily life. Materialism is actually a philosophy, an overall approach to life, or a way of life that is divorced from spirituality and religion. This is likely why Shoghi Effendi, in a letter to Western Bahá'ís, cautions them of the "prevailing spirit of modernism, with its emphasis on a purely materialistic philosophy, which, as it diffuses itself, tends increasingly to divorce religion from man's daily life."[7]

People with a materialistic perspective, such as the Cartesian-Newtonian worldview, regard the physical world to be the true reality, and consequently, they regard the material aspects of their lives to be of primary importance. This is contrary to a spiritual perspective, such as the Bahá'í worldview, in which the physical world is seen as a false reality—a mirage or an illusion that is projected from a deeper, truer spiritual reality. Within this Bahá'í perspective, humans are to be regarded as being, first and foremost, spiritual entities (souls) that happen to be experiencing a physical realm. In essence, this physical world is intended to assist us (as souls) to exercise and test our spiritual attributes. In this way, we may hopefully become prepared for the true life that will occur when our bodies die and our souls move on to the spiritual worlds of God (the true reality). One of the main purposes of religion is to help people to become awakened to the deeper spiritual reality. We can catch glimpses of the spiritual world through prayer, good deeds, spiritual contemplation and meditation, certain dreams, and so forth. The point here is that the soul cannot be nourished by physical things alone. People who believe that they are mostly a physical body and that the material world is the "be all, end all" will perceive their mission in life very differently than people who believe that they are just passing through this "physical classroom for the soul" and that God has an overall divine plan that gives meaning and purpose to human life. Ultimately, one's perception of true reality determines the goals and the overall trajectory of one's life.

As such, Bahá'ís are encouraged to detach from the physical world and to cultivate a deep understanding that real happiness and liberation are to be found in the development of spiritual virtues such as humility, generosity, compassion, contentment, forgiveness, self-sacrifice, and a service orientation. Thus the Bahá'í worldview is contrary to the prevailing Western worldview, which encourages people to chase after happiness through the incessant pursuit of physical wealth and status. Such a lifestyle promises happiness and peace, but instead delivers anxiety, fear, and depression as exemplified by the shattered lives of many of our pop culture icons. Ultimately, the thirst for worldly power, the attachment to physical pleasures, and the unmitigated craving for the instant gratification of ever-increasing personal wants and desires are all contrary to spiritual wisdom. Such a self-indulgent, materialistic approach to life helps to breed immoralities of every sort including government and corporate corruption, sexual irresponsibility, substance abuse, theft, dishonesty, greed, envy, selfishness, incessant competition, and criticism of others as well as poor relations between people including racial prejudice.

In *The Advent of Divine Justice*, a book aimed primarily at the American Bahá'í community, Shoghi Effendi notes that there are three "spiritual prerequisites" for the success of the American Bahá'ís in all their endeavors including their efforts to teach the Bahá'í Faith, to maintain financial solvency, and to build their Temples. He names these three as: "a high sense of moral rectitude," "absolute chastity in their individual lives," and "a complete freedom from prejudice in their dealings with peoples of a different race, class, creed, or color."[8]

Shoghi Effendi explains that the first prerequisite is especially but not exclusively aimed at the elected representatives of the Bahá'í community, and it implies a sense of fair-mindedness, equity, justice, truthfulness, trustworthiness, and reliability. This rectitude must be present in all business dealings, in all the verdicts of the elected representatives, and in all service and employment activities. It must also manifest in an aloofness from partisan political controversies, and in an impartiality of Bahá'ís toward enemies of the Faith.

The second prerequisite (holiness and chastity) is especially, but not exclusively, aimed at the youth of the Bahá'í community, who are called to live a pure life that, as stated by Shoghi Effendi, rises above the "indecencies, the vices, the false standards" that the "deficient moral code tolerates." In this way, the youth will contribute "decisively" to "the driving force" of the community and will play a key role in determining its future orientation and overall trajectory. Bahá'ís of all ages, however, have the responsibility of maintaining holiness and chastity as controlling principles in their lives, and this implies clean-mindedness; modesty; temperance; marital fidelity; a control of one's carnal desires; an aloofness from misdirected pleasures such as drug use; as well as moderation in language, dress, amusements, and all literary and artistic avocations.

The third prerequisite (overcoming prejudice) is aimed at all members of the American Bahá'í community irrespective of class, color, age, or experience. All members must face the challenge of fulfilling this prerequisite in all aspects of their activities inside and outside of the Bahá'í community, and according to Shoghi Effendi, none can claim "however much he may have progressed along this line, to have completely discharged the stern responsibilities which" this prerequisite demands. Shoghi Effendi states that every Bahá'í community has the "first and inescapable obligation to nurture, encourage, and safeguard every minority belonging to any faith, race, class, or nation within it." Indeed, if members have equivalent qualifications for any office or position, or if an equal number of ballots are cast in an election, then "priority should unhesitatingly be accorded the party representing the minority, and this for no other reason except to stimulate and encourage it, and afford it an opportunity to further the interests of the community."[9]

With the above three "spiritual prerequisites" in mind, Shoghi Effendi calls on the American Bahá'ís to take part in a "double crusade" aimed at ridding themselves and their fellow countrymen of the "patent evils" that "an excessive and binding materialism" has "engendered within" their nation. He states,

A rectitude of conduct which . . . offers a striking contrast to the deceitfulness and corruption that characterize the political life of the nation and of the parties and factions that compose it; a holiness and chastity that are diametrically opposed to the moral laxity and licentiousness which defile the character of a not inconsiderable proportion of its citizens; an interracial fellowship completely purged from the curse of racial prejudice which stigmatizes the vast majority of its people—these are the weapons which the American believers can and must wield in their double crusade, first to regenerate the inward life of their own community, and next to assail the long-standing evils that have entrenched themselves in the life of their nation.[10]

The Bahá'í Faith encourages moderation, contentment, and the reduction of wants and desires as the route to true peace, harmony, and happiness. The writings, however, do not encourage asceticism or an "excessive and bigoted puritanism." Sadly, as mentioned earlier, various studies show that today's American children and adolescents—one of the most prosperous generations in history—are suffering from very high, and in many cases escalating, rates of suicide, homicide, depression, drug abuse, mental illness, sexually transmitted diseases, anxiety disorders, addictions, and various forms of violent behavior. Along these lines, in a cautionary message to the American Bahá'í community, Shoghi Effendi refers to the American people's "attachment to worldly things that enshrouds" their "souls," to the "fears and anxieties that distract their minds," and to "the pleasure and dissipations that fill their time." He asserts that the American Bahá'ís must overcome such "formidable obstacles" so that they can fulfill their sacred task involving the "redemption" of their "own countrymen."[11] In short, the American Bahá'ís are constantly confronting an American worldview that is antithetical to the teachings of Bahá'u'lláh. *Century of Light*, a book prepared under the supervision of the Universal House of Justice, contains a highly lucid and compelling passage that essentially summarizes the various characteristics of the Western worldview:

There has not been a society in the history of the world . . . that did not derive its thrust from some foundational interpretation of reality. Such a system of thought reigns today virtually unchallenged across the planet, under the nominal designation "Western civilization." Philosophically and politically, it presents itself as a kind of liberal relativism; economically and socially, as capitalism—two value systems that have now so adjusted to each other and become so mutually reinforcing as to constitute virtually a single, comprehensive worldview. Appreciation of the benefits—in terms of the personal freedom, social prosperity and scientific progress enjoyed by a significant minority of the Earth's people—cannot withhold a thinking person from recognizing that the system is morally and intellectually bankrupt. It has contributed its best to the advancement of civilization, as did all its predecessors, and, like them, is impotent to deal with the needs of a world never imagined by the eighteenth century prophets who conceived most of its component elements. . . . Tragically, what Bahá'ís see in present-day society is unbridled exploitation of the masses of humanity by greed that excuses itself as the operation of "impersonal market forces" [capitalism]. What meets their eyes everywhere is the destruction of moral foundations vital to humanity's future, through gross self-indulgence masquerading as "freedom of speech." What they find themselves struggling against daily is the pressure of a dogmatic materialism, claiming to be the voice of "science," that seeks systematically to exclude from intellectual life all impulses arising from the spiritual level of human consciousness. . . . And for a Bahá'í the ultimate issues are spiritual. . . . The process of transformation it has set in motion advances by inducing a fundamental change of consciousness, and the challenge it poses to everyone who would serve it is to free oneself from attachment to inherited assumptions and preferences that are irreconcilable with the Will of God for humanity's coming of age.[12]

The quote above highlights the understanding that a culture's perception or interpretation of reality (its worldview) is critical because it establishes the trajectory of the society, and it determines the meaning, purpose, and goals of the people. The quote also eloquently reinforces the idea that Western civilization currently holds a powerful grip on the rest of the globe—a "system of thought" that is reigning "virtually unchallenged across the planet." The passage explains that this "system" has resulted in some noteworthy benefits, but that these benefits are primarily enjoyed by a "minority of the Earth's people." Significantly, the passage asserts that Western civilization, despite its benefits, is essentially a "morally and intellectually bankrupt" system.

The above quote also notes that most of the West's "component elements" (social, economic, and political elements as well as the philosophical underpinnings of these elements) were conceived in Europe particularly by "eighteenth century prophets." This is likely a reference to the philosophers, scientists, and intellectuals of the eighteenth century—a time known as the Age of Enlightenment. As will be explained in the next section, Cartesian-Newtonian materialistic science thrived and greatly proliferated during the Enlightenment. The results of this proliferation are still evident in our society today—it shows up as the daily "pressure of a dogmatic materialism, claiming to be the voice of 'science.'" Contrary to the obsolete, mechanistic theories and philosophies inherited from the eighteenth century thinkers, the quote explains that the issues of the day are essentially spiritual struggles that must be overcome through a fundamental change in human spiritual consciousness. In this regard, the teachings of the Bahá'í Faith are noteworthy in that they can help to induce this shift in consciousness. Along these lines, the passage emphasizes that anyone who would like to serve the Cause of God must remain unattached to the "inherited assumptions and preferences" of Western civilization that are "irreconcilable with the Will of God for humanity's coming of age." According to the Bahá'í teachings, the core essence of the will of God for this age is the unification of humankind and the creation of a spiritually enlightened planetary civilization, the Kingdom of God on earth.

The Bahá'í critiques of Western civilization and America contained in this section share much in common with the views of a diversity of people worldwide who are deeply aware of and increasingly concerned with the defective nature of the Western-dominated global system. Of particular relevance here are the views of an emerging international movement of scholars from various disciplines who reject the prevailing mechanistic worldview and who believe that what is needed is a paradigm shift into a holistic view of reality. Consistent with the Bahá'í perspective, these holistic scholars assert that the necessary shift in worldview requires the recognition of the oneness of humanity, and indeed, the oneness of the universe. Also, in accord with Bahá'í teachings, the proponents of the holistic paradigm believe in the unity of mind, body, and spirit, and moreover, they emphasize that scientific truths should be integrated with religious truths in order to gain a fuller, more accurate view of reality. Along these lines, Fritjof Capra, a distinguished physicist, author, and holistic advocate, states,

> I have come to believe that today our society as a whole finds itself in a . . . crisis . . . an energy crisis, a crisis in health care, . . . environmental disasters, a rising wave of violence and crime. . . . These are all different facets of one and the same crisis, . . . this crisis

is essentially a crisis in perception . . . it derives from the fact that we are trying to apply the concepts of an outdated worldview— the mechanistic worldview of Cartesian-Newtonian science—to a reality that can no longer be understood in terms of these concepts. . . . What we need, then, is a new "paradigm"—a new vision of reality; a fundamental change in our thoughts, perceptions, and values. The beginnings . . . of the shift from the mechanistic to the holistic conception of reality, are already visible in all fields.[13]

My first book, *Faith, Physics, and Psychology: Rethinking Society and the Human Spirit*, provides a detailed view of how the Bahá'í Faith— though distinct in its origin, history, and teachings—shares much in common with the emerging holistic movement. Indeed, several of the core teachings of the Faith, especially its emphasis on the oneness and interconnectivity of everything in the cosmos as well as the principle of the harmony of science and religion, are consistent with the central views of the overall holistic movement. It must be noted, however, that the holistic movement is not formally organized or orchestrated in any fashion. It is made up of individuals who share similar values, theories, beliefs, and perspectives pertaining to holism. It includes scholars within diverse fields of knowledge such as quantum physics, philosophy, psychology, religious studies, economics, education, medicine, ecology, and cosmology. As such, Bahá'ís who work in a diversity of fields and occupations often find themselves working hand in hand with other holistic advocates to pursue common goals related to the development of a spiritually enlightened, peaceful, unified, and just global order.

Significantly, Bahá'í and non-Bahá'í proponents of holism share the common belief that humanity is already naturally evolving toward a holistic paradigm through transformations in human spiritual consciousness. In other words, the movement toward a holistic worldview in all fields of human endeavor is not coerced, but rather, evolutionary in nature. Along these lines, Ron Miller, a distinguished educator, author, and holistic advocate, states,

Holism holds that human beings are essentially spiritual beings, individual expressions of a transcendent creative source that we do not fully comprehend. Our long, sorry history of violence, greed, and oppression reflects ignorance of our spiritual nature and its suppression, not an innate drive toward evil. Humanity's development is not finished and may never be; we are still evolving morally, culturally, and spiritually. The holistic approach strives to develop our latent capacity for cooperation and community, and asserts that there need not be "losers" in a just and caring society.[14]

It is worth noting that, to my knowledge, educator Ron Miller and physicist Fritjof Capra (quoted earlier) are not enrolled members of the Bahá'í Faith, and yet, a significant portion of their philosophical and theoretical work seems consistent with the Bahá'í worldview. Because of commonalities in worldview, the Bahá'í teachings would likely be generally appealing to both of these scholars.

In short, it would be a mistake to view the Bahá'í Faith as an isolated religious movement with only a narrow appeal. As discussed above, the Bahá'í perspective is quite consistent with the views of a worldwide diverse movement of people who are increasingly questioning the limited materialistic view of reality that is promoted by Western civilization. The next section takes a closer look at the characteristics of modern Western civilization.

"A System of Thought" that Reigns "Virtually Unchallenged Across the Planet"

The passage quoted earlier from the Bahá'í book, *Century of Light,* maintains that Western civilization is "a system of thought" that "has contributed its best to the advancement of civilization" and it is now "impotent to deal with the needs of a world never imagined by the eighteenth century prophets [Western scientists, scholars, and philosophers]" who helped to develop it. The passage further states that "everyone who would serve" the Bahá'í Faith must accept the challenge "to free oneself from attachment to inherited assumptions and preferences that are irreconcilable with the Will of God for humanity's coming of age." Keeping the above in mind, in this section, we will take an in-depth look at the Cartesian-Newtonian worldview that lies at the foundation of modern Western civilization. As we explore the origin and characteristics of this dominant "system of thought," we will also simultaneously critique this system from a Bahá'í perspective.[15] Related to this, the Universal House of Justice issued the following guidance to Western Bahá'í scholars:

There are many aspects of western thinking which have been exalted to a status of unassailable principle in the general mind, that time may well show to have been erroneous or, at least, only partially true. Any Bahá'í who rises to eminence in academic circles will be exposed to the powerful influence of such thinking.[16]

Along similar lines, Shoghi Effendi maintains:

If long-cherished ideals and time-honored institutions, if certain social assumptions . . . have ceased to promote the welfare of the generality of mankind . . . let them be swept away. . . . For legal standards, political and economic theories are solely designed to safeguard the interests of humanity as a whole, and not humanity to be crucified for the preservation of the integrity of any particular law or doctrine.[17]

Please note that this section's description of the origin and characteristics of the Cartesian-Newtonian worldview is not comprehensive. *Faith, Physics, and Psychology: Rethinking Society and the Human Spirit,* has detailed information (almost 500 pages) regarding this worldview's pervasive influence within Western culture as well as information regarding the groundbreaking efforts that are being undertaken to find holistic alternatives to this worldview.

The Cartesian-Newtonian worldview has its earliest roots in the Scientific Revolution that started in Europe in the mid-1500s with the brilliant work of Nicolas Copernicus, Tycho Brahe, William Gilbert, Johannes Kepler, Galileo Galilei, Francis Bacon, Rene Descartes, and

Isaac Newton. The worldview is named after Descartes, who did much of his work during the early 1600s, and Newton, who did much of his work in the late 1600s and early 1700s. As will be seen, the Cartesian-Newtonian worldview then rapidly spread and thrived throughout the 1700s (the eighteenth century is known as the Age of Enlightenment). As mentioned earlier in the quote from *Century of Light*, this was when the "prophets of the eighteenth century" conceived most of the component elements of modern Western civilization.

One of the salient features of the Cartesian-Newtonian perspective is that it promotes a mechanistic view of human beings and the universe. It pictures people as being essentially biological machines. It similarly views the universe as being a huge machine made up of separate parts. Descartes (1596–1650), a highly influential French philosopher, scientist, and mathematician was the first to picture the universe as a perfect machine, essentially a clockwork universe that is governed by exact mathematical laws of cause and effect. Newton (1642–1727), an illustrious English scientist and mathematician, liked the idea of a mechanical universe, and he was able to invent differential calculus, which allowed him to formulate his famous mathematical laws and principles of the mechanical universe. As will be explained, the thinking of these two men in particular had dramatic consequences in all fields of study, and it laid the groundwork for the way that we currently view reality in the United States and the West in general.

Rene Descartes developed an entire philosophy in which he argued that the universe is made up of matter and that matter is devoid of any spirit, life, or purpose. In this way, he introduced a very strong split between spirit and matter. He also introduced a strong split between mind and body. He argued that there is nothing in the mind that pertains to the body and nothing in the body that pertains to the mind. This Cartesian approach of separating spirit and matter as well as mind and body is readily apparent in present-day fields of study within the West. For instance, this approach is obvious in the psychological schools of psychoanalysis and behaviorism, both of which reject the spiritual dimensions of human nature. For instance, Sigmund

Freud, the founder of psychoanalysis, ridiculed the idea of the human soul and instead insisted that, at its core, human nature is dominated by lower instincts, especially sexual drives and fears. He stated that religion itself is just "an obsessive-compulsive neurosis of mankind" and a manifestation of unresolved psychosexual conflicts from an infantile developmental level. Similarly, John Watson, the founder of behaviorism, not only rejected the soul but also even rejected the existence of human consciousness itself. He reduced human beings to complex animals that mindlessly respond to environmental stimuli. He stated, "Man is an animal different from other animals only in the types of behaviors he displays."

It almost goes without saying that the manifestly degraded views of human nature proposed by both of the above Western schools of psychology bear absolutely no semblance to the Bahá'í perspective regarding the spiritual nobility of the human reality. The Bahá'í writings explain that man has two natures, a lower bodily nature and an exalted, spiritual higher nature. The *true* nature of a person is the spiritual nature—the human soul that is created at the moment of conception. The soul is the seat of a person's consciousness, self, and personality. Within the soul lie innate divine traits such as the ability for self-sacrificing love or altruism, the power of reason, the love of God, willpower, as well as many virtues such as generosity, compassion, justice, truthfulness, humility, and forgiveness. These qualities and virtues, however, lie latent in the human soul and must be developed before they can be properly expressed in the physical realm. Regarding this, Baha'u'llah declared,

> Upon the reality of man . . . He [God] hath focused the radiance of all of His names and attributes, and made it a mirror of His own Self. Alone of all created things man hath been singled out for so great a favor, so enduring a bounty. . . . These energies with which the . . . Source of heavenly guidance hath endowed the reality of man lie, however, latent within him, even as the flame is hidden within the candle and the rays of light are potentially present in the lamp.[18]

The Bahá'í Faith rejects religious and philosophic doctrines that postulate that human beings have original sin or that they have innate evil elements in their nature. Even the bodily lower nature is not regarded as evil. The lower nature has the same physical needs, desires, and sufferings that are common to all other animals such as thirst, hunger, sexual drive, fear, anger, and pain. Spiritual progress is hampered when a person becomes overly preoccupied with these physical passions of the lower nature. In short, a person's physical needs, desires, and sufferings are not inherently bad or evil. However, if a person becomes enslaved by one or more of these physical promptings, then the latent virtues of the soul remain underdeveloped, and this leads to evil actions. Along these lines, Bahá'u'lláh wrote, "Man is even as steel, the essence of which is hidden: through admonition and explanation, good counsel and education, that essence will be brought to light. If, however, he be allowed to remain in his original condition, the corrosion of lusts and appetites will effectively destroy him."[19]

In addition to errantly promoting a degraded view of human nature as described above, Descartes' philosophical understandings had other negative consequences. He also zealously emphasized the power of human reason, and, based on his understandings, he contended that the only route to certain, evident knowledge—to absolute truth— was science. Interestingly, prior to the emergence and consolidation of the Cartesian-Newtonian worldview, most Europeans believed in the interdependence of physical and spiritual phenomena. However, the views of the Europeans, particularly those of the early scientists, were radically altered as they internalized the mechanistic philosophy of Descartes. To this day, many scientists keep their distance from religion. Scientists who do happen to believe in God and religion are usually afraid to publicly admit their faith for fear of being ostracized by the scientific community, which tends to pigeonhole religion with various superstitions and myths of the past. In contrast, the Bahá'í Faith supports a holistic perspective in which the discovered truths of science along with the revealed truths of religion are both necessary in order to get an accurate picture of reality. 'Abdu'l-Bahá affirms this position in the following quote:

Religion and science are the two wings upon which man's intelligence can soar into the heights, with which the human soul can progress. It is not possible to fly with one wing alone! Should a man try to fly with the wing of religion alone he would quickly fall into the quagmire of superstition, whilst on the other hand, with the wing of science alone he would also make no progress, but fall into the despairing slough of materialism.[20]

Descartes also was the first to introduce the analytic method as a scientific tool. This method is based on the assumption that, if you break something into its component parts, and if you study the parts separately, then you can understand the whole thing. The Cartesian analytic approach to scholarship shows up today in our universities, which are broken into rigid disciplines and into a myriad of departments and sub-departments that are often busy studying only a "part" of society. It also shows up in the government's attempts to analyze and solve the overall breakdown in our society by creating categories such as education problems, health care problems, environmental problems, immigration problems, and so forth rather than recognizing that practically any problem that exists in our society today is a complex interaction of the social, political, economic, and spiritual dimensions. For instance, if we truly want to solve the issue of under-performing schools, then we must also deal with problems associated with immorality, the breakdown of families, the lack of affordable health care, unemployment, poor race relations, teenage depression, mindless consumerism, crime, addictions, and so forth. Yet, we have legions of education experts who are myopically (in Cartesian-Newtonian fashion) attempting to solve the issue of underperforming schools by solely focusing on school changes such as: adding computers and other expensive technologies, changing textbooks, adopting lockstep education standards and rigid "one size fits all" reading and math curriculums, extensively utilizing standardized tests along with punitive consequences for those who fail, firing teachers and principles and having the government take over underperforming schools, as well as other measures. This will not work because it does not deal with any of the other societal problems (mentioned above) that are negatively impacting the education of students.

The Cartesian analytic method has been very successful at producing breakthroughs in various scientific areas such as the ability of highly specialized experts to pinpoint the causes and remedies of various diseases and certain genetic deformities or maladies. However, this "old science" approach has also limited the ability of many Westerners to see the overall bigger picture and to connect the mountain of information from the various disciplines into a consistent, comprehensive view of reality. Along these lines, quantum physics now shows that you cannot gain a true understanding of the whole just by studying its parts because when the parts come together, they create something much more complex than the sum of the individual effects of each part. Along these same lines, all of the various economic, political, social, and spiritual problems have now combined with each other and have interacted in unpredictable ways to create a society (the whole) that is much more lethal and dysfunctional that any of its individual problems. Indeed, as discussed in chapter two, the Bahá'í writings make it clear that humanity has "strayed too far and suffered too great a decline to be redeemed" even through the devoted efforts and concerted actions of its best rulers, statesmen, economists, and moralists. In short, a piecemeal approach to resolving societal problems is ultimately an exercise in futility.[21]

The Bahá'í teachings, in contrast to the Cartesian analytic method, offer a holistic approach to life that encourages people to remain cognizant of the various spiritual, psychological, scientific, social, economic, and political factors that are influencing any given situation. The Bahá'í teachings also maintain that, not only do well-functioning parts influence the overall whole, but also just as importantly, a well-functioning whole can have a positive, alleviating effect on the parts. For instance, an overall healthy body can have a healing effect on smaller parts of the body such as the skin or teeth, which may sometimes become afflicted with infections. Similarly, a well-functioning, healthy society can have a positive effect on its constituent parts including even some unhealthy individuals who may be inclined to do evil. Unfortunately, due to the analytic method, some present-day scholars are almost solely focused on fixing the economic, social, and/ or political structures of the external society, while on the opposite end, some modern professionals are almost solely focused on resolving the personal issues of individuals. The Bahá'í Faith calls for a holistic approach that addresses both the inward life of the individual as well as the outward structures of society. This holistic approach is shown in the following Bahá'í passage:

> We cannot segregate the human heart from the environment outside us. . . . Man is organic with the world. His inner life moulds the environment and is itself also deeply affected by it. The one acts upon the other and every abiding change in the life of man is the result of these mutual reactions. . . . No movement in the world directs its attention upon both these aspects of human life and has full measures for their improvement, save the teachings of Bahá'u'lláh. . . . We need a change of heart, a reframing of all our conceptions and a new orientation of our activities. The inward life of man as well as his outward environment have to be reshaped if human salvation is to be secured.[22]

The Cartesian-Newtonian worldview can essentially be characterized by the word separation rather than the word integration. For instance, this perspective breaks apart mind, body, and soul. This is especially obvious in today's medical field where Western doctors still attempt to cure the body of the patient but pay little, if any attention, to the condition of the patient's mind and soul. Similarly, biologists and other scientists often attempt to reduce the divine human reality, the mysterious inner workings of a human being, to mechanical interactions between various cells, neurons, genes, chemical compounds, and hormones. This worldview also puts the powers of reason and the intellect on a pedestal while alienating human beings from their emotional, spiritual, and moral faculties. Furthermore, its emphasis on separation, when applied at the societal level, promotes a rabid individualism where people are not encouraged to see themselves as interconnected parts of one whole. Regarding this, a passage from the Bahá'í book, *Century of Light*, states that "it is not surprising to find at the very heart of the current crisis of civilization a cult of individualism that increasingly admits of no restraint . . ." This worldview typically creates mutually exclusive categories or dichotomies such as science versus religion, reason versus faith, logic versus intuition, White versus Black, man versus woman, and so forth. This reflects an "either/or" mentality instead of a "both/and" holistic perspective. In contrast to such separations and dichotomies, Bahá'u'lláh's teachings promote the oneness of the universe, the oneness of humanity, the harmony of science and religion, the equality of men and women, as well as the unity of mind, body, and spirit. The Bahá'í writings state, "Earthly and heavenly, material and spiritual . . . appearance and reality and the essence of all things, both inward and outward—all of these are connected one with another and are interrelated."[23]

It is fascinating to note that the Bahá'í view of reality has many similarities to the theories and perspectives that have been put forth by some modern quantum physicists. The theoretical work of David Bohm, a world-renowned quantum physicist, is particularly consistent with the Bahá'í perspective on reality. Bohm is famous for his holographic theory of the universe by which he proposes that the universe itself is like an enormous holographic image—a projection from a higher, non-manifest reality. A holographic projection looks almost exactly like a real physical object, but it is actually just an intangible three-dimensional image of an object. It is even possible to walk around a holographic projection and to view it from different angles just like a real object. Science writer Michael Talbot states the following in his acclaimed book, *The Holographic Universe:* "One of Bohm's most startling assertions is that the tangible reality of our everyday lives is really a kind of illusion, like a holographic image. Underlying it is a deeper order of existence, a vast and more primary level of reality that gives birth to all the objects and appearances of our physical world in much the same way that a piece of holographic film gives birth to a hologram."[24]

Along these same lines, the Bahá'í writings assert that the physical world is just a manifestation or projection from a deeper, truer spiritual reality. 'Abdu'l-Bahá wrote, "Know thou that the Kingdom [spiritual realm] is the real world, and this nether place [physical universe] is only its shadow stretching out. A shadow hath no life of its own; its existence is only a fantasy, and nothing more; it is but images reflected in water, and seeming as pictures to the eye." Furthermore, in a talk he gave in 1911 (many years before Bohm's holographic theory), 'Abdu'l-Bahá stated, "Whatever objects appear in this world of existence [physical world] are the outer pictures of the world of heaven [spiritual world]."[25]

The Bahá'í writings assert that the physical world and the spiritual world ultimately merge into each other and can be considered one interconnected realm. Likewise, Bohm asserts that the non-manifest higher reality and the manifest holographic universe merge together, and he proposes a concept known as "unbroken wholeness" in which everything in the cosmos, including human consciousness, is considered to be "a seamless extension of everything else." Indeed, akin to the Bahá'í teachings, Bohm states, "Deep down the consciousness of mankind is one." Thus, Bohm and the Bahá'í Faith propose complementary views of reality that are not in accord with Rene Descartes' model of a mechanical universe composed of unconnected physical matter devoid of any consciousness, life, and spirit.[26]

The work of Descartes contributed greatly to the development of classical science, but by the end of his life, he was still unable to formulate the mathematical laws and principles that could describe his mechanical model of the universe. This was left for Isaac Newton, a seventeenth century scholar who is considered by many to be the preeminent Western scientist of all time. As a physicist, Newton invented a new math, differential calculus, which enabled him to formulate mathematical laws and principles that seemed to describe, quite accurately, the workings of the so-called clockwork universe. Indeed, by applying Newton's deterministic approach along with his mathematical laws, early scientists were incredibly successful in describing and predicting the motion of planets, comets, moons, and tides. They were also able to develop other mathematical principles and laws pertaining to the temperature and pressure of gases, the vibrations of elastic bodies, the behavior of heat and sound, and many other things. These scientific successes reinforced the idea that the universe was indeed a machine governed by mathematical laws of cause and effect. Unfortunately, the early scientific successes at defining and manipulating phenomena also led to the West's compulsive emphasis on prediction and control. This overemphasis on manipulating physical phenomena has made Western culture quite dismissive regarding the spiritual concepts of faith and the will of God. For instance, it is unlikely that one may ever hear a scientist on the news state that a space shuttle will make it safely into orbit— "God willing." In contrast, the Bahá'í writings exhort us to prepare appropriately for material circumstances, but to ultimately place our trust and reliance in God and to accept the will of God even if God's will is contrary to our own wishes. Along these lines, 'Abdu'l-Bahá stated the following regarding the sinking of the Titanic:

> We are living in a day of reliance upon material conditions. Men imagine that the great size and strength of a ship, the perfection of machinery or the skill of a navigator will ensure safety, but these disasters sometimes take place that men may know that God is the real Protector. . . . These events happen in order that man's faith may be increased and strengthened. . . . Let no one imagine that these words imply that man should not be thorough and careful in his undertakings . . . he must provide and surround himself with all that scientific skill can produce . . . yet, withal, let him rely upon God. . . . If God protects, nothing can imperil man's safety; and if it be not His will to safeguard, no amount of preparation and precaution will avail.[27]

Additionally, the Cartesian-Newtonian idea of deterministic mathematical laws has also resulted in the West's overemphasis on quantitative data, on numbers such as GNP (Gross National Product), profit margin, SAT scores, temperature, weight, and so forth. Numbers, however, can only tell part of the story. Spiritual, psychological, and emotional qualities and circumstances are qualitative aspects that cannot be quantified with numbers. Thus Western quantitative evaluations of phenomena typically do not account for spiritual, psychological, and emotional factors. For instance, nations with very high GNPs (a dollar measure of economic productivity) are considered successful even though they may be riddled with suicides, homicides, addictions, divorces, lawsuits, prejudice, anxieties, and fears. What dollar values can one place on joy, courage, justice, truth, generosity, and so forth? Can we place a dollar amount on a happy marriage or a joyful, well-adjusted teenager? Furthermore, governments and corporations often conduct economic cost-benefit analyses that are primarily centered on monetary gains and losses while ignoring the true social and environmental costs of doing business. For instance, experts claim that they can figure out the monetary costs of running a coal-fired, electrical generating plant. But, again, can we place a dollar amount on the clean air that is lost by this activity? This is why, contrary to most of today's Western research methods, situations should be evaluated by both quantitative and qualitative standards.

Based on the early scientific successes of Newtonian physics, many early scientists believed that they could apply the same Cartesian-Newtonian concepts toward the study of human nature and human society. Some believed that they could create a "social physics." For instance, John Locke (1632–1704), a famous English philosopher, believed that just as there are mathematical laws that govern the mechanical universe, there are also natural laws that govern human relationships and human society. This signaled the beginning of what we now call the social sciences such as economics, political science, sociology, psychology, and so forth. Unfortunately, these social sciences are also steeped in the Cartesian-Newtonian paradigm and are thus characterized by the following: a mechanistic view of human beings and of human society; the belief that science is the only route to absolute knowledge, and a dismissive attitude toward religion; an emphasis on logic and the power of human reason, and a rejection of emotions and mystical intuition or inspiration; the assumption that human society, just like the universe, is deterministic—that it is governed by the natural laws of cause and effect that can be defined mathematically; a dependence on the analytic method—a tendency to first break apart topics or issues before studying them; the tendency to separate rather than integrate such as by creating mutually exclusive categories or dichotomies; an overemphasis on prediction and control; and an overemphasis on quantitative data. Thus even though this worldview began as a paradigm within the "hard sciences" (such as physics and chemistry), it then spread to the "soft sciences" (such as political science, economics, and psychology). The obvious problem here is that there is a difference between studying the interactions of chemicals in a test tube within a controlled laboratory setting and studying the interactions of human beings in a society. Unfortunately, social scientists eventually applied their faulty theories to the actual organization of society, and consequently, the Cartesian-Newtonian worldview spread rapidly throughout the governmental, business, legal, educational, and other social institutions of Western civilization.

The philosophical work of John Locke contributed significantly to the promulgation of the Cartesian-Newtonian paradigm within the social sciences. Prior to developing his own theories, Locke had been heavily influenced by Descartes' emphasis on the power of human reason and also by Descartes' belief that science is the only route to absolute truth. Similar to the way that Descartes and Newton had pictured the universe as a machine, Locke pictured human society as a machine made up of separate individuals who are primarily motivated by self-interest. Furthermore, in the same way that Newton spoke of the force of gravity, Locke spoke of the "force of self-interest." Locke also asserted that the primary purpose of government should be to protect individual private property. The following philosophical ideas of Locke all played a major role in the creation of capitalism: self interest as a primary force in society, the law of supply and demand, private property rights, individualism, free markets, and government noninterference. Locke also believed that human beings are born as blank slates and that we gain knowledge only through the power of human reason coupled with the use of the five senses. Not surprisingly, he challenged the idea of divine sources of knowledge, and thus, he rejected the belief in faith, mystical inspiration, intuition, and divinely revealed scriptures. He also argued against the concept of the divine right of kings whereby kings claimed that they had the authority to rule based on the divine authority of the Church.

The influential philosophy of Locke contributed to the West's positive movement toward representative government and toward increased individual freedom in the political and economic domains; however, it also had several negative long term consequences. For instance, his philosophy contributed to the rabid, self-centered individualism that is pervasive in our society. Based on Locke's principles, the West developed an economic science that is based on a dark cynical view of human nature. Western classical economists, for instance, promote the following assumptions: human beings have insatiable desires that should be fulfilled; people are primarily motivated by self-interest; and people will first choose to maximize their own profit. This is an economic science that promotes the idea that the primary goal of a society is the production of material wealth, not the advancement of emotional, psychological, moral, and spiritual health. Ultimately, Locke's philosophy contributed heavily to the anti-spiritual, anti-religion tenor of Western civilization's underlying worldview. Related to this, in *The Secret of Divine Civilization*, 'Abdu'l-Bahá provides a detailed explanation of the difference between a true, divinely inspired civilization and a false, manmade, godless civilization. He explains that the West has the latter form of civilization:

. . . the peoples of Europe, notwithstanding their vaunted civilization, sink and drown in this terrifying sea of passion and desire, and this is why all the phenomena of their culture come to nothing. . . . Human happiness consists only in drawing closer to the Threshold of Almighty God, and in securing the peace and well-being of every individual member, high and low alike, of the human race. . . . A superficial culture, unsupported by a cultivated morality, is as . . . external luster without inner perfection. . . . Be just: can this nominal [Western] civilization, unsupported by a genuine civilization of character, bring about the peace and well-being of the people or win the good pleasure of God? Does it not, rather, connote the destruction of man's estate and pull down the pillars of happiness and peace?[28]

Most importantly, John Locke spearheaded what we now call the Age of Enlightenment, which started in the late 1600s and then encompassed the entire eighteenth century. During this time period the Scientific Revolution really flourished. Many of the influential thinkers of that era are well known, such as Voltaire, Rousseau, David Hume, Immanuel Kant, Adam Smith, Thomas Jefferson, and others. This era is also known as the Age of Reason because most of the intellectuals of that time emphasized the power of human reason as opposed to faith, and they encouraged the separation of science and religion. Many of these intellectuals, including Jefferson and Voltaire were deists who believed God had created the machine universe and mechanical people, and had then left them to function on their own. In other words, they believed that God was no longer involved in the day-to-day matters of human beings. Jefferson enshrined this deist perspective in the United States constitution with language that created a separation between church and state. Other intellectuals of this era were agnostics or outright atheists.

During the Age of Enlightenment, capitalism was officially born. In 1776, Adam Smith, an English economist, published *An Inquiry into the Nature and Causes of the Wealth of Nations.* In this famous book, Smith promulgated many of the ideas of John Locke, and he additionally argued that people who are left free (without government interference) to compete for their own wealth and to pursue their own self-interest will be ultimately guided as if by an "invisible hand" to enrich the whole society. Of course, Smith was referring to physical riches and not to spiritual, moral, or psychological wealth. Smith's exuberant promotion of unmitigated self-interest and unrestricted economic activity (laissez-faire) as positive values ultimately led to the exploitation of countless workers as industrial slaves, the destitution of many families at the whim of powerful businesses, and the destruction of major portions of the environment.

The philosophical ideas of the Enlightenment also later influenced other Western economists such as Karl Marx, a German economist and the primary architect of communism. Marx was a staunch atheist who called religion the opiate of the people. Like the philosophers of the Enlightenment, Marx had a faith in natural laws. He argued that humanity is ruled by the law of economic determinism (people are defined by their economic circumstances) and the law of class struggle (conflict between the "haves" and the "have-nots"). In order to deal with the injustice and inequality that capitalism had produced, he advocated violent class warfare to overthrow the "haves" and to establish a classless dictatorship of the "have-nots." His ideas ultimately led to the creation of the totalitarian Soviet Union, an abysmal failure on practically all fronts that resulted in great harm to people and the environment. It must be made clear that both capitalism and communism are products of the Cartesian-Newtonian worldview. Both of these defective, Western economic systems are the end result of the anti-spiritual, godless philosophies of John Locke and other Western philosophers. As such, the Bahá'í Faith equally rejects both of these economic systems.[29]

The Cartesian-Newtonian thinking of the Age of Enlightenment sparked other major movements that significantly shaped Western civilization during the nineteenth century. The scientific theories and advances of the 1700s, for instance, set off the Industrial Revolution in the early 1800s. The Industrial Age essentially enshrined the machine in the psyches of Western peoples and further reinforced the idea that we live in a mechanical universe. Moreover, in 1859, Charles Darwin, the famous English naturalist, published his revolutionary book, *The Origin of Species*, which did much to bolster Rene Descartes' idea that the universe is made up of matter and that matter is devoid of any spirit or purpose. The Darwinian theory of evolution completely does away with the idea that God played any role in the origin of humanity. Unlike this theory, the Bahá'í teachings maintain that the evolutionary process did indeed occur, but that this process was initiated and guided by God. In essence, according to the Bahá'í teachings, God created humankind through a slow process of evolution. In contrast, Darwinian theory asserts that life on earth started as a result of random mutations without the help of any deity or external intelligence of any kind. As such, this theory is not in accord with all the spiritual traditions that assert that humanity has a divine purpose that is linked to an eternal plan of God. Darwinian theory, if carried to its logical conclusion, means that life is devoid of any purpose—life started by accident. This theory also maintains that all life forms are locked into a struggle or an eternal competition for existence where only the fittest survive. This concept of "survival of the fittest" significantly influenced Western society especially when it combined with capitalist ideology, which emphasizes competition, individualism, and government noninterference. Considerable numbers of Americans, for instance, still believe that the competition between individuals in society is virtuous because it results in the selection of the "fittest" human beings, whether it be in business, government, education, or other social arenas.

The godless, manmade theories and philosophies of John Locke, Adam Smith, Karl Marx, Charles Darwin, and other Western intellectuals had a major impact on the people of Europe and the United States. The "classical science," mechanistic perspectives promulgated by such intellectuals radically altered the Western people's view of spirituality and religion. Throughout the Western world, science achieved major dominance as the ultimate authority in defining reality. Based on its achievements, classical science claimed to be the voice of absolute truth (just as Rene Descartes, one of its founders, had asserted much earlier). Furthermore, science claimed that religion could no longer exercise any jurisdiction over physical matters. This marked the split between science and religion that is one of the chief characteristics of today's Cartesian-Newtonian worldview. This split shows up in our society as a strong division between the secular (business, government, or scientific) aspects of life on the one hand, and the sacred (religious or spiritual) aspects of life on the other. A good example of this is shown by the tendency of many Westerners to reduce religion to something that is done on Sundays when Christian church is attended. Such an attitude toward religion is not in accord with the Bahá'í teachings, which exhort believers to practice their faith on a moment by moment basis in all aspects of life. Indeed, in 1994, the Universal House of Justice sent a letter to the members of the National Spiritual Assembly of the Bahá'ís of the United States to warn them (and the American Bahá'ís in general) that their attitudes and actions are in danger of being infected by the rabidly secular United States culture:

> You live in a society [U.S.] caught in the tightening grip of moral decadence on a vast scale. . . . It is the unavoidable consequence of a pervasive godlessness; its symptoms and repercussions were described in painful detail by Shoghi Effendi in several of his letters to the Western friends. Inevitably, the American Bahá'í community is affected by this condition to some extent. The corrosive influence of an overbearing and rampant secularization is infecting the style of administration of the Faith in your community and threatening to undermine its efficacy. The aggressiveness and competitiveness which animate a dominantly capitalist culture . . . the cynical disregard of the moderating principles and rules of civilized human relationships resulting from an excessive liberalism and its immoral consequences—such unsavory characteristics inform entrenched habits of American life, which imperceptibly at first but more obviously in the long run have come to exert too great a sway over the manner of management of the Bahá'í community and over the behavior of portions of its rank and file in relation to the Cause. This unwholesome influence must be arrested by immediate, deliberate effort . . .[30]

This guidance from the Universal House of Justice has helped to keep the American Bahá'í community on track. Such letters from the supreme governing body will likely be periodically necessary so long as American Bahá'ís are still living, working, and worshipping in the midst of an "overbearing and rampant" secular-based culture.

The next section takes a detailed look at the tragic events that unfolded when European colonists immigrated to America and started interacting with the American Indian peoples, who had been living relatively unmolested on this continent for tens of thousands of years. As will be seen, a monumental clash of worldviews occurred when European colonists (many of whom were imbued with a Cartesian-Newtonian worldview) encountered a people with a holistic view of reality who perceived no separation between the secular and the sacred or between the material and the spiritual. The tragedy that unfolded between these two different cultures will forever remain a startling and haunting example that serves to vividly demonstrate the crucial importance of worldview. Indeed, as will be shown, a people's view of reality can largely determine whether they will follow the path of love, unity, and justice or follow the path of hatred, division, and iniquity.

The American Indians and the European Colonists: A Clash of Worldviews

We live in what has been termed the Age of Information. Indeed, information abounds everywhere—on the internet, television, radio, and print media. Moreover, the expansion of information within the various fields of study is advancing at an incredible rate. However, the nagging question remains: if information is increasing at an almost exponential rate, is wisdom also increasing? Sadly, judging by the severity and scope of our global problems, it seems that wisdom is actually decreasing. Wisdom can be defined as a keen sense of personal discernment or judgment that springs from one's ability to integrate intellectual, spiritual, physical, and emotional information in order to get a comprehensive view of reality. By definition, wisdom requires the integration of the powers of mind, body, and spirit. It also requires the ability to bring together different and often seemingly conflicting bodies of knowledge (such as science and religion) in order to apprehend a truer, deeper sense of reality. In other words, wisdom should not be equated with the mere act of filling one's head with an assortment of disconnected facts and figures. In my view, any society that widely disseminates information without also cultivating wisdom is on a dangerous path. Along these lines, E. F. Schumacher, a Rhodes scholar in economics and one of the founders of the modern environmental sustainability movement, states,

> There is . . . the need to transmit know-how but this must take
> second place for it is obviously somewhat foolhardy to put great
> powers into the hands of people without making sure that they
> have a reasonable idea of what to do with them. At present, . . . the
> whole of mankind is in mortal danger, not because we are short
> of scientific and technological know-how, but because we tend to
> use it destructively, without wisdom. More education can help us
> only if it produces more wisdom.[31]

Ironically, many modern Westerners have been brought up to believe that scientific know-how will save humankind from annihilation. However, as suggested by Schumacher, science must be coupled with wisdom (based on the integration of intellectual, emotional, physical, and spiritual knowledge), or else, it itself can become a destructive power. Since religion is a major repository of spiritual knowledge, it is important that it play an important role in science.

The monumental conflict that occurred in early America between the American Indians and the White European settlers is a quintessential example of the deadly outcomes that can transpire when Cartesian-Newtonian technological know-how is divorced from spiritual knowledge. The White settlers were obviously much more technologically advanced than the indigenous peoples; however, I have no evidence to suggest that the White settlers were also more spiritually advanced than the Indians. To the contrary, it seems the settlers' extensive technological knowledge outpaced their spiritual ability to use this knowledge morally. Using their technological superiority to its full dreadful extent, the White settlers, as a group, executed an immoral campaign of physical and cultural genocide against the indigenous peoples that will continue to stain the pages of American history for many years to come. In one of his writings, Dr. Martin Luther King,

Jr. referred to the tragic history of Indian-White relations, and he emphasized the importance of studying this history:

> Our nation was born in genocide when it embraced the doctrine that the original American, the Indian, was an inferior race. Even before there were large numbers of Negroes on our shores, the scar of racial hatred had already disfigured colonial society. . . . We are perhaps the only nation which tried as a matter of national policy to wipe out its indigenous population. Moreover, we elevated that tragic experience into a noble crusade. Indeed, even today we have not permitted ourselves to reject or to feel remorse for this shameful episode. . . . For too long the depth of racism in American life has been underestimated. The surgery to extract it is necessarily complex . . . it is important to X-ray our history and reveal the full extent of the disease.[32]

It is my belief that America continues to be haunted by its brutal past. Until it comes to terms with this past and truly understands it, it will never redeem itself and it will never achieve its true calling and destiny. A crucial question here is: How could a nation that was ostensibly founded on the principles of justice, equality, democracy, and liberty, possibly lower itself to the barbaric level of practicing human genocide (as well as slavery)? As will be shown below, it is my belief that the Cartesian-Newtonian materialistic worldview of many of the early White colonists played a key role in the tragic events that unfolded on this continent. Sadly, as I have abundantly demonstrated in this book and in my first book, this situation has still not been remedied. The same cultural paradigm that led to genocide and other atrocities is still intact. Indeed, many Americans (even many modern Indians) continue to vainly look for solutions within the same materialistic paradigm that generated the problems. Both Indians and non-Indians are increasingly experiencing the breakdown of their communities. We should all try to find solutions in alternative paradigms such as the traditional Indian holistic worldview, the Bahá'í Faith, and the modern holistic movement.

In terms of understanding the central theme of this book, which is the redemption of America and the awakening of Americans to their true sacred calling, it would be instructive to spend a brief moment here covering some history, especially as it pertains to the early founding of America. Indeed, some of the problems that we are currently experiencing in America, particularly racial disunity, environmental destruction, gender inequality, and socioeconomic inequality, are rooted in the actual founding of this nation. It is my belief that the American Indians possessed a holistic view of reality that could have helped the early Americans to create a better nation. Unlike European societies that were broken into all forms of unequal socioeconomic classes (monarchy, titled nobles, landed gentry, peasants, and so forth), native societies in general were known for the equal and just relationships that existed between the various Indian members. Also, in contrast to patriarchal European societies, where women were literally treated as the property of men, Indian women enjoyed surprisingly high levels of freedom, respect, equality, and democratic participation within Indian nations (some Indian nations were even matriarchal). Moreover, in Indian societies, land was not owned by any individual but was instead held in common so that all could benefit from it. This was unlike all the European societies of that time where members of the monarchy and the aristocracy owned virtually all of the land such as in Spain where ninety-five percent of the land was owned by two percent of the population.[33]

Furthermore slavery was not practiced among the native peoples, and in contrast to European societies that were constantly racked by religious warfare, Indians in general did not fight over religious differences. Many Indian societies were also known for their democratic processes by which power was held by group decision-making councils that were selected by the people (women in many cases could also vote). This is in contrast to the European government structures of that time where power rested solely with the king and a few landed nobles who received such power based on inheritance (in 1776, for instance, only five percent of the people in England were allowed to vote, and women had absolutely no legal or political rights). It is very

telling that, in 1797, Thomas Paine, a famous American revolutionary, stated the following regarding the egalitarian and just nature of
Indian societies: "The fact is, that the condition of millions in every
country in Europe, is far worse than if they . . . had been born among
the Indians of North America at the present day."[34]

Ultimately, the physical clash that occurred between the White
European settlers and the American Indians was rooted in a conflict
in worldviews (their views of reality were different). The various
Indian peoples that occupied the Americas prior to the arrival of
Europeans had different languages, foods, homes, and modes of
dress; however, they all shared a common holistic view of reality.
The traditional Indian holistic perspective was most obvious in the
belief that the natural environment was sacred and that humankind
was a part of an interconnected sacred web of life. This holistic view
of reality was also evident in the Indian belief that the Creator, in
His non-manifest Essence, transcended all created forms and stood
independent of any limitations, and yet at the same time, the Creator was omnipresent within all physical things. Thus in the traditional Indian holistic perspective there was no separation between
the secular material realm and the sacred spiritual realm. This view
is evident in the following quote by Black Elk (1863–1950), a La-
kota Indian medicine man, who witnessed the Battle of the Little
Bighorn against the U.S. army's seventh cavalry:

> We regard all created beings as sacred. . . . We should understand
> well that all things are the works of the Great Spirit [God]. We
> should know that He is within all things; the trees, the grasses,
> the rivers, the mountains, and all . . . animals; . . . even more
> important, we should understand that He is also above all these
> things and peoples.[35]

Similarly, Chief Luther Standing Bear (1868–1939) stated, "From . . .
the Great Spirit, there came a great unifying life force that flowed in
and through all things. . . . Thus all things were kindred. . . . All were
of one blood, made by the same hand, and filled with the essence of
the Great Mystery [God]."[36]

In contrast to the above, many Europeans, around the time that they started migrating to America were imbued with a view of reality that was based on Cartesian-Newtonian materialistic science. This despiritualized perspective is obvious in the expressed views of Francis Bacon, a famous early European scientist, who wrote that nature should be "hounded in her wanderings," "bound into service," and made a "slave." He also wrote that the goal of the scientist is to "torture nature's secrets from her."[37] Such views were utterly inconsistent with the Indian conception of the "Mother Earth" as a sacred entity that was not separate from the Great Spirit.

The influential Francis Bacon also developed what is known as the empirical method of science, which is based on the assertion that knowledge can be obtained only through physical experimental procedures. This method had the effect of limiting truth to only that knowledge that could be discovered through man's five senses or through technological extensions of the five senses, such as the telescope and the microscope. This method of science became highly popular, especially among the European and American intellectuals of the 1600s and 1700s, such as the famous English philosopher John Locke, who adopted Bacon's empirical method. Locke founded the philosophical school of empiricism, which promoted the idea that true knowledge could only be obtained through physical experience involving the five senses and the power of human reason. Locke's philosophical ideas, as already described earlier, had a huge impact on European and American intellectuals, such as Thomas Jefferson, Voltaire (French philosopher who influenced many American revolutionaries), and Adam Smith (the preeminent founder of capitalism).

Not surprisingly, Voltaire and Thomas Jefferson, as well as many of Jefferson's contemporaries in the early U.S. government, subscribed to the rational philosophy known as deism. They believed that God was no longer involved in the day-to-day affairs of humankind. Deists believed that God was like a mechanic who had created the mechanical universe and had then walked away. Along these lines, *A History of Civilization*, a textbook on Western civilization, states, "The ideas of Locke . . . were as well known and as much respected in North America as they were in Europe. They underlay the Declaration of

Independence. . . . The opening paragraph of the Declaration . . . expressed the concept of a world-machine . . ." Almost needless to say, Bacon's, Locke's, and Jefferson's views of knowledge were definitely not in accord with the traditional Indian holistic perspective that maintained that the attainment of truth should be based not only on the five physical senses and the power of human reason, but also on spiritual intuition (dreams, meditation, contemplation, and other spiritual arts) and the apprehension of divinely revealed sacred truths (as expressed by holy prophets or messengers).[38]

Related to the discussion above, some people have come to believe the mythology that the U.S. government was built on a Biblical worldview. Obviously, Christians have always constituted the majority of the American religious population, but this fact alone should not be taken to mean that American social, economic, and political institutions are a reflection of Biblical ideals. In actuality, pragmatic skepticism, empiricism (reliance on verifiable observation and experience rather than faith), and deism shaped the religious beliefs of many of the early American founders and government administrators. As noted above, Thomas Jefferson and many of his colleagues in the early U.S. government were deists who did not subscribe to any particular religion. Jefferson, like many of his Enlightenment contemporaries, was essentially a religious skeptic who openly doubted even the existence of God. Along these lines, Jefferson stated, "Question with boldness even the existence of God; because, if there be one, he must more approve the homage of reason than of blindfolded fear."[39]

Undoubtedly, the influential ideas of Jefferson and other unconventional religious thinkers cleared the way for other Americans, even conventional Christians, to begin to question their own religious customs and beliefs. Like Jefferson and his deist colleagues, the early American Christians seem to have readily accepted the establishment of a secular state, possibly the first secular government in the history of humanity. Regarding this, Jerome Weeks, a journalist who reviewed Susan Jacoby's book, *Freethinkers: A History of American Secularism*, states, "Our country was the first established

without recourse to divine authority: Nowhere in the Constitution
. . . is God invoked to justify our rights or government. The highest
authority is 'we the people.'"[40]

Along these same lines, one of the preeminent founding fathers,
John Adams, the second president of the United States, signed the
following statement in a 1797 treaty that was also ratified by the U.S.
Senate: "the Government of the United States is not, in any sense,
founded on the Christian religion."[41]

Thus the United States was set up as a secular state, and the guiding
overarching principle became the "separation of church and state."
This had the positive effect of allowing for greater religious tolerance;
however, there was a heavy price to pay in terms of exacerbating the
Cartesian-Newtonian division between the sacred and the secular.
This contributed greatly to an overall societal movement toward what
I have termed secular Christianity, which is a form of Christianity that
has an underlying predominantly secular and materialistic worldview.
Secular Christianity is dominated by a myriad of Cartesian-Newtonian values, beliefs, and assumptions all of which run counter to any
authentic Biblical worldview. Operating within this framework, it is almost impossible to live a life of Christian love, humility, self-sacrifice,
generosity, compassion, and charity, as is encouraged by the Bible,
especially if one is living (like many Americans) a life of competitive,
self-centered individualism and science-dominated materialism—the
"religion of secularism." In essence, as individual Christians became
caught in the grip of secular science, secular government, and secular
capitalist economics, the American Christian community as a whole
lost its Biblically inspired moral power as a potential autonomous
force of love and reconciliation.

Related to the discussion above, Richard Thomas, a professor of
history and urban affairs at Michigan State University, asserts that
the American Christian community in general could have done
much (based on Biblical ideals) to alleviate the oppression against
the American Indians. Unfortunately, this was not the case. In
his very well researched book, *Racial Unity: An Imperative For Social
Progress*, Thomas states,

The American churches failed abysmally in protecting the human rights of Indians. . . . American churches in general failed to confront the ideology and beliefs of white racial manifest destiny. . . . By its refusal to use its moral forces to combat racial oppression against Indians . . . the white American Christian community lost its soul and the opportunity to be in the spiritual vanguard of the progressive forces supporting racial unity and justice as a means of universal social progress.[42]

The fundamentalist Puritanical form of Christianity that was practiced by some of the colonists was also problematic. The Puritans claimed to be upholders of a pure form of Christianity, and yet, their actions greatly contributed to hatred and intolerance, especially since they contorted the Bible to justify brutality, alienation, and treachery against the "pagan" Indians. In short, both secular Christianity and fundamentalist Puritanical forms of Christianity were detrimental to the Biblical and moral commitments of many American Christians.

In contrast to secular Christianity and Puritanism, the traditional Indian holistic view of reality is consistent with the primary understandings of the modern holistic movement. Indeed many present-day holistic advocates have high regard for native traditional teachings. The following passage from Deganawidah, considered by the Iroquois Indians to be a divine messenger of the Creator, is an incredibly beautiful example of timeless Indian wisdom:

I carry the Mind of the Master of Life, and my message will bring an end to the wars between east and west. The word that I bring is that all peoples shall love one another and live together in peace. This message has three parts: Righteousness and Health and Power—*Gaiihwiyo, Skenno, Gashedenza.* And each part has two branches. Righteousness means justice practiced between men and between nations; it means also a desire to see justice prevail. Health means soundness of mind and body; it also means peace, for that is what comes when minds are sane and bodies cared for. Power means authority, the authority of law and custom, backed by such force as is necessary to make justice prevail; it also means religion, for justice enforced is the will of the Holder of the Heavens and has His sanction. It will take the form of the Longhouse, in which there are many fires, one for each family, yet all live as one household under one Chief Mother. Hereabouts are Five Nations, each with its own Council Fire, yet they shall live together as one household in peace. They shall be the Kanonsiónni, the Longhouse. They shall have one mind and live under one law. Thinking shall replace killing, and there shall be one Commonwealth.[43]

It is not surprising to me that the traditional Indian holistic perspective is in accord with some important tenets of the Bahá'í Faith. This is especially true as it relates to the idea of oneness—the oneness of God, the oneness of humanity, and the oneness of the universe. This is in contrast to the Cartesian-Newtonian materialistic worldview, which is in many ways antithetical to the Bahá'í worldview.

Significantly, as noted earlier in this book, the Bahá'í writings maintain that the Indians of the Americas have the potential to play a key part in the redemption of humanity. 'Abdu'l-Bahá compared the American Indians to the pre-Islamic Arabs who proceeded to create a very advanced civilization after accepting the revelation of Muḥammad. However, 'Abdu'l-Bahá stated that "in comparison" to the barbaric nature of the pre-Islamic Arabs, the "Indians of America were as advanced as a Plato [highly acclaimed philosopher of ancient Greece]." He prophesied that if the Indians become "educated and guided" in the teachings of Bahá'u'lláh, "there can be no doubt that they will become so illumined as to enlighten the whole world."[44] Similarly, in some communications, Shoghi Effendi underscores the importance of sharing the message of Bahá'u'lláh with the indigenous peoples throughout North, Central, and South America. For instance, one of his letters states,

As you know, the Master attached the utmost importance to the teaching of the Indians. . . . [Hopefully] your Assembly will devote considerable energy to this most important matter so that contacts are made with Indians in all of the Countries . . . and some of these Indians become confirmed in the Faith. . . . If the light of Divine Guidance enters properly into the lives of the Indians, it will be found that they will arise with a great power and will become an example of spirituality and culture to all of the people in these countries. . . . The Master has likened the Indians in your Countries to the early Arabian Nomads at the time of the appearance of Muḥammad. Within a short period of time they became the outstanding examples of education, of culture and of civilization for the entire world. The Master feels that similar wonders will occur today if the Indians are properly taught and if the power of the Spirit properly enters into their living."[45]

No comparable statement is made in the Bahá'í writings concerning any other people.

Tragically, the differences in worldview between the White colonists and the American Indians ultimately led to conflict, but this conflict did not necessarily have to lead to open warfare and eventually to genocide. Historian D'Arcy McNickle states,

. . . in fact Indian tribes across the continent acted in positive ways to reach accommodation with the incoming stranger [Whites]. The Indian experience had placed at the core of Indian life a respect for what each man stood for; warfare was not the initial or usual reaction to intrusion. . . . Unfortunately for the Indians, who on their own had settled two continents, the Europeans had the technology and very soon the power to impose their view of reality.[46]

Based on the evidence, it is highly likely that many of the White settlers literally did not have the necessary spiritual perspective and aptitude to appropriately transcend and resolve conflict. Ultimately, the Whites relied on their superior technological strength in order to get their way. As discussed earlier, science must be coupled with spiritual knowledge (usually religion), or else it can become a highly destructive force. Ultimately, the seeds for genocide (and environmental destruction) were first planted when White Europeans made a conscious choice to divorce their science and technology from religion and morality.

In many cases, the indigenous peoples of the past practiced a level of spirituality and morality that far surpassed the forces of treachery and greed that were arrayed against them. For instance, in a 1657 letter, a French Jesuit missionary wrote about the high character traits of the Indians that he met:

> No hospitals [poorhouses] are needed among them . . . because there are neither mendicants nor paupers as long as there are any rich people among them. Their kindness, humanity, and courtesy not only makes them liberal with what they have, but causes them to possess hardly anything except in common. A whole village must be without corn, before any individual can be obliged to endure privation.[47]

Indeed, in the first documented encounter between Europeans and Indians, Christopher Columbus, in a letter to Spain, wrote about the high virtue of the Indian people, but he then proceeded to make a very chilling statement, which in a nutshell lays bare the genocidal nature of European-Indian relations that would play out for almost the next 500 years:

> They [Indians] are very . . . honest. . . . They exhibit great love toward all others in preference to themselves. They also give objects of great value . . . and content themselves with very little or nothing in return. . . . I [found] men of great deference and kindness. . . . Should your Majesties command it, all the inhabitants could be taken away to . . . [Spain], or made slaves on the island. With 50 men we could subjugate them all and make them do whatever we want.[48]

Despite the friendly Indian reception, Columbus went on a fourteen-year murderous campaign that resulted in the deaths of over three million Arawak Indians from warfare and slavery.[49]

One can only guess how much further along we would all be if the White European colonists had interacted with the American Indians on an equal and just basis. What if the early colonists had adopted some of the spiritual wisdom of the Indians and then merged it with their own technological genius? This wisdom could have enriched these White colonists and their American descendants more than any of the gold and land that they eventually seized by conquest and treachery. Alas, the White settlers, due to a superiority consciousness, were blind to the philosophical and spiritual wisdom of the many Indian peoples that they encountered.

It is heartening to know that, even in the face of blind hatred, some Indian peoples never gave up on the power of love. Along these lines, Chief Joseph (1840–1904), a leader of the Nez Perce Indians, uttered the following incredibly enlightened and inspiring words even after having witnessed the deaths of many of his people at the hands of White settlers and U.S. army troops:

We shall all be alike—brothers of one father and one mother, with one sky above us and one country around us, and one government for all. Then the Great Spirit Chief who rules above will smile upon this land, and send rain to wash out the bloody spots from the face of the earth that were made by brothers' hands. For this time the Indian race is waiting and praying. I hope that no more groans of wounded men and women will ever go to the ear of the Great Spirit Chief above, and that all people may be one people.[50]

Some modern Indians are still committed to furthering the noble legacy of Chief Joseph and of other Indian ancestors who never lost their spiritual core in spite of the incredible hatred and ignorance that were unleashed against them. As a person of Mexican/American Indian ancestry I also wish to continue this legacy. In short, we must all rise to a high spiritual vantage point where the struggle between Whites and

American Indians can be transcended. It is here that the true battle becomes apparent—the moral battle that all peoples must now wage against the evils of greed, ignorance, hatred, and poverty. Within this spiritual context, America can (and will) collectively redeem itself for its cruel history of genocide, and as prophesied by 'Abdu'l-Bahá, it can (and will) become the nation that will lead all nations spiritually.

Increasing Signs of Global Collapse

Many believed that the expansion of Western culture and technology throughout the globe would result in the resolution of humankind's problems in a straightforward way through Western-style technological and economic development. Such an optimistic view, however, is now completely incongruous with what is actually happening. The fact is that we are presently facing a collapsing global order. Some of the problems include: extremes of wealth and poverty, government and corporate corruption, environmental degradation, rising violence and terrorism, racial and ethnic animosity, escalating addictions and mental health issues, social disorder and immorality, as well as economic malaise.

The recent worldwide economic collapse is currently the most salient feature of the failing Cartesian-Newtonian global paradigm. In an April, 2009 report, the International Monetary Fund stated that the latest collapse in the world economy is "by far the deepest global recession since the Great Depression." Similarly, an Associated Press news report asserted that the global downturn will have "appalling consequences for nations large and small—trillions of dollars in lost business, millions of people thrust into hunger and homelessness and crime on the rise." Meanwhile, in an April, 2008 report, Josette Sheeran, the executive director of the World Food Program, warned that a "silent tsunami" of hunger is sweeping the planet especially hurting the world's most desperate countries. Furthermore, in an October, 2008 report, the Organization for Economic Cooperation and Development (OECD) reported that the gap between the rich and the poor is actually getting bigger in the world's developed nations. In this report, Angel Gurria, secretary general of the OECD, noted that the increasing gap in wealth "polarizes societies, it divides regions within countries, and it carves up the world between the rich and the poor." This underscores the fact that the developed nations are having great difficulty resolving their own socioeconomic issues and are thus not in a good position to help resolve the problems in the developing Third World countries of the globe.[51]

Ironically, the current worldwide downturn started in the United States, the very Western nation that was supposed to be leading and uplifting the rest of the world toward new heights of economic development. The United States' recession primarily began with a crisis in the subprime mortgage sector, an industry that was later shown to be rife with profiteering and with the unethical brokering of loans. As scores of borrowers began to default on their loans, foreclosures started skyrocketing. Because of a lack of proper government oversight, many banks invested heavily and recklessly in unregulated financial products known as mortgage-backed securities that were later called worthless "toxic assets." Such banks were hurt badly when home prices precipitously dropped and foreclosures reached record levels. This caused a catastrophic meltdown in the U.S. financial sector as huge, highly prestigious banks and institutions such as Bear Stearns, AIG, Lehman Brothers, Merrill Lynch, Goldman Sachs, Fannie Mae and Freddie Mac, Washington Mutual, and Wachovia either went bankrupt, were "bailed out" with massive infusions of taxpayer government money, or were simply taken over by other institutions or the U.S. government. The U.S. stock market then experienced a monumental drop, which also led to massive drops in other world markets such as in Japan, Hong Kong, South Korea, Britain, Germany, France, and Russia. Amazingly, as a result of this turmoil, the nation of Iceland itself essentially went bankrupt. It could no longer afford to pay its external debts, and its currency became valueless in all other parts of the world. Meanwhile, unemployment escalated in the United States and throughout the globe to record levels. Scores of businesses in the United States and elsewhere went bankrupt including, amazingly, even business titans such as General Motors and Chrysler corporations. Moreover some American states, such as California, admitted that they were essentially insolvent.

The American people were devastated by the economic turmoil. Many individual investors who invested in Wall Street were left with vastly eroded retirement accounts. Not surprisingly, after the economic collapse, it was discovered that some Wall Street portfolio managers had been involved in long term corrupt schemes that defrauded investors of enormous sums of money. Furthermore, countless Americans lost all the equity in their homes while many millions lost their jobs (unemployment remains high). Also, it is projected that U.S. taxpayers will be left with an astronomical bill because, in the end, the government will have spent several trillion dollars of taxpayer money to avert a complete meltdown of the entire global economy. In an October 20, 2008 letter to the Bahá'ís of the world, the Universal House of Justice reflected on the breathtaking turn of global events:

. . . financial structures once thought to be impregnable have tottered and world leaders have shown their inability to devise more than temporary solutions, a failing to which they increasingly confess. Whatever expedient measures are adopted, confidence has been shaken and a sense of security lost. Surely such developments have caused the believers in every land to reflect on the lamentable condition of the present order and have reinforced in them the conviction that material and spiritual civilization must be advanced together.[52]

The last phrase—"material and spiritual civilization must be advanced together" is especially pertinent to this chapter's discussion regarding the "staggering responsibility" of the American Bahá'ís. As noted earlier, the World Order of Bahá'u'lláh "can never be reared unless and until" the United States and the generality of its citizens have "been already purged from the divers ills, whether social or political, that now so severely afflict" them. Regarding this, the American Bahá'ís, as a part of their mission, are expected to exercise their "staggering responsibility" to help purge the generality of the American people from these "divers ills." It must be emphasized that the United States, almost by definition, is presently incapable of promoting the mutual advancement of "material and spiritual civilization" due to its secular, materialistic cultural worldview. This then means that the American Bahá'ís must become deeply aware of the nature of the Cartesian-Newtonian worldview, which is hindering the tandem development of material and spiritual civilization. This despiritualized perspective affects our perception of "true reality" and this, in turn, alters our ability to discern our true meaning, purpose, and goals in life.

In an earlier section, we covered some pertinent aspects of the Cartesian-Newtonian worldview that are acting as barriers to the establishment of the New World Order and must therefore be challenged and overcome by the American Bahá'ís. Along these lines, it is important for us to recognize that many of the social, economic, political and environmental crises facing us today, such as the global economic meltdown, are just symptoms of a still larger crisis—a crisis in the materialistic Cartesian-Newtonian worldview. Indeed, it is my belief that the Bahá'í book *Century of Light* (a publication commissioned by the Universal House of Justice) alludes to this in the following passage:

Inspiring these political, social and economic crises was the inexorable rise and consolidation of a disease of the human soul infinitely more destructive than any of its specific manifestations. . . . Fathered by . . . European thought . . . materialism emerged . . . as a kind of universal religion claiming absolute authority in both the personal and social life of humankind. Its creed was simplicity itself. Reality—including human reality and the process by which it evolves—is essentially material in nature. . . . Whether as worldview or simple appetite, materialism's effect is to leach out of human motivation—and even interest—the spiritual impulses that distinguish the rational soul. . . . In the absence of conviction about the spiritual nature of reality and the fulfillment it alone offers, it is not surprising to find at the very heart of the current crisis of civilization a cult of individualism that increasingly admits of no restraint and that elevates acquisition and personal advancement to the status of major cultural values. . . . It is here that one would find the root cause of such apparently unrelated problems as the pollution of the environment, economic dislocation, ethnic violence, spreading public apathy, the massive increase in crime, and epidemics that ravage whole populations. However important the application of legal, sociological or technological expertise to such issues undoubtedly is, it would be unrealistic to imagine that efforts of this kind will produce any significant recovery without a fundamental change of moral consciousness and behavior.[53]

In the next chapter we will take a close look at capitalism, an ideology that is one of the most destructive manifestations of materialism. As we shall see, capitalism promotes some of the things that are condemned in the quote above, such as a despiritualized view of reality, a "cult of individualism," and the elevation of "acquisition and personal advancement to the status of major cultural values."

Chapter Six

CAPITALISM: A BARRIER TO AMERICA'S EXALTED DESTINY

In the previous chapter, we examined the origin, salient characteristics, and negative ramifications of the Cartesian-Newtonian worldview. As noted previously, the Cartesian-Newtonian worldview spawned two completely different and yet equally defective economic models—capitalism (also known as the free market or free enterprise system) and communism. It must be emphasized that both of these economic systems are end products of the godless, anti-spiritual philosophies of seventeenth and eighteenth century Western thinkers, and thus, are antithetical to true religion. As such, Shoghi Effendi confirms that the Bahá'í Faith equally rejects capitalism and communism as "two antagonistic schools of thought which, however divergent in their ideologies, are to be commonly condemned by the upholders of the standard of the Faith of Bahá'u'lláh for their materialistic philosophies and their neglect of those spiritual values and eternal verities on which alone a stable and flourishing civilization can be ultimately established."[1]

With the demise of the Soviet Union in 1989, communism lost most of its power as a cultural influence. Capitalism, however, continues to act as a potent force that influences the thinking and actions of most Americans. Capitalist ideology powerfully shapes all areas of American culture including governmental, business, educational, and sadly even religious institutions. Indeed, this ideology has spread so widely throughout the planet that we now live in the era of what has been termed global capitalism or simply "globalization." In this chapter, we will take a brief look at the tragic outcomes and the very real human costs of the global capitalist system, and where appropriate, we will also critique this prevailing world order from a Bahá'í perspective. As will be shown, the capitalist system has reduced untold numbers of human beings to grinding poverty and misery and has induced widespread gross violations of human rights. It is critical that Americans understand the serious deficiencies of capitalism, and indeed, it is my belief that, before America can attain its true glorious destiny, it must first rise above its slavish attachment to this banal, materialistic economic model.

Century of Light, a book written under the supervision of the Universal House of Justice, states the following regarding the capitalist global order:

In the perspective of Bahá'u'lláh's teachings, the greatest danger of both the moral crisis and the inequities associated with globalization in its current form is an entrenched philosophical attitude that seeks to justify and excuse these failures. . . . [A] system of thought reigns today virtually unchallenged across the planet, under the nominal designation 'Western civilization.' . . . It presents itself as . . . relativism [no moral absolutes] . . . and . . . as capitalism—two value systems that have now so adjusted to each other and become so mutually reinforcing as to constitute virtually a single, comprehensive worldview. . . . The system is morally and intellectually bankrupt. . . . Tragically, what Bahá'ís see in present-day society is unbridled exploitation of the masses of humanity by greed that excuses itself as the operation of 'impersonal market forces' [free market capitalism]."[2]

As discussed in the previous chapter, according to the Bahá'í writings, the American Bahá'ís have a "staggering responsibility" to cleanse themselves from the "faults, habits, and tendencies which they have inherited from their own nation" and then to help eradicate "such evil tendencies" from the lives of their fellow American citizens. It is my belief that capitalism, a manifestation of the materialistic Cartesian-Newtonian worldview, is a quintessential example of an "evil tendency" that must be acknowledged and properly redressed before America can assume its exalted destiny as the nation that "will lead all nations spiritually" as prophesied by 'Abdu'l-Bahá. This is why I consider this topic to be of critical importance. Unfortunately, many Americans actively promote the spread of capitalism throughout the world. This is especially true of the significant numbers of Americans who have strong nationalist tendencies and who stridently believe in the superiority of the United States and its dominant socioeconomic system.[3]

A Theory That Promotes
a Materialistic View of Reality

A major problem with the theory of capitalism is that it defines the highest good as the creation of material wealth, not the advancement of moral, psychological, and spiritual development. Thus, in contrast to the Bahá'í perspective, capitalism promotes a materialistic view of reality where the physical world is perceived to be true reality and the material aspects of one's existence are considered to be of primary importance. Within this context, capitalist economic theory mistakenly presumes that the central goal of a society should be to fulfill as many human desires as possible, whatever they may be. Contrary to this, the various spiritual traditions assert that true happiness and inner peace are based on a reduction of personal desires and a commitment to practicing contentment. Due to its materialistic perspective, capitalist economic theory ultimately promotes a degraded, cynical view of human nature. As noted earlier, Western classical economics is based on the theoretical assumptions that human beings are primarily motivated by self-interest, that they have insatiable desires, and that they will first choose to maximize their own profit.

Furthermore, Adam Smith, the preeminent founder of capitalist theory, promoted the concept known as *laissez-faire,* which is the belief that government should not interfere with economic affairs beyond the minimum necessary for the maintenance of security and private property rights. According to Smith, individuals should be given unhampered freedom to seek their own self-interest and to compete for their own wealth. As mentioned in the previous chapter, during the 1800s and early 1900s at the height of *laissez-faire* capitalism, industrial barons built up incredible fortunes while masses of workers (including child laborers) in Europe and the United States were reduced to the status of industrial slaves who were subjected to subhuman working conditions with abysmal pay, excessively long hours, safety hazards, cruel discipline, and squalid housing. In retrospect, it can easily be argued that if government institutions and trade unions had not interfered in the *laissez-faire* capitalist system, then most Americans and Europeans, to this day, would still be eking out an abject existence as industrial slaves at the mercy of powerful corporate barons. Contrary to such capitalist theoretical notions, Shoghi Effendi explains that the Bahá'í teachings on economics encourage a proper balance between the freedom of the individual and the preservation of the collective:

In the Bahá'í economic system of the future, private ownership will be retained, but will be controlled, regulated, and even restricted. Complete socialization is not only impossible but most unjust, and in this the [Bahá'í] Cause is in fundamental disagreement with the extreme socialists or communists. It cannot also agree with the other extreme tendency represented by the 'Laissez-faire" or individualistic school of economics which became very popular in the late eighteenth century. . . . For absolute freedom, even in the economic sphere, leads to confusion and corruption, and acts not only to the detriment of the state, or the collectivity, but inevitably results in the end in jeopardizing the very interests of the individual himself. Individualism and socialism, therefore do not offer the right solution to the economic problem. . . . The [Bahá'í teachings] can . . . maintain the right balance between the two tendencies of individualism and collectivism."[4]

Capitalist economic theory also erroneously stipulates that the chief measure of the worth of anything is based on its monetary market value or the amount of profit that can be derived from the particular person (employee) or thing (land, food, or product). This means that the theory does not recognize the worth of the nonmonetary and spiritual aspects of the overall socioeconomic system. For instance, it is impossible to put a price on clean air, on vibrant ecosystems, on loving and just relations between people, and on well-functioning unified families. Therefore the theory does not recognize the worth of these and other precious essentials that make for a healthy world. This explains why, when it comes to business and government decisions, monetary profits are often placed ahead of human relationships and the environment. Within this context, labor (i.e., human beings) and land are not perceived as sacred entities. Instead, they are treated like lowly commodities to be bought and sold in the market at a price determined by supply and demand, irrespective of the detrimental effects on families and the ecosystem. Indeed, governments and corporations often conduct economic cost-benefit analyses that primarily account for monetary gains and losses while ignoring the true spiritual, social, and environmental costs of doing business.

Moreover, capitalist economic theory argues that it is value-free or value neutral (that it does not entail moral value judgments between things or that it is not promoting certain values over others). This means that, for example, it is not permissible for economists to make value judgments between alcohol and food or between pornography and good literature. From a hypothetical standpoint, economists would treat the purchase of one hundred dollars of egregiously violent video games as being essentially the same as the purchase of one hundred dollars of children's text books. In actual economic calculations, economists currently treat such purchases as equivalent positive entries that increase the nation's gross national product (GNP). Even the attorney fees and other litigation costs associated with acrimonious divorce proceedings are currently treated by economists as contributions to the nation's GNP. Additionally, according to the theory, it is not permissible for economists to make distinctions between naturally occurring and manmade goods or between renewable and nonrenewable resources. Thus, since economists make the specious claim that their "scientific" models are value-free, the monetary market value is the sole criterion that they use to judge the relative value of goods and services. This essentially means that the free enterprise system reduces all values to the criterion of profit.

Ultimately, in theory and practice, capitalism has consistently undermined the spiritual values of compassion, justice, moderation, humility, and love, and has encouraged a worldview that equates meaning and purpose with the individualistic pursuit of material wealth, power, and status. Capitalist ideology is not consistent with the teachings of the numerous religious traditions, including the teachings of the Bahá'í Faith, which assert that the path to true liberation is based on self-sacrificial spiritual transformation and detachment from the vanities and desires of the physical world. Moreover, these spiritual teachings maintain that an individual's worth is based on his or her character, deeds, and relationship with God and not on his or her potential for monetary profit. In practice, capitalism has led to rampant consumerism, self-indulgent individualism, and invidious competition and profiteering between individuals, groups, and nations.

Widespread Rising Poverty
Amidst Incredible Concentrations of Wealth

As we take a closer look at the world's current socioeconomic situation, especially as it pertains to hunger and poverty, we get a clear view of the workings of a cruel economic machine. For any person of moral conscience, it is hard to come to grips with the fact that we live on a planet in which staggering numbers of people are literally dying of hunger. About one billion people on the globe are at or near starvation. Almost half of the world's children live in a state of debilitating poverty and malnutrition. If our real world could be reduced to a hypothetical village containing only one hundred people, then the following would be true: sixty people in the village would always be hungry (twenty-six of these being severely undernourished); sixteen people would go to bed hungry at least some of the time while only twenty-four people within the village would always have enough to eat. This reveals the true callous nature of the prevailing global order in which only twenty-four percent of the Earth's people have enough to eat. It must be emphasized here, that if food was properly distributed and shared, there would be plenty for everyone on the planet. Food is readily available; however, many of the world's poor cannot pay the market price, and thus, sometimes even huge surpluses of food are allowed to rot away.

Additionally, about one billion people worldwide have no access to clean water and half of the world's people have no access to sanitation (sewage, flushing toilets, etc.). This lack of clean water and sanitation leads to health problems and to the easy spread of disease. It also results in a waste of time and energy because the poor spend several hours each day collecting water from distant areas.[5]

Kevin LaMastra, an educator, explains that young people expressed much sympathy for Haiti after an earthquake recently devastated it, but he asserts that teachers must now help students to "move from talking about charity to working for justice." LaMastra has spent the past four summers leading groups of teachers to Haitian migrant camps in the Dominican Republic, and he maintains that "Haiti [the poorest nation in the Western Hemisphere] is also the victim of disasters caused by humans." He states,

We visit free trade zones established through international agreements. There we meet Dominican workers earning just 60 cents an hour. Managers warn them not to ask for more because Haitians will do the work for less. Trade should alleviate poverty, but here trade seems to deepen poverty. Textbooks rarely discuss this aspect of globalization, but students need to know about it. Unable to sustain themselves in Haiti, many migrants cross the Dominican border to find employment . . . living in . . . ramshackle shelters ... with dirt floors, no running water, and no toilets . . . people continue to come because, unbelievably, life in Haiti can be even worse.[6]

In contrast to the grim reality described above, it is significant to note that the Bahá'í writings are very passionate regarding the loving care and just protection that should be shown to the world's poor. For instance, Bahá'u'lláh declares,

> Know ye that the poor are the trust of God in your midst. Watch that ye betray not His trust, that ye deal not unjustly with them. . . . Ye will most certainly be called upon to answer for His trust on the day when the Balance of Justice shall be set, the day when unto every one shall be rendered his due, when the doings of all men, be they rich or poor, shall be weighed.[7]

The apparent cruelty of the existing global order is especially demonstrated by the fact that the people living in the wealthy developed nations (only about twenty percent of the Earth's population) consume a disproportionate share of the world's resources and goods each year, including about seventy percent of the world's energy, about seventy-five percent of its metals, about eighty-five percent of its timber, and about eighty-six percent of its goods. The United States has the highest consumption levels per capita in the globe. Along these lines, on August 28, 2005, an article in the *San Diego Union Tribune* reported that Americans alone spend "$1.9 billion more a day on imported clothes and cars and gadgets than the entire rest of the world spends on its goods and services." Similarly, eighty-five percent of the Earth's water is used by a mere twelve percent of the world's people who live in the wealthy developed nations. In addition to consuming a disproportionate share of the Earth's food, resources, and goods, the rich countries of the globe are claiming an ever-increasing ratio of the world's wealth. In 1950, the income gap between the people living in the wealthy developed nations and the people living in the poorest nations was thirty-five to one. By 1997, in less than fifty years during the worldwide expansion of capitalism, this income gap increased to seventy-four to one. In contrast to this situation, Bahá'u'lláh exhorts all peoples to "Be generous in prosperity. . . . Be a treasure to the poor, an admonisher to the rich, an answerer to the cry of the needy."[8]

The gap between the rich countries and the poor countries of the world is rapidly increasing as noted above; however, equally disconcerting is the fact that the gap between the rich and poor is also increasing within the United States itself. It may surprise some to know that the United States now has the most unequal income distribution of any industrialized country. Alarmingly, super-rich Americans who represent the top one percent of the U.S. population control forty percent of America's total wealth. Meanwhile, the top twenty percent of Americans, as a group, control eighty-three percent of America's total wealth. This means that the overwhelming majority of Americans are competing for only the remaining seventeen percent of the wealth after the super-rich and the rich take their lion's share.[9]

Over the past four decades, in the face of major government deregulation, corporate downsizing, and the dissolution of trade unions, American workers have experienced a significant erosion of protections, benefits, income, and freedoms. Additionally, over this same period of time, American multinational corporations have made a massive transfer of capital, factories, and labs to Third World countries with the weakest workplace safety and environmental laws, the toughest anti-union laws, and the lowest wages and taxes. Not surprisingly, as shown by the statistics above, wealth has been upwardly distributed—indeed, approximately ninety percent of the increase in U.S. income over about the past twenty-five years has gone to the rich people at the top of the socioeconomic pyramid (the top twenty percent of Americans). As a result of all of this, rising numbers of Americans are joining the ranks of what has been termed the "working poor." This is a reference to the millions of Americans who are working year-round, full-time, for poverty-level wages (based on government guidelines). Some have to live in their cars or have to work two full-time jobs just to pay the rent and to buy enough food for their children. Some experience constant pain because they cannot afford medical treatment and are unable to miss any work because they lack sick leave. The reality is that the U.S. economy is not producing enough living-wage jobs to accommodate all Americans. Sadly, in the United States, about one in three children under the age of twelve are hungry or at risk of hunger. All of this once again demonstrates the grim dehumanized nature of this system.[10]

Survival of the Fittest Class Consciousness

Interestingly, in spite of the gross maldistribution of wealth in the United States, many Americans do not protest because they still feel fortunate in comparison to the vast numbers of people in the Third World who live on the brink of real starvation. As such, the maldistribution of wealth (a salient feature of capitalism) results in a pyramid-shaped hierarchy that stratifies people into socioeconomic classes ranging from the American super-rich elites at the top of the pyramid down to the lowliest peasant classes in the Third World. The rich upper classes use their wealth strategically to promote and to protect their economic and political interests often at the expense of the middle and lower classes. Through the use of gifts, grants, and contributions to government officials, churches, universities, foundations, think tanks, and a variety of other organizations, the elites exert tremendous influence on all aspects of society including governmental, business, religious, legal, educational, media, law enforcement, and military institutions. Indeed, the scandalous amount of money that the American upper classes spend on political campaigns to maintain their power is truly an affront to democracy. The corrupting influence of money, however, is not the only thing that maintains the unjust status quo. The system is also kept in order because capitalist ideology itself fosters a "survival of the fittest" mentality in which individuals perceive each other as competitors in a struggle for survival (Social Darwinism). This promulgates the faulty belief that the best people rise to the top and that the lower classes are inferior and possibly even morally and/or intellectually deficient. Thus class prejudices play a major role in maintaining the system.

Interestingly, many lower and middle class Americans often willingly support such an iniquitous economic model because they subscribe to the capitalist inspired notion that someday they too can climb to the top of the socioeconomic hierarchy. However, the current deep economic recession involving major job losses, the collapse of the housing market, and the massive loss of personal investments and savings has caused some Americans to realize that they are indeed vulnerable to the iniquities of the free market system. Moreover, with banks and credit card companies being increasingly tight on loans and credit, the recession has stoked serious concerns among average Americans who have become accustomed to living counterfeit "middle class" lifestyles based on staggering levels of debt. Meanwhile, due to the high surplus of desperate unemployed Americans, companies now have the capability to fire well-paid employees and to easily replace them with "cheaper" workers. The current job market situation in the United States is radically different in comparison to the job market of the mid-1940s through the mid-1960s when U.S. industrial firms were manufacturing about half of all of the world's products. As noted above, over the past few decades, the U.S. economy has lost huge numbers of well-paid manufacturing jobs due to capitalist "free trade" policies that have allowed American multinational corporations to simply close entire factories and ship them off to the Third World where they can easily exploit entire populations. Additionally, many American families in the past could make an adequate living on only one income. This is no longer the case. In today's families, both parents typically have to work to make ends meet. In light of all of this, many Americans are starting to realize that they are potentially only a few paychecks away from poverty and potentially even homelessness. Thus, increasing numbers of Americans are coming to the painful recognition that the so-called American dream of never-ending upward mobility is coming to an abrupt end. Of course, for some Americans, the thought of upward mobility has always been nothing more than a fleeting fantasy, especially for inner-city minorities living in blighted urban centers with high unemployment rates, eroded tax bases, and a lack of social infrastructure (poor medical care, substandard housing, and indeed, even a lack of grocery stores).

The Extremes of Wealth and Poverty as an Impediment to Peace and Spiritual Growth

Ironically, as mentioned above, in the face of widespread rising poverty in the United States and throughout the globe, astonishing levels of wealth are nonetheless being amassed and increasingly concentrated in the hands of a very small cadre of super-rich, powerful individuals. In the United States, the gap in wealth distribution is currently greater than at any other time since 1929, the year of the Great Depression. Similarly, practically every Third World country has a small cadre of rich elites (oligarchs) who live lavish lifestyles amidst the abject debilitating poverty of their fellow citizens. Related to this, the Universal House of Justice warns that the widening gap between the rich and the poor throughout the world is a major impediment to peace: "The inordinate disparity between rich and poor, a source of acute suffering, keeps the world in a state of instability, virtually on the brink of war."[11] Along similar lines, 'Abdu'l-Bahá states the following regarding wealth:

If a judicious and resourceful individual should initiate measures which would universally enrich the masses of the people, there could be no undertaking greater than this. . . . Wealth is most commendable, provided the entire population is wealthy. If, however, a few have inordinate riches while the rest are impoverished, and no fruit or benefit accrues from that wealth, then it is only a liability to its possessor. If, on the other hand, it is expended for the promotion of knowledge, the founding of elementary and other schools, the encouragement of art and industry, the training of orphans and the poor—in brief, if it is dedicated to the welfare of society—its possessor will stand out before God and man as the most excellent of all who live on earth and will be accounted as one of the people of paradise."[12]

It would be accurate to say that one of the defining features of capitalism is that it encourages individuals to concentrate wealth. Capitalism also lacks any moral constraints that admonish and encourage individuals to expend such wealth for the benefit of others. This alone practically guarantees that 'Abdu'l-Bahá's above admonition will remain unheeded within the current economic paradigm. He asserts that wealth that is not utilized for the benefit of the overall society is actually "a liability to its possessor." I believe that this is a reference to the spiritual deficits (deficits in the virtues of generosity, compassion, justice, humility, and love) that likely multiply in the souls of any individuals who devote their time and energy to selfishly amassing physical treasures while, at the same time, showing little concern for the general welfare of the community. It is probably the case that such individuals may outwardly appear prosperous, and yet, they may actually be experiencing spiritual starvation and a poverty of the soul.

Keeping the World Safe for Capitalism

Such a poverty of the soul is clearly evident in the corrupt social, political, and economic arrangements of the global order. These prevailing arrangements are based on blatant physical power and control and are not mediated in any sense by moral or spiritual constraints. Indeed, physical wealth is the chief mediating force in global politics and economics. Wealthy elites are able to exercise tremendous power not only within their own nations, but also beyond their respective nations' borders. Elites may live in different countries, but they often collaborate with one another to exert extreme control over the resources and governmental institutions of the planet in order to maintain the prevailing unjust global order. Within the United States, big business interests (American multinational corporations, huge investment banks, and rich owners/investors) hold a powerful sway over the government. Through the instrumentality of the U.S. government as well as through American-dominated international bodies such as the International Monetary Fund, the World Bank, and the World Trade Organization, big business entities project their power onto the global stage where they consistently promote economic, political, and military policies and actions that make the world safe for capitalism (actually, safe for the easy exploitation of the masses). Such U.S.-led policies and actions effectively preserve the privileged position of American big business interests throughout the planet as well as protect the positions of elites within impoverished countries where ruthless oppression is often used to maintain the gap between the rich and the poor.

The control of agitated hungry populations typically requires the use of military force. Not surprisingly, in order to maintain the global arrangements described above, the United States has been, and continues to be, the leading supplier of weapons on the planet. By the end of the 1990s, the United States accounted for seventy percent of the commerce in weapons to the Third World. Significantly, even after the fall of the Soviet Union and the end of the Cold War in 1989, the United States continued to flood the world with weapons. For instance, it provided arms or military technology to belligerent parties in ninety percent of the fifty most significant conflicts that occurred between 1993 and 1994.[13] In November 13, 2006, *The Boston Globe* reported the following:

> . . . it is the United States that by far remains the top purveyor of high-tech arms to areas where . . . the likelihood of armed conflict remains highest. A study last year by the progressive World Policy Institute found that the United States transferred weaponry to 18 of the 25 countries involved in an ongoing war. . . . [M]ore than half of the countries buying U.S. arms . . . were defined as undemocratic. . . . "The U.S. would be significantly affected if there was an arms treaty that took into account human rights abuses and conflict areas," added William Hartung [World Policy Institute]. . . . "The U.S. government still wants to be able to do covert and semi-covert arms transfers."[14]

The findings above are very significant considering the fact that many contemporary outbreaks of famine are related to armed struggles and civil wars such as the recent conflict in Somalia. Thus, arms transfers and U.S. military aid to the Third World contribute considerably to world hunger because they help keep famine-inducing armed conflicts alive.

It is ironic that the United States has often touted itself as the prime promoter of worldwide democracy when, as noted above, a myriad of undemocratic governments have received military aid and weapons from the United States. Some of these governments have essentially acted as American-influenced puppets that have served to maintain political and economic conditions that are favorable to the United States and to American-based multinational corporations. During the 1800s and 1900s, the United States established such governmental arrangements throughout the world in a variety of countries in Central and South America, Africa, Asia, the Middle East, and the Pacific region. Indeed, these arrangements were cultivated especially in Third World countries where profits could be made through the exploitation of cheap labor and/or the exploitation of natural resources such as oil, copper, silver, gold, diamonds, timber, minerals, and so forth. Along these lines, sociologist James Loewen states, "From 1815 on, instead of spreading democracy . . . we [Americans] sought hegemony over Mexico, the Philippines, much of the Caribbean basin, and other nations." In many instances, the U.S. government blatantly worked hand in hand with wealthy Third World oligarchs to actually create puppet regimes.[15]

Overthrowing Democracy in the Name of Capitalism

Especially during the Cold War period (1946–1989), the United States financed and sometimes installed numerous dictatorships in the Third World. The aforementioned Bahá'í publication, *Century of Light*, explains that the West (the United States and its allies) used development aid to influence governments during the Cold War, but "wherever" this "failed to retain the loyalties of recipient populations" the West resorted "to the encouragement and arming of a wide variety of authoritarian regimes." This publication further states that such political and economic manipulations contributed to "gross violations of human rights" and led to "the rise of opportunistic elites who saw in the suffering of their countries only openings for self-enrichment."[16]

An almost endless stream of documentation now exists that affirms the accuracy of the statements quoted above from *Century of Light*.[17] For instance, John Stockwell, a former Central Intelligence Agency (CIA) officer and author of *The Praetorian Guard: The U.S. Role in the New World Order*, does a masterful and courageous job of document-

ing the almost unimaginable horrors and atrocities that were committed by various U.S. sponsored dictatorships during the twentieth
century. As a CIA officer, Stockwell helped to manage "secret wars"
in Africa and Southeast Asia. Stockwell points out that, over many
decades, the United States designed a worldwide military system of
control to protect capitalist interests throughout the globe:

> With a brief interruption during World War II, the creation of
> military oligarchies became a standard U.S. policy of control. We
> set up schools and eventually trained tens of thousands of military
> and police officers in countries all over Latin and Central America,
> in Africa . . . and in Asia. We . . . armed them . . . and created a
> military fraternity of people in power in these countries who were
> more closely identified with our own military, and hence, U.S.
> national interests and capitalist values, than they were with the
> people of their own countries."[18]

Utilizing its international military fraternity, the U.S. government
has sponsored coups in a variety of countries throughout the globe.
Indeed, in 1954, the United States sponsored a coup that overthrew
the democratically elected government of Guatemala. The coup occurred at the urging of Guatemalan wealthy landowners and U.S.-
based corporations with business operations in Guatemala, such as the
United Fruit Company. In relation to this, Walter LaFeber, a professor
of history and author of the book, *Inevitable Revolutions: The United
States in Central America*, states,

> Guatemala has historically been the most economically powerful
> nation in Central America, but half the population average only
> $81 income each year. This half are the pure-blooded Indians
> (descendants of the great Mayans) who are among the poorest
> and most isolated people in the hemisphere. . . .They and other
> exploited Guatemalans became the targets of a 20,000-man army
> trained and largely supplied by the United States. That army runs

the government, and it is a direct descendant of a regime placed in power by a U.S.-planned *golpe* (or coup) in 1954 that overthrew the constitutionally elected, reformist Arbenz government.[19]

It is indeed disturbing to note that, mostly from 1954 through the 1980s, a series of Guatemalan military dictatorships that were backed and financed by the United States executed what was essentially a modern-day campaign of genocide against American Indians. The Historical Clarification Commission, a commission sponsored by the United Nations, stated that the Guatemalan military had committed "acts of genocide" in which 200,000 people (mostly Mayan Indians) were killed. Along these same lines, in an article titled, "Indians Fight Modern Conquistadores," Deborah Menkart explains that, in order to suppress growing resistance among the poor starving peasants, the Guatemalan military took part in the mass killings of Mayan Indians, destroyed fields of crops and forests, raped and tortured countless women and children, sadistically amputated the limbs of many Indians and then abandoned them in holes to suffer alone, fouled water supplies, slaughtered livestock, demolished hundreds of villages, and desecrated Mayan sacred places and cultural symbols. A 1999 United Nations report stated that the Guatemalan army demonstrated "an aggressive racist component of extreme cruelty that led to extermination en masse of defenceless Mayan communities, including children, women and the elderly, through methods whose cruelty has outraged the moral conscience of the civilised world." Mass graves containing the bodies of murdered people were uncovered. Also, over a million people, primarily Mayan Indians, were displaced and forced at gunpoint to move into so-called "model villages" (militarized concentration centers) where the government maintained oppressive control.[20]

It is interesting to note that the Bahá'í book *Century of Light* mentions the tragic history of Latin America. This publication alludes to the long-standing dominating role of the United States and corporations in Latin America: "The coming agony of Latin America was all too clearly prefigured in the suffering of Mexico, large sections of which had been annexed by its great northern neighbor [the U.S.], and whose natural resources were already attracting the attention of avaricious foreign corporations."[21]

Multinational Corporations

A cursory review of the literature pertaining to global capitalism quickly reveals that multinational corporations are at the epicenter of many of the problems that we are currently experiencing both in the United States and throughout the world. Possibly because of this, the Bahá'í writings envisage that corporations (trusts) will no longer exist in the future: "No more trusts will remain in the future. The question of the trusts will be wiped away entirely."[22] Many multinational corporations, as they currently exist, are manifestations of a Cartesian-Newtonian value system that places the maximization of profits ahead of all other goals—often to the exclusion of even ethical and moral considerations. Along these lines, history professor Howard Zinn, author of the highly acclaimed *A People's History of the United States*, notes that the prevailing unscrupulous activities of multinational corporations are built upon a long history of corporate abuse in the Third World:

> The relationship of these global corporations with the poorer countries had long been an exploiting one. . . . Whereas U.S. corporations in Europe between 1950 and 1965 invested $8.1 billion and made $5.5 billion in profits, in Latin America they invested $3.8 billion and made $11.2 billion in profits, and in Africa they invested $5.2 billion and made $14.3 billion in profits.[23]

Corporations wield incredible power, and indeed, are beyond the control of any one government. Of the world's 100 largest economies, fifty-one are now multinational corporations while only forty-nine are nations. Currently, there is no body of national or international law to deal effectively with such corporate "states." Corporations are not democratic institutions, and they often make it clear that their only obligation is to deliver profits to shareholders.

In the United States, corporate lawyers have used the courts to carve out an entire body of case law including language that declares that corporations (also known as trusts) are legal persons entitled to First Amendment free speech rights and also to the protection of life, liberty, and property. Moreover, case law grants corporations legal immunity, which means that corporate executives cannot be held fully accountable for their activities. As such, corporations enjoy the *rights* of individuals without having to assume the *responsibilities* of individuals. Along these lines, Noreena Hertz, a Cambridge University economist and author of *The Silent Takeover: Global Capitalism and the Death of Democracy*, contends that multinational corporations pose a grave threat to democracy itself because of their ever growing capacity to manipulate governments with legal and illegal methods. She maintains that corporations, almost by design, do not currently serve the world's political and social needs, but rather, mostly serve the interests of profit-motivated investors.[24]

In contrast to the prevailing laissez-faire global capitalism model, the Bahá'í teachings stipulate that all business enterprises should be well regulated by international codes of law that set effective, fair, and just guidelines pertaining to global wages, working conditions, environmental protections, property issues, capital-labor relationships, restrictions on the concentration of wealth, and the sharing of natural resources. Furthermore, according to the Bahá'í teachings, businesses should be democratically run with workers and owners mutually participating in the decision-making process at all levels and workers also enjoying a percentage of the profits. All people, including the disabled, should be employed in some capacity. Moreover, in order to avoid the harmful speculation in currencies that currently exists, Bahá'ís believe that there should be one uniform worldwide monetary currency. 'Abdu'l-Bahá wrote, "When the laws He [Bahá'u'lláh] has instituted are carried out, there will be no millionaires possible in the community and likewise no extremely poor."[25]

In their perpetual efforts to find, control, and exploit natural resources, corporations have caused much damage to the environment and have also caused much harm to indigenous communities with close ties with the land. The Bahá'í Faith recognizes that the constant struggle to seize and dominate natural resources has often resulted in major wars and conflicts between nations, groups, and enterprises. In light of this, the Bahá'í writings envisage that, in the future, all of the earth's natural resources will be placed under public control, under the auspices of a world super-state (a world federation of nations). According to the Bahá'í writings, the world super-state will exercise full authority over the planet's resources including oceans, forests, oil deposits, copper, silver, gold and other metals, diamonds, minerals, natural gas, coal, and so forth. It is believed that the super-state will protect, coordinate, and organize the planet's resources so that all peoples and countries may benefit equitably from these natural riches.[26]

Western-Style Development in the Third World

An overwhelming body of evidence now shows that Western-style economic development, the kind that is promoted by multinational corporations, has led to highly destructive outcomes in the Third World. Indeed, a common theme among critics of globalization is that the multinational corporations and the wealthy First World nations (especially the United States) have been using international financial and trade institutions—such as the World Bank, the International Monetary Fund (IMF), and the World Trade Organization (WTO)—to their advantage and to the detriment of poor Third World nations. For instance, Joseph Stiglitz, winner of the 2001 Nobel Prize in economics and author of *Globalization and Its Discontents*, contends that the IMF has consistently placed the interests of the United States and the rich industrialized countries above the interests of the impoverished developing countries. Similarly, economist Biplab DasGupta, author of *Structural Adjustment, Global Trade, and the New Political Economic Development*, asserts that the global economic policies of the IMF and the WTO are harmful to poor countries and primarily reflect the interests of the wealthy countries of the Northern Hemisphere.[27]

Third World debt has become a major driving force in international relations. During the 1970s and 1980s, First World banks found that it was profitable to lend money to Third World governments. Indeed, such banks have managed to collect exorbitant interest on the long-term debt. As it has become evident that some countries might default on their loans, the IMF (ultimately funded by public taxpayers) has stepped in to save the private banks by assuming some of the Third World debt. The IMF and the World Bank, however, have increasingly pressured impoverished nations to enact economic austerity measures or face penalties. These measures are formally known as structural adjustment programs, and they typically require countries to: devalue their currency, which results in a dramatic reduction in the purchasing power of the poor; sell state-run enterprises to private parties (usually corporations); sell state-owned communally held lands to private parties (usually wealthy landowners or agribusiness corporations); severely cut state spending on social programs such as education, health care, and food subsidies for the poor; radically reduce the employment of civil servants in the government sector, which results in massive government layoffs; remove subsidies and price supports for small farmers who consequently can no longer compete with agribusiness corporations; stop producing food crops (such as corn and beans) for the hungry local population and start producing cash crops (like coffee, cotton, and tobacco) for export and sale to wealthy countries; deregulate economic activity (repeal minimum wage laws, gut environmental protection laws, etc.); and other changes. The measures described above have had the overall effect of transferring wealth and power from the public sphere (governments and the people) to private entities (rich elites and multinational corporations).[28]

Loans have done almost nothing to alleviate the distress of Third World populations. To the contrary, they have done much to increase this distress while at the same time augmenting the coffers of multinational corporations and First World banks. Amazingly, poor countries now spend over twenty-five dollars on debt repayment for every one dollar in aid that they receive from wealthy nations. Dennis Brutus, a professor of Africana Studies at the University of Pittsburgh, states,

One of the central mechanisms by which this recolonization [of Africa] . . . is carried out is the loan system through structural adjustment programs. . . . [M]any of the countries that received loans . . . have not seen their economies improve. Quite the opposite. Some are in a far worse economic position and more indebted than they were prior to taking the loans . . . more bankrupt . . . more impoverished. . . . It is hardly imaginable that anyone could knowingly devise such a ruthless, heartless system that is entirely devoted to increasing profit and largely indifferent to its human cost. This, however, is the system that is shaping life in Africa today, and it is the system that we must challenge.[29]

Taking Water Away
From the Bolivian Indians

In January 2000, the city of Cochabamba, the third largest city in the country of Bolivia with a population of 500,000, became the scene of a crisis that attracted worldwide attention and that, to this day, serves as a quintessential example of the destructive policies of "survival of the fittest" Darwinian capitalism. The crisis in Cochabamba was first sparked when the IMF approved a loan for Bolivia and then proceeded to pressure Bolivian government officials to privatize (to sell off) all state owned enterprises including public oil refineries and Cochabamba's municipal water system. In September, 1999, in closed door negotiations that involved only one bidder, Bolivia signed a forty-year contract that handed over Cochabamba's water system to Aguas del Tunari (a company managed by International Water Limited, a subsidiary of U.S.-based Bechtel corporation). Within a few months of taking over, without having made any appreciable investments in the system, Aguas del Tunari dramatically hiked up water rates. As a result of these rate hikes, the water bills of the residents doubled and tripled. This sparked almost immediate protests from the residents who united together in peaceful demonstrations and marches beginning in January of 2000. A grassroots organization of concerned Bolivians (mostly Indians), The Coalition for the Defense of Water and Life (La Coordinadora), began to coordinate some of the rallies.[30]

To understand the true dimensions of this crisis it is necessary to recognize that Bolivia is the most impoverished nation in Latin America (based on per capita GNP) and the second poorest country in the Western Hemisphere, after Haiti. American Indians make up between sixty and seventy percent of Bolivia's population. The three primary indigenous languages that are spoken are Aymara, Guarani, and Quechua. For these impoverished indigenous people, access to affordable water is a top priority. Water and food are absolute necessities. Steep increases in the price of either of these represent a mortal threat. More money spent on water means that less money is available for other necessities, including food.[31]

Eventually, demonstrations spread from Cochabamba to La Paz and to other cities and outlying rural villages. In April 2000, the Bolivian government declared a "state of siege." The "state of siege" (like martial law) allowed police to arrest and detain many people and to impose curfews and travel restrictions. Unfortunately, the April demonstrations became violent, leaving six people dead and many injured. On April 10, 2000, the government signed an agreement with the leader of The Coalition for the Defense of Water and Life. This agreement revoked the contract with the Bechtel corporation subsidiary and granted control of the Cochabamba municipal water system to the grassroots coalition. It also repealed water privatization legislation as well as provisions that would have charged people for drawing water from local wells.

It is amazing to note that, after losing its contract, Bechtel Corporation sued the nation of Bolivia for $25 million in damages and an additional $25 million in lost potential profits (money the corporation argues that it could have earned if it had been able to keep the water system). It must be recognized here that, in 2000, Bechtel's revenues were more than $14 billion while the entire national budget of Bolivia was merely $2.7 billion. Oscar Olivera, the leader of The Coalition for the Defense of Water and Life stated, "With the $25 million [in damages] they are seeking, 125,000 people could have access to water."[32]

Fortunately, in January 2006, Bechtel finally decided to drop its suit after being subjected to four years of sustained international pressure. Organizations and citizens groups from throughout the world coordinated their efforts to apply pressure on Bechtel to drop its case. The company was bombarded with emails, and concerned groups used the international media to bring attention to Bechtel's attempts to profiteer at the expense of the poor people in Bolivia. Oscar Olivera declared, "Multinational corporations want to turn everything into a market. . . . For indigenous people water is not a commodity, it is a common good. For Bolivia this retreat by Bechtel means that the rights of the people are undeniable."[33]

Shipping Toxic Waste to the Third World

The issue of Third World toxic waste lays bare a picture of callous inhumanity and blatant cruelty that is truly shocking in its scope. It has now been widely reported that the First World is exporting its toxic waste to impoverished developing nations. Not only is such waste being shipped to the Third World, some corporations have actually found a way to profit from this deadly transaction.

The "ship breaking business" is a case in point of corporate behavior that can be characterized as nothing short of criminal. Ten shipping corporations dominate the global merchant cargo trade. When these corporations want to dispose of an old vessel, they send it to a ship breaking yard where it is dismantled for scrap metal. Probably the largest ship breaking yard in the world is in Bangladesh (a hunger-ravaged nation) where massive tanker ships, some as long as three football fields and as tall as twenty stories high, have been run aground in the Bay of Bengal. Workers (cutters) use blow torches to cut ships to pieces. From high above, gigantic plates of metal, some weighing several tons, are cut from ships and then fall dangerously to the ground. Crews of workers then carry the plates on their shoulders as they step in unison to the rhythm of a leader's chant. The National Labor Committee (NLC), a U.S.-based worker rights organization, investigated the industrial atrocities at the Bengal shipyard. An NLC article titled "Where Ships and Workers Go to Die," states,

The kids usually help the cutters or remove asbestos [a known carcinogen]. They smash the asbestos with a hammer, shovel it into a plastic bag and remove it from the ship. . . . Dismantled ships are toxic to workers and the environment. Each ship contains an average of 15,000 pounds of asbestos and ten to 100 tons of lead paint. Besides asbestos and lead [which can cause kidney damage and brain impairment in children], workers are exposed to mercury, arsenic, dioxins, solvents, toxic oil residues and carcinogenic fumes from melting metal and paint. Environmental damage to beaches, ocean and fishing villages is extensive.[34]

Charles Kernaghan, director of the National Labor Committee, calls the Bengal ship breaking yard "hell on earth." Thirty thousand workers, some as young as ten years old, dismantle ships at a nonstop pace for twelve hours a day, seven days a week, for the equivalent of twenty-two to thirty-six cents an hour with no sick days or holidays. Workers live in utter squalor in stifling hot rooms without windows and without refrigerators. Each tiny room is packed with four people who sleep on the floor with only old sheets and rags for bedding. While doing their incredibly dangerous tasks, the workers are not given any safety gear by the ship-owners. Baseball caps serve as hard hats, and in the absence of steel-toed shoes, young workers are seen handling heavy sheets of metal wearing only flip-flops. Filthy bandanas serve as respiratory masks, and when using dangerous blow torches, sunglasses are used in place of safety visors. Kernaghan states, "Last year, a 13-year-old child his very first day on the job was hit in the head with a heavy piece of metal and he just died immediately." Kernaghan eerily adds, "the ship-owners don't document anything, they don't investigate the killings and the injuries, they just throw the people back into their villages and in some cases, we've heard that they throw the dead bodies into the water."[35]

The heinous disregard for human life and the environment that is described above is the end result of an insidiously reckless capitalist order that has thrown away all moral restraint. In a Law Review article titled, "Beyond Eco-Imperialism: An Environmental Justice Critique of Free Trade," Carmen Gonzalez, a law professor, provides a highly detailed and well-researched view of the environmental justice issues that have emerged as a result of globalization. Her article states,

[I]nternational trade promotes environmental degradation in developing countries and threatens the physical health, cultural integrity and economic well being of the Southern [Third World] poor. . . . [T]he North [First World] reaps the benefits of liberalized trade while exporting the environmental costs to the South. . . . [This] article . . . identifies the North's resource-intensive, consumption-oriented lifestyle as the primary cause of global environmental degradation. . . . This lifestyle can only be maintained through the ongoing appropriation of the natural resources of the South.[36]

Earlier in this chapter a section titled "Widespread Rising Poverty Amidst Incredible Concentrations of Wealth," provided statistics that show that the people living in the wealthy developed nations (only about twenty percent of the world's population) consume a disproportionate share of the globe's food, resources, and goods. Indeed, the United States has the highest consumption levels per capita in the globe with Japan and Western Europe not being far behind. Gonzalez uses similar statistics in her article to support her thesis (as expressed in the quote above). A group of researchers in the Center for Sustainability Studies in Xalapa, Mexico, created a concept known as the "ecological footprint" in order to study the amount of resources, "natural capital," that a country must have (or must appropriate from others) in order to maintain its level of consumption. The researchers discovered that "the Netherlands, United States, Belgium, Germany, Switzerland, United Kingdom, Japan, and Israel were among the highest per capita importers of natural capital." This means that these countries, in particular, are using many more resources than they actually possess, and that the First World "is living far beyond its ecological means," and the developing nations cannot catch up "without exceeding the limits of the global ecosystem." Indeed, if everyone in the world adopted and tried to maintain a Western level of consumption, then, instead of just one world, it would actually be necessary to have ten worlds to satisfy everyone's needs. Gonzalez contends that there is a great need for legal scholarship in the area of researching and creating international laws that address the problem of over-consumption.[37]

Gonzalez further asserts that, for many years, the U.S. environmental movement has been perceived to be a middle class, White, suburban phenomenon that has been primarily interested in the protection of endangered species, wilderness areas, and parks, but it has not shown sufficient interest in environmental justice issues related to racism, poverty, and societal antidemocratic processes and policies. She cites a variety of studies that show that "poor people and racial and ethnic minorities suffer disproportionately high levels of exposure to toxic substances while whites residing in more pristine suburban neighborhoods reap the benefits of environmental protection." This unjust dynamic within the United States shows up in the choice of location for hazardous waste facilities and also in the selective enforcement of laws and standards pertaining to water and air pollution, as well as waste disposal.[38]

Similar to the dynamic described above, Gonzalez maintains that, when it comes to the international arena, environmentalists from the Northern wealthy nations have been mainly concerned with protecting global natural areas. As such, they have been slow to recognize that socioeconomic justice issues are a direct cause of global pollution and resource depletion. In contrast, environmentalists from the poor Southern nations are increasingly asserting that international environmental degradation is directly linked to justice issues related to international inequality and to the struggle for democracy, self-determination, economic sufficiency, and cultural rights. Along these lines, the Southern environmentalists contend that the primary causes of international pollution and resource depletion are the excessive consumption patterns of wealthy nations as well as "the world economic order" that "has institutionalized Southern poverty, which places additional stress on the environment."[39] Along these lines, Gonzalez states,

Indeed, one prominent Southern environmentalist has argued that the South is bearing a disproportionate share of the environmental consequences of globalization, and has described this phenomenon as environmental apartheid. . . . The allegations of Southern environmentalists have been supported by studies commissioned by the United Nations Development Program, [specifically related to] the export of hazardous wastes and deforestation.[40]

Gonzalez points out that there is a need for the development of international human rights laws that "link the environmental struggle with the struggle for social justice."

Unfortunately, the hazardous waste trade is flourishing. Illegal shipments destined from the United States to other nations (Mexico, Ecuador, Haiti, Sri Lanka, Malaysia, and others) have continued to be intercepted. Even recycling efforts that seem innocent on the surface can actually be deadly in Third World environments where there are not appropriate safeguards. A prime example of this is the shipment of used car batteries to poor countries in order to recover and recycle the lead. Lead is extremely hazardous and typically causes all forms of problems for the poor. Along similar lines, the Bangladesh ship breaking yard described above is extremely toxic to the people and to the environment, and yet the ship-owners would likely try to defend it as a good venture that recovers and recycles scrap metal. Gonzalez states, "Environmentalists have rightfully denounced" such practices "as 'toxic colonialism.'"[41]

Rearranging the Deck Chairs on the Titanic

A few words should be said regarding the Bahá'í idea of civilization. Bahá'u'lláh wrote, "All men have been created to carry forward an ever-advancing civilization."[42] Obviously, the civilization that is intended here is not the kind of civilization that was first conceived by Rene Descartes, Isaac Newton, John Locke, Adam Smith, Charles Darwin, and other Western intellectuals who promulgated an anti-spiritual mentality. Indeed, in the following passage, Bahá'u'lláh uses the words "infernal engine" in reference to Western civilization:

In all matters moderation is desirable. If a thing is carried to excess, it will prove a source of evil. Consider the civilization of the West, how it hath agitated and alarmed the peoples of the world. An infernal engine hath been devised, and hath proved so cruel a weapon of destruction that its like none hath ever witnessed or heard. The purging of such deeply rooted and overwhelming corruptions cannot be effected unless the peoples of the world unite in pursuit of one common aim and embrace one universal faith.[43]

In relation to the quote above, it is significant to note that capitalism, if anything, actually encourages immoderation. For instance, it encourages the ideas of unbridled competition, insatiable desires, unrestricted individualism, boundless accumulation of wealth, and absolute freedom (*laissez-faire*). It also promotes the cynical assumption that self-interest and profit motivation are the primary forces between individuals in society. This ultimately leads to self-indulgence and greed.

In relation to the above discussion, it is sad to say that capitalist ideology has made major inroads even into the realm of religion. Indeed, the underlying worldview of significant numbers of Christians has become intermixed with a myriad of capitalistic values, beliefs, and assumptions, most of which run counter to any authentic biblical outlook. This uncertainty in worldview has resulted in confusion regarding goals and priorities. While operating within this capitalistic perspective, it is extremely difficult to live a life of Christian compassion, humility, charity, and love as is encouraged by the Bible.

Fortunately, some Christians have begun to recognize that, in order to maintain a biblical perspective, they must challenge and transcend, in thoughts and actions, the existing socioeconomic materialistic paradigm. For instance, Ron Sider, a professor of theology, holistic ministry, and public policy at Eastern Baptist Theological Seminary, states,

We need to ask, "Are we really biblical?" . . . Cheap grace results when we reduce the gospel to forgiveness of sins only . . . when we embrace the individualism and materialism and relativism of our current culture. . . . [E]mbracing Jesus . . . means embracing [Him] as Lord as well as Savior. . . . [I]t means beginning to live as a part of his new community where everything is being transformed. . . . [T]he mission of the church is both to do evangelism and to do social ministry. . . . That means . . . a concern for justice for the poor. It will mean concern for creation care [care for the environment], for human rights, and for peacemaking."[44]

In his recent book, *The Scandal of the Evangelical Conscience: Why Are Christians Living Just Like the Rest of the World?*, Sider maintains that many Christians have conformed their thinking and actions to the prevailing un-biblical materialistic paradigm. This, he asserts, has seriously compromised their worldview and has crippled their ability to transform the society around them based on the Word of Christ. Indeed, Sider cites a plethora of studies, polls, and statistics showing that many Christians live very much like the general American population in terms of materialism, hedonism, racism, sexual immorality, and other traits. For instance, he shows that, even though today's American Christians are the wealthiest generation of Christians in world history, their charitable giving, as a percentage of income, has gone down. Sider also asserts that, as a group, they do not take care of the poor. He points out that, in particular, the tithing of Christian Evangelicals (the group most likely to attend church regularly) has gone down every year for several decades. He argues that these negative conditions will persist so long as mammon (money) remains on the throne as the idol of worship.[45]

It is also troubling to note that considerable numbers of Christians now subscribe to a point of view that merges their religious beliefs with a staunchly nationalist, capitalist ideology that often promotes and defends the American-dominated global economic order even at the expense of other nations and peoples. Regarding this, S. R. Shearer, an Evangelical Christian who runs his own ministry, points out that it is truly disturbing and ironic that capitalist ideology enjoys a significant amount of support from Christian Americans.[46] He maintains that it is virtually impossible for Christians to justify the immorality of the American-dominated capitalist global order [he calls it the "American New World Order System"], especially in light of the following passages from the Bible:

Lay not up for yourselves treasures upon the earth. . . . But lay up for yourselves treasures in heaven. . . . For where your treasure is, there will your heart be also . . .[47]

[I]f thou wilt be perfect, go sell (all) that thou hast, and give it to the poor, . . . and come and follow me [Christ].[48]

No servant can serve two masters: for either he will *hate* the one, and love the other; or else he will hold to the one, and despise the other. Ye *cannot* serve God and mammon [material wealth or possessions].[49]

Many Americans, including many religious believers, may believe that our cultural paradigm is fundamentally sound and that we can resolve our global problems simply by implementing an assortment of reforms, adjustments, and tweaks to the system here and there. Such attempts to reform the system, however, without confronting the underlying destructive materialistic worldview are tantamount to rearranging the deck chairs on the Titanic. Solutions to our global problems cannot be found within the same despiritualized system that created these problems.

Based on information provided in this chapter, it should be evident that some of the people who have been most negatively impacted by the immoderation of Western civilization have been the indigenous peoples of the Americas. Indeed, countless indigenous cultures have been decimated by the relentless wayward march of the West. This destructive process has continued even into modern times. For instance, the genocide against the Guatemalan Mayan Indians and the "water wars" against the Indian people of Bolivia (both of these situations were described earlier) are good examples of this destructive process.

It is important to note that many Latin American nations have very large populations of American Indians, and in fact, in some countries, Indians make up the majority of the population. Unfortunately, Indians throughout Latin America continue to face deeply ingrained racism on the part of Whites (people of European descent) who still wield disproportionate levels of economic, political, and social power.

In light of the information above, it is truly fascinating that, as noted earlier, 'Abdu'l-Bahá prophesied that if the Indians become "educated and guided" in the teachings of Bahá'u'lláh, "there can be no doubt that they will become so illumined as to enlighten the whole world."[50] Considering the fact that the indigenous people of the Americas are now some of the most impoverished and marginalized peoples in the world, this prophetic passage seems truly remarkable. This may be a case of God using the downtrodden and dispossessed to show the true power of spirituality to positively transform the material world.

In 1977, a group of Indian people presented three papers to some of the nongovernmental organizations of the United Nations located in Geneva, Switzerland. In these documents, the American Indian authors raised "a call for a consciousness of the Sacred Web of Life in the Universe." The passage below is an excerpt from one of these documents. Please note the similarity between the sentiments expressed by Bahá'u'lláh in the quote above and the sentiments expressed by the indigenous authors of the statement below:

Today the species of Man is facing a question of the very survival of the species. The way of life known as Western Civilization is on a death path on which their own culture has no viable answers. When faced with the reality of their own destructiveness, they can only go forward into areas of more efficient destruction. The appearance of Plutonium [nuclear technology] on this planet is the clearest of signals that our species is in trouble. It is a signal which most Westerners have chosen to ignore. . . . The air is foul, the waters poisoned, the trees dying, the animals are disappearing. We think even the systems of weather are changing. Our ancient teaching warned us that if Man interfered with the Natural Laws, these things would come to be. When the last of the Natural Way of Life [traditional Native way of life] is gone,

all hope for human survival will be gone with it. And our Way of
Life is fast disappearing, a victim of the destructive processes. . . .
Our essential message to the world is a basic call to consciousness.
The destruction of the Native cultures and people is the same
process which has destroyed and is destroying life on this planet.
The technologies and social systems which have destroyed the
animal and the plant life are also destroying the Native people.
And that process is Western Civilization. . . . The traditional
Native peoples hold the key to the reversal of the processes in
Western Civilization which hold the promise of unimaginable
future suffering and destruction. Spiritualism is the highest form
of . . . consciousness. And we, the Native peoples of the Western
Hemisphere, are among the world's surviving proprietors of that
kind of consciousness. We are here to impart that message.[51]

True solutions will have to be based upon perspectives, ideas, values, and assumptions that lie outside the confines of the prevailing
Western view of reality. In this regard, Bahá'ís believe that the teachings of Bahá'u'lláh are intended to create an entirely new peaceful,
just, and unified global order that will wipe away, at their very root,
the maladies of the current age. The following passage from the Bahá'í
writings eloquently enunciates this concept of renewal:

The call of Bahá'u'lláh is primarily directed against all forms
of provincialism, all insularities and prejudices. If long-
cherished ideals and time-honored institutions, if certain social
assumptions and religious formulae have ceased to promote
the welfare of the generality of mankind, if they no longer
minister to the needs of a continually evolving humanity, let
them be swept away and relegated to the limbo of obsolescent
and forgotten doctrines. Why should these, in a world subject
to the immutable law of change and decay, be exempt from
the deterioration that must needs overtake every human
institution? For legal standards, political and economic theories
are solely designed to safeguard the interests of humanity as a

whole, and not humanity to be crucified for the preservation of the integrity of any particular law or doctrine.[52]

Moving Toward a Holistic View of Reality

When one considers the egregious levels of abuse, corruption, and exploitation prevalent in the world today, it becomes quite clear that it is impossible to build a well-functioning world order on the defective foundation of global capitalism. As stated in the Bahá'í publication, *Century of Light*, Western civilization has erected a capitalist-based global system that is "morally and intellectually bankrupt."[53] Fortunately, the Bahá'í Faith is not alone in recognizing this. Indeed, as detailed in my first book, *Faith, Physics, and Psychology: Rethinking Society and the Human Spirit*, a diversity of movements from various fields of study (including economics, psychology, physics, religious studies, history, medicine, education, sociology, political science, and others) have started to challenge the underlying ideologies, theories, and philosophies of Western civilization. Within this context, capitalism itself, the golden idol of many modern people, has come under intense scrutiny and criticism.

The various movements that are challenging the Western paradigm are based on worldviews that are radically different from the Cartesian-Newtonian worldview. Like the Bahá'í perspective, these movements maintain that, before we can resolve the major social, economic, political, and environmental problems facing us, we must leave behind the false, materialistic, Cartesian-Newtonian view of reality. Also, like the Bahá'í Faith, such movements assert that we need to adopt a holistic view of reality that is capable of recognizing the oneness of humanity and the oneness of the cosmos and of integrating science and religion, as well as acknowledging the unity of mind, body, and spirit. Along these lines, Theodore Roszak, a well-known advocate of the holistic paradigm, asserts,

It is as Schumacher [a Rhodes Scholar in economics, and a highly respected holistic advocate] tells us: "when the available 'spiritual space' is not filled by some higher motivations, then it will necessarily be filled by something lower—by the small, mean, calculating attitude to life which is rationalized in the economic calculus." If that is so, then we need a nobler economics that is not afraid to discuss spirit and conscience, moral purpose and the meaning of life, an economics that aims to educate and elevate people, not merely to measure their low-grade behavior.[54]

In short, any global order that aspires to honor the exalted nature of the human soul must be able to integrate the spiritual and the sacred with the material and the secular. This is something that the capitalist paradigm, almost by definition, cannot achieve. Thus, it has planted the seeds of its own ultimate destruction because it is virtually incapable of truly edifying and inspiring the human soul—the real source of power for any sustainable economic system.

Since spiritual transformation and material transformation must go together, it is essential for individuals to remain cognizant of the economic, political, social, and environmental state of the world. People of faith must also be directly engaged in helping to transform the world rather than retreating into comfortable "spiritual enclaves." Bahá'u'lláh states, "Be anxiously concerned with the needs of the age ye live in, and center your deliberations on its exigencies and requirements."[55]

In essence, a faith without physical deeds is dead. According to the Bahá'í Faith, some of the noblest of all human beings are those who have been educated, trained, and spiritually inspired for a life of service to humanity. Along these lines, 'Abdu'l-Bahá's following statement regarding the importance of service is highly pertinent to the discussion in this chapter regarding the plight of many who are currently being held in the claws of tyranny and oppression:

Without action nothing in the material world can be accomplished. . . . It is not through lip-service only that the elect of God have attained to holiness, but by patient lives of active service they have brought light into the world. . . . Therefore strive that your actions day by day may be beautiful prayers. Turn towards God, and seek always to do that which is right and noble. Enrich the poor, raise the fallen, comfort the sorrowful, bring healing to the sick, reassure the fearful, rescue the oppressed, bring hope to the hopeless, shelter the destitute! . . . If we strive to do all this, then are we true Bahá'ís, but if we neglect it, we are not followers of the Light, and we have no right to the name.[56]

Related to the discussion above, the Bahá'í teachings assert that humanity is involved in an evolutionary process that is inevitably moving humankind toward maturity and away from destructive ways of thinking and acting. This, however, does not mean that individuals should sit idly by and just wait for the process to take its natural evolutionary course. Indeed, this process seems to be an interactive, mutually reinforcing, synergistic progression—the more that individuals strive for spiritual transformation and the more that individuals strive to implement spiritual virtues and deeds in the material world, the greater the evolutionary shifts for the overall society. Conversely, any positive shifts in the overall society help people to make further internal changes as individuals.

Many holistic advocates believe that we are already beginning to experience a paradigm shift toward holism and away from the Cartesian-Newtonian worldview (and its capitalistic system). Similar to the Bahá'í perspective, such holistic advocates believe that humanity is presently undergoing an evolutionary jump toward holism as a result of major leaps in human spiritual consciousness. Indeed, Bahá'ís and holistic advocates both believe that the paradigm shift toward a holistic view of reality is not coerced, but rather, it is a natural process of spiritual transformation that is moving humanity from its adolescent stage of development to its stage of maturity (the coming of age of humanity). Along these lines, the Bahá'í publication *Century of Light* states,

And for a Bahá'í the ultimate issues *are* spiritual. The Cause [Bahá'í Faith] is not a political party nor an ideology, much less an engine for political agitation against this or that social wrong. The process of transformation it has set in motion advances by inducing a fundamental change of consciousness, and the challenge it poses to everyone who would serve it is to free oneself from attachment to inherited assumptions and preferences that are irreconcilable with the Will of God for humanity's coming of age. Paradoxically, even the distress caused by prevailing conditions that violate one's conscience aids in this process of spiritual liberation. In the final analysis, such disillusionment drives a Bahá'í to confront a truth emphasized over and over again in the Writings of the Faith: "He hath chosen out of the whole world the hearts of His servants and made them each a seat for the revelation of His glory. Wherefore, sanctify them from every defilement, that the things for which they were created may be engraven upon them."[57]

Thus as agents of spiritual and material transformation we all have the responsibility to purify ourselves from "every defilement" and "to free" ourselves "from attachment to inherited assumptions and preferences that are irreconcilable with the Will of God for humanity's coming of age." The sentiments expressed in the quote above bring us full circle to the concept of responsibility that we discussed at the beginning of this chapter—according to the Bahá'í writings, the American Bahá'ís in particular have a "staggering responsibility" to cleanse themselves from the "faults, habits, and tendencies which they have inherited from their own nation" and then to help eradicate "such evil tendencies" from the lives of their fellow American citizens. Indeed, the Bahá'í writings emphasize that America will not manifest its exalted destiny until this "staggering responsibility" is fulfilled. It is my hope that this chapter has made it plainly evident that, capitalism, a manifestation of the materialistic Cartesian-Newtonian worldview, is an "evil tendency" that must be acknowledged and properly redressed so that America can assume its exalted destiny as the nation that "will lead all nations spiritually" as prophesied by 'Abdu'l-Bahá.[58]

Chapter Seven

A "SPIRITUALLY BLESSED AND ENVIABLE NATION"

As described in detail in chapter four, the United States and the American Bahá'í community will both play uniquely special roles in the creation of the World Order of Bahá'u'lláh—a unified, just, and peaceful global commonwealth of nations "whose life is sustained by its universal recognition of one God and by its allegiance to one common Revelation [the Bahá'í Faith]." Unlike any Messenger of the past, Bahá'u'lláh, as the Promised One of all ages, conceived of this World Order of universal laws and institutions that will ultimately lead to the establishment of a glorious world civilization—the Kingdom of God on earth. The establishment of the World Order of Bahá'u'lláh still lies in the distant future; however, the "embryonic form" of the future World Order already exists in the worldwide administrative and governance system (the Administrative Order) of the Bahá'í Faith. Indeed, the American Bahá'ís were endowed with the God-given mission to build, improve, and consolidate this Administrative Order, which will ultimately serve as "the nucleus," "the precursor," and "the very pattern" of the future New World Order. They were also given the mission to utilize this worldwide administrative structure to promulgate the teachings of Bahá'u'lláh throughout the planet. Meanwhile, the U.S. government and its citizens were endowed with the God-given destiny to take part in actions that will unwittingly and indirectly promote the establishment of national and international institutions that will, in turn, help to establish the World Order of Bahá'u'lláh. Again here, it must be emphasized that the United States and its people were given this special distinction not because of any inherent excellence. To the contrary, Shoghi Effendi states that the American nation was given this special bestowal precisely because of the "patent evils" as well as the social and political "divers ills" that exist in the United States. By such means, Bahá'u'lláh can best demonstrate the transformative power of His teachings to change vice to virtue, corruption to purity, and shame to glory.[1]

In a previous chapter, it was made clear that the future establishment of the World Order of Bahá'u'lláh cannot occur "unless and until" the American Bahá'ís (as a part of their mission) successfully "weed out" the "faults, habits, and tendencies which they have inherited from their own nation," and then, in turn, help to eradicate these same "evil tendencies" and "divers ills" from the lives of the entire body of their American fellow-citizens. In the *Advent of Divine Justice*, Shoghi Effendi calls this the "staggering responsibility" of the American Bahá'ís. In this same book, he calls on them to take part in a "double crusade" to "first regenerate the inward life of their own community, and next to assail the long-standing evils that have entrenched themselves in the life of their nation." As explained in detail earlier, it is my belief that the American "patent evils," "divers ills," "evil tendencies," "long-standing evils," "godlessness," "enervating materialism," and "irreligion," as well as the American "faults, habits, and tendencies" that are condemned in the Bahá'í writings are all related to the materialistic Cartesian-Newtonian worldview that lies at the foundation of American culture. Thus in order to fulfill their God-given mission, the American Bahá'ís must, in my view, confront and overcome this mechanistic, secular Western perspective.[2] Along these lines, Shoghi Effendi states,

> Indeed, the chief reason for the evils now rampant in society is a lack of spirituality. The materialistic civilization of our age has . . . absorbed the energy and interest of mankind. . . . The spirit of the age, taken on the whole, is irreligious. Man's outlook upon life is

too crude and materialistic to enable him to elevate himself into the higher realms of the spirit. It is this condition, so sadly morbid, into which society has fallen, that religion seeks to improve and transform. For the core of religious faith is that mystic feeling that unites man with God.[3]

The Western, materialistic view of reality splits apart science and religion; views human beings as soulless biological machines; emphasizes dichotomies and separation rather than integration and oneness; promotes self-indulgence rather than self-sacrifice; encourages profit motivation rather than service orientation; creates societies that exalt individualism, rabid competition, and self-interest; and in far too many instances, ultimately militates against the existence of God Himself. In essence, American Bahá'ís must continue to be directly and compassionately engaged in their communities without conforming to the existing corrupt paradigm in the sense that they refuse to partake in what Shoghi Effendi described as "the shifts, shams and compromises that characterize the present age." This is akin to the early heroes of the Christian dispensation, who refused to engage in the excesses and decadence of the tottering Roman Empire. This means that, if Bahá'ís are to remain faithful to the teachings of Bahá'u'lláh, they must examine all prevailing scientific, economic, social, political, educational, and legal theories (the assumptions, values, beliefs, and ideas of such viewpoints) through the lens of the Bahá'í writings.[4]

Indeed, the process of overcoming the faulty, Western "system of thought" will strengthen the faith of the American Bahá'ís; will bolster their steadfast exertions to obey the laws, ordinances, and commandments of the Bahá'í writings; and will energize their efforts to spread the teachings of Bahá'u'lláh as mapped out in the current plans of the Universal House of Justice. This cleansing process will ultimately help the American believers to establish a clear identity as the noble, pure, valiant disciples of a new message of God that bears no semblance to the "exploded theories" and debased, fragmented doctrines of modern man. This, in turn, will equip the American Bahá'ís for the exalted role that they will play in helping to transform America and in continuing to build and consolidate the Administrative Order as "the champion-builders of the mightiest institutions of the Faith of Bahá'u'lláh." The American Bahá'ís are essentially being called to become "living sacrifices" for the Cause of God. This means that if they aspire to fulfill the true purpose of their physical existence in this material world, they must be willing to sacrifice their personal wills for the will of God as expressed by His supreme Messenger, Bahá'u'lláh.

As described earlier, in order to live a life of true meaning and purpose, one must recognize that this physical realm is not true reality but merely an illusion—a projection from an unseen true or deeper reality. The Bahá'í writings use metaphors to describe this physical world as a "mirage," a "vapor," a "distorted image," or as "drifting shadows" stretching out from reality. The spiritual worlds of God are the "true reality." God temporarily placed us in the false reality of this physical world so that we may learn unique lessons and prepare our souls for the true life that begins only after our bodies die and our souls wing their way to their real habitation or home—the glorious spiritual worlds of God. If an individual spends his or her life primarily chasing after the false reality—pursuing material wealth, power, and status as well as indulging in the delights and entertaining distractions of the physical world, he or she will ultimately find emptiness, utter loss, and lamentation. Tests and trials are a natural part of this physical "classroom for the soul," but even in the face of earthly tribulations, one can still build a life of true, inner peace, happiness, meaning, and purpose if one follows the will of God. Along these lines, Bahá'u'lláh declares,

Follow not, therefore, your earthly desires, and violate not the Covenant of God, nor break your pledge to Him. With firm determination, with the whole affection of your heart, and with the full force of your words, turn ye unto Him, and walk not in the ways of the foolish. The world is but a show, vain and empty, a mere nothing, bearing the semblance of reality. Set not your affections upon it. Break not the bond that uniteth you with your Creator, and be not of those that have erred and strayed from His ways. Verily I say, the world is like the vapor in a desert, which the thirsty dreameth to be water and striveth after it with all his might, until when he cometh unto it, he findeth it to be mere illusion. It may, moreover, be likened unto the lifeless image of the beloved whom the lover hath sought and found, in the end, after long search and to his utmost regret, to be such as cannot fatten nor appease his hunger."[5]

In contrast to the Bahá'í paradigm of true reality, the Western secular worldview encourages people to incessantly pursue the false reality of this physical world. Ultimately, in order to rise above such a banal and meaningless view of existence, it is important for the American Bahá'ís (and indeed for all people) to constantly keep in mind a clear view of true reality. In essence, all souls can approach true reality not only in the next world but also in this physical world through prayer and meditation on the Word of God, good deeds, self-sacrificial service to humanity, and adherence to the ordinances, laws, and commandments of the Messenger of God for this age, Bahá'u'lláh. By maintaining this spiritual view of reality, the American Bahá'ís can begin to reprioritize the use of their personal energy, time, money, and resources for maximum effect in fulfilling their God-given mission. Essentially, they must prevent their lives from becoming enmeshed and circumscribed by the American cultural traps of jobs, careers, consumption, debt, and the obsessive pursuit of various distractions (TV, movies, sports, games, sex, overeating, alcohol, drugs, gambling, and so forth).

Following the teachings of Bahá'u'lláh will not necessarily lead to "success," "popularity," and a charmed life of "good fortune" as defined by American culture. To the contrary, in a letter to the American Bahá'ís, Shoghi Effendi makes it clear that they will suffer significant persecutions, and he quotes 'Abdu'l-Bahá, who prophesied that "many a test will be visited upon you. Troubles will befall you, and suffering afflict you." In this same letter, Shoghi Effendi further states that the American Bahá'ís will face "the fury of conservative forces, the opposition of vested interests, and the objections of a corrupt and pleasure-seeking generation" but these "must be reckoned with, resolutely resisted, and completely overcome." Additionally, the American Bahá'ís may have to suffer through "storms of abuse and ridicule, and campaigns of condemnation and misrepresentation." Such tests, troubles, sufferings, and persecutions have always been the lot of the heroes and heroines who arise to steadfastly and courageously promote the teachings of a new Messenger of God. This was true at the time of Moses, Christ, and Muḥammad, and it is still true now. Shoghi Effendi explains that, ironically, the persecution of the American Bahá'í community will actually help the Bahá'í Faith to thrive, grow, and to win over its detractors.[6]

As a part of his sacred Tablets of the Divine Plan, 'Abdu'l-Bahá lovingly exhorts the American Bahá'ís to steadfastly and courageously arise to fulfill their God-given mission: "Be not concerned with the smallness of your numbers, neither be oppressed by the multitude of an unbelieving world. . . . Exert yourselves; your mission is unspeakably glorious. Should success crown your enterprise, America will assuredly evolve into a center from which waves of spiritual power will emanate, and the throne of the Kingdom of God, will, in the plenitude of its majesty and glory, be firmly established."[7]

In a hope-filled message, Shoghi Effendi, in a letter to the American Bahá'ís, asserts that their sacred efforts to distinguish themselves from the larger American society have already started an inspiring "spiritual renaissance" in the United States as foretold by 'Abdu'l-Bahá. In this letter, he lays out a stunning view of the luminous mission of the American Bahá'ís and enumerates the noteworthy ways in which they have already distinguished themselves:

Can our eyes be so dim as to fail to recognize in the anguish and turmoil which . . . are now afflicting the American nation, evidences of the beginnings of that spiritual renaissance which . . . [the] pregnant words of 'Abdu'l-Bahá so clearly foreshadow? The throes and twinges of agony which the soul of a nation in travail is now beginning to experience abundantly proclaim it. Contrast the sad plight of . . . this great Republic of the West, with the rising fortunes of that handful of its citizens [American Bahá'ís], whose mission, if they be faithful to their trust, is to heal its wounds, restore its confidence and revive its shattered hopes. Contrast the dreadful convulsions, the internecine conflicts, the petty disputes, the outworn controversies, the interminable revolutions that agitate the masses, with the calm new light of Peace and of Truth which envelops, guides and sustains those valiant inheritors of the law and love of Bahá'u'lláh. Compare the disintegrating institutions, the discredited statesmanship, the exploded theories, the appalling degradation, the follies and furies, the shifts, shams and compromises that characterize the present age, with the steady consolidation, the holy discipline, the unity and cohesiveness, the assured conviction, the uncompromising loyalty, the heroic self-sacrifice that constitute the hallmark of these faithful stewards and harbingers of the golden age of the Faith of Bahá'u'lláh.[8]

In a letter to the American Bahá'ís, Shoghi Effendi eloquently testifies that mysterious spiritual powers are at the disposal of every "warrior in the service of Bahá'u'lláh." However, every individual Bahá'í must first take the initiative to act now and to continue to act. Indeed, Shoghi Effendi states that there are "unseen legions, standing rank upon rank, and eager to pour forth from the Kingdom on high the full measure of their celestial strength on the individual participants of this incomparably glorious Crusade," but first, each individual must valiantly and steadfastly "rush into the arena of service ready to sacrifice his all for the Cause he is called upon to champion."[9]

In regard to the special God-given destiny of the American nation, Shoghi Effendi explains that the Bahá'í revelation has already infused the United States with "potencies" that are "insensibly shaping, under the impact of world political and economic forces, the destiny of that nation, and are influencing the lives and actions of both its government and its people."[10] He further majestically declares that the United States, in spite of the woes that will afflict it, will remain undefeatable until it attains its glorious destiny:

Whatever the Hand of a beneficent and inscrutable Destiny has reserved for this youthful, this virile, this idealistic, this spiritually blessed and enviable nation, however severe the storms which may buffet it in the days to come in either hemisphere, however sweeping the changes which the impact of cataclysmic forces from without, and the stirrings of a Divine embryonic Order [the Administrative Order] from within, will effect in its structure and life, we may, confident in the words uttered by 'Abdu'l-Bahá, feel assured that that great republic—the shell that enshrines . . . [the American Bahá'í community]—will continue to evolve, undivided and undefeatable, until the sum total of its contributions to the birth, the rise and the fruition of that world civilization, the child of the Most Great Peace and hallmark of the Golden Age of the Dispensation of Bahá'u'lláh, will have been made, and its last task discharged.[11]

Herein, within the beauty, power, and poetry of such words, lies the true monumental scope of the epic mission of the American Bahá'ís and the glorious destiny of the United States—"two simultaneous processes" that, as promised by the Bahá'í writings, are "destined to culminate, in the fullness of time, in a single glorious consummation"—the World Order of Bahá'u'lláh and the establishment of the Kingdom of God on earth.

Then will the Everlasting Covenant be fulfilled in its completeness. Then will the promise enshrined in all the Books of God be redeemed, and all the prophecies uttered by the Prophets of old come to pass, and the vision of seers and poets be realized. Then will the planet, galvanized through the universal belief of its dwellers in one God, and their allegiance to one common Revelation, mirror, within the limitations imposed upon it, the effulgent glories of the sovereignty of Bahá'u'lláh, shining in the plenitude of its splendor in the Abhá Paradise, and be made the footstool of His Throne on high, and acclaimed as the earthly heaven, capable of fulfilling that ineffable destiny fixed for it, from time immemorial, by the love and wisdom of its Creator.[12]

NOTES

Preface

1. Gregg Easterbrook, *Progress Paradox*, p. 146; Patrick Morley, *The Man in the Mirror*, pp. 19–43; Gregg Easterbrook, *Progress Paradox*, pp. 163–65; Juliet Schor, *Born to Buy*, pp. 173–75; Michael Gurian, *The Good Son*, pp. 43, 52–53.

2. 'Abdu'l-Bahá, *Paris Talks*, no. 44.17–26.

3. Shoghi Effendi, *The World Order of Bahá'u'lláh*, p. 202.

4. Bahá'u'lláh, cited in Shoghi Effendi, *The World Order of Bahá'u'lláh*, p. 169; The Universal House of Justice, *Messages from the Universal House of Justice, 1963–1986*, no. 55.5; Shoghi Effendi, *The Promised Day is Come*, p. 116.

Chapter 1: The End of the World as We Know It

1. Charles Van Doren, *A History of Knowledge*, p. 96.

2. Ibid., p. 94.

3. Ibid; Shoghi Effendi, *The World Order of Bahá'u'lláh*, pp. 156, 155; Shoghi Effendi, *Citadel of Faith*, p. 56.

4. Shoghi Effendi, *The World Order of Bahá'u'lláh*, p. 183; Shoghi Effendi, quoted in Ruḥíyyíh Rabbani, *The Priceless Pearl*, p. 355; Shoghi Effendi, *The Advent of Divine Justice*, ¶45.

5. John Medina, *Faith, Physics, and Psychology*, pp. 2, 3–5, 363–65, 456; Adam Liptak, "U.S. Prison Population Dwarfs That of Other Nations," www.nytimes.com/2008/04/23/world/americas/23iht-23prison.

6. Azadeh Moaveni, *Lipstick Jihad: A Memoir of Growing Up Iranian in America and American in Iran*, p. 81.

7. Shoghi Effendi, *Messages to Canada*, p. 67.

8. Shoghi Effendi, in *Fire and Gold*, p. 99; The Universal House of Justice, in *Fire and Gold*, pp. 124–25.

9. Shoghi Effendi, in *Fire and Gold*, p. 99.

10. Shoghi Effendi, *Citadel of Faith*, p. 32.

11. Bahá'u'lláh, *Gleanings from the Writings of Bahá'u'lláh*, no. 46.4; Bahá'u'lláh, Hidden Words, Persian, no. 12.

Chapter 2: Bahá'u'lláh, the Supreme Manifestation of God

1. Shoghi Effendi, *The Promised Day is Come*, p. 3.

2. Ibid., p. 4.

3. Ibid., p. 3.

4. Shoghi Effendi, quoted in *Political Noninvolvement*, pp. 7, 8.

5. Ibid., p. 8.

6. The Universal House of Justice and Bahá'u'lláh, quoted in ibid., p. 9.

7. Bahá'u'lláh, quoted in Shoghi Effendi, *The World Order of Bahá'u'lláh*, p. 107; Shoghi Effendi, *The Advent of Divine Justice*, ¶70, 72.

8. Shoghi Effendi, *The Advent of Divine Justice*, ¶71–72.

9. Baha'u'llah, quoted in ibid., p. 77; 'Abdu'l-Bahá, quoted in Shoghi Effendi, *God Passes By*, p. 99.

10. Bahá'u'lláh, *Summons of the Lord of Hosts*, no. 1.50.

11. Bahá'u'lláh, quoted in Shoghi Effendi, *God Passes By*, p. 99; Baha'u'llah quoted in Shoghi Effendi, Ibid; Shoghi Effendi, *Letters from the Guardian to Australia and New Zealanad*, p. 41; From a letter written on behalf of Shoghi Effendi to an individual believer, October 19, 1947, *Lights of Guidance*, no. 1552.

12. Adib Taherzadeh, *The Revelation of Bahá'u'lláh, vol. 4*, p. 134.

13. Bahá'u'lláh, *Epistle to the Son of the Wolf*, p. 47.

14. Bahá'u'lláh, quoted in Shoghi Effendi, *The World Order of Bahá'u'lláh*, p. 103.

15. Shoghi Effendi, letter dated July 23, 1936, to an individual, cited in Adib Taherzadeh, *The Covenant of Bahá'u'lláh*, p. 39.

16. Shoghi Effendi, *The World Order of Bahá'u'lláh*, p. 166.

Chapter 3: The Dawning of a New Spiritual Cycle

1. Bahá'u'lláh, quoted in Shoghi Effendi, *Citadel of Faith,* p. 95; Bahá'u'lláh, Kitáb-i-Íqán, ¶272; The Báb, quoted in Bahá'u'lláh, *Epistle to the Son of the Wolf,* p. 155; The Báb, *Selections from the Writings of the Báb,* no. 3:32:1; The Báb, quoted in Bahá'u'lláh, *Epistle to the Son of the Wolf,* p. 152.

2. The Báb, *Selections from the Writings of the Báb,* no. 3:15:3.

3. 'Abdu'l-Bahá, *The Promulgation of Universal Peace,* p. 95.

4. The Báb, *Selections from the Writings of the Báb,* no. 3:35:2; Bahá'u'lláh, "Tablet of Aḥmad," *Bahá'í Prayers,* p. 310.

5. Adib Taherzadeh, *The Covenant of Bahá'u'lláh,* p. 54.

6. Shoghi Effendi, *The Advent of Divine Justice,* ¶75.

7. Karen Armstrong, *Muḥammad: A Biography of the Prophet,* p. 10.

8. 'Abdu'l-Bahá, *Some Answered Questions,* pp. 18–21.

9. Shoghi Effendi, in *Lights of Guidance,* no. 1664.

10. Jared Diamond, *Guns, Germs, and Steel: The Fates of Human Societies,* p. 409.

11. John Medina, *Faith, Physics, and Psychology,* pp. 160–65.

12. 'Abdu'l-Bahá, *Some Answered Questions,* pp. 18–21.

13. Karen Armstrong, *Muḥammad: A Biography of the Prophet,* p. 165.

14. Ibid., p. 168.

15. Ibid.

16. 'Abdu'l-Bahá, *Some Answered Questions,* pp. 20–21.

17. Charles Smith as cited by John Medina, *Faith, Physics, and Psychology,* p. 165; Karen Armstrong, *Muḥammad: A Biography of the Prophet,* pp. 190–92; John Medina, *Faith, Physics, and Psychology,* pp. 162–65; 'Abdu'l-Bahá, *Some Answered Questions,* p. 21; F. Roy Willis, *World Civilizations,* p. 356.

18. Karen Armstrong, *Muḥammad: A Biography of the Prophet,* p. 191.

19. Ibid.

20. Ibid., p. 26; Charles Smith, "A Clash of Civilizations?" *Arizona Alumnus,* 82, no. 3, (Spring 2005), p. 5; Azadeh Moavani, *Lipstick Jihad,* p. 159.

21. Thomas Aquinas, quoted in Janet and Peter Khan, *Advancement of Women,* p. 32.

22. Karen Armstrong, *Muḥammad: A Biography of the Prophet,* p. 22.

23. Ibid., p. 40.

24. Ibid., p. 264.

25. 'Abdu'l-Bahá, *Some Answered Questions,* pp. 20–23.

26. From a letter written on behalf of Shoghi Effendi, February 27, 1938, in "Living the Life," *Compilations of Compilations,* vol. 2, p. 7; Bahá'u'lláh, Hidden Words, Persian, no. 5; Bahá'u'lláh, *Gleanings,* no. 125.3.

27. Shoghi Effendi, in *Lights of Guidance,* no. 697.

28. Ibid., nos. 699, 683, 705.

29. Shoghi Effendi, cited in William Hatcher and Douglas Martin, *The Bahá'í Faith,* p. 77.

30. The Báb, in Nabíl-i-A'ẓam, *The Dawn-Breakers,* p. 92.

31. Shoghi Effendi, *God Passes By,* p. 100.

32. Bahá'u'lláh, Kitáb-i-Íqán, ¶28.

33. Ibid.

34. The Báb, *Selections from the Writings of the Báb,* no. 3:24:3.

35. Ibid., no. 3:8:3.

36. Ibid., no. 3:8:3–4.

37. Bahá'u'lláh, *Gleanings from the Writings of Bahá'u'lláh,* no. 34.6.

38. 'Abdu'l-Bahá, *The Promulgation of Universal Peace,* pp. 322–23.

39. Bahá'u'lláh, *Tablets of Bahá'u'lláh,* p. 10.

Chapter 4: The Nation That
"Will Lead All Nations Spiritually"

1. 'Abdu'l-Bahá, quoted in Shoghi Effendi, *Citadel of Faith,* pp. 35, 31; 'Abdu'l-Bahá, quoted in Shoghi Effendi, *The Advent of Divine Justice,* ¶89; 'Abdu'l-Bahá, quoted in Shoghi Effendi, *Citadel of Faith,* pp. 35, 132.

2. Shoghi Effendi, *The Advent of Divine Justice,* ¶26; Shoghi Effendi, *Citadel of Faith,* pp. 31, 33, 66; 'Abdu'l-Bahá, quoted in Shoghi Effendi, *The Advent of Divine Justice,* ¶23, 89.

3. Shoghi Effendi, *The Advent of Divine Justice,* ¶32.

4. Ibid.

5. Shoghi Effendi, *Citadel of Faith,* p. 32.

6. Ibid., p. 126.

7. Shoghi Effendi, *World Order of Bahá'u'lláh,* p. 203.

8. Bahá'u'lláh, *Gleanings from the Writings of Bahá'u'lláh,* no. 119.5.

9. Shoghi Effendi, *The Promised Day is Come*, p. 123.

10. Ibid.

11. Shoghi Effendi, *The World Order of Bahá'u'lláh*, p. vi; Shoghi Effendi, *The Advent of Divine Justice*, ¶15.

12. Shoghi Effendi, *The Promised Day is Come*, p. 123.

13. Shoghi Effendi, *Citadel of Faith*, pp. 31, 32, 33.

14. 'Abdu'l-Bahá, cited in Shoghi Effendi, *The Advent of Divine Justice*, ¶119.

15. Shoghi Effendi, *Citadel of Faith*, p. 35.

16. Ibid., pp. 32, 36, 33.

17. Ibid., p. 32.

18. Shoghi Effendi, *The Advent of Divine Justice*, ¶118.

19. Shoghi Effendi, *The World Order of Bahá'u'lláh*, p. 145.

20. Shoghi Effendi, *The Advent of Divine Justice*, ¶117; Shoghi Effendi, *Citadel of Faith*, p. 38; Shoghi Effendi, *The World Order of Bahá'u'lláh*, pp. 144, 19.

21. Shoghi Effendi, *The Advent of Divine Justice*, ¶117.

22. Shoghi Effendi, *Citadel of Faith*, p. 66; William Hatcher and Douglas Martin, *The Bahá'í Faith*, p. 66.

23. Shoghi Effendi, *Citadel of Faith*, pp. 34, 31; Shoghi Effendi, *The Advent of Divine Justice*, ¶32; Shoghi Effendi, *The World Order of Bahá'u'lláh*, p. 53.

24. Shoghi Effendi, *Citadel of Faith*, pp. 32, 34, 35, 123.

25. Shoghi Effendi, cited in Barron Harper, *Lights of Fortitude*, p. 201.

26. 'Abdu'l-Bahá, quoted in Shoghi Effendi, *Citadel of Faith*, p. 16; Shoghi Effendi, *Citadel of Faith*, p. 16.

27. Shoghi Effendi, in *Lights of Guidance*, no. 1776.

28. Shoghi Effendi, quoted in Barron Harper, *Lights of Fortitude*, p. 98.

29. Shoghi Effendi, *The World Order of Bahá'u'lláh*, p. 19.

30. Shoghi Effendi, *Citadel of Faith*, p. 34.

31. Shoghi Effendi, *The Advent of Divine Justice*, ¶100.

32. Shoghi Effendi, *God Passes By*, pp. 308, 386.

33. Ibid., p. 386.

34. Queen Marie of Romania, cited in Shoghi Effendi, *God Passes By*, p. 390.

35. Shoghi Effendi, *God Passes By*, p. 388.

36. Ibid., p. 388.

37. Ella Bailey, cited in O. Z. Whitehead, *Portraits of Some Bahá'í Women*, p. 135.

38. A Bahá'í friend of Ella Bailey, cited in ibid., p. 137.

39. Committee for the Training and Teaching of Children, cited in ibid., p. 138.

40. Ella Bailey, quoted in ibid., p. 140; Shoghi Effendi, quoted in ibid, p. 142.

41. Shoghi Effendi, *Citadel of Faith*, p. 165.

42. Gwendolyn Etter-Lewis and Richard Thomas, *Lights of the Spirit*, p. 262.

43. Ibid., p. 255.

44. Ibid., p. 59.

45. Ibid., pp. 251–63.

46. Bahá'u'lláh, Kitáb-i-Aqdas, ¶1, 3.

47. The Universal House of Justice, Riḍván Message, 2010, ¶5.

48. Ibid., ¶26.

49. Shoghi Effendi, *God Passes By*, p. 212.

50. Ibid., pp. 212–13.

51. Shoghi Effendi, *The Promised Day is Come*, p. 123; Shoghi Effendi, *World Order of Bahá'u'lláh*, p. 19.

52. Shoghi Effendi, *The Advent of Divine Justice*, ¶118; Shoghi Effendi, *Citadel of Faith*, p. 32.

53. Shoghi Effendi, *Citadel of Faith*, pp. 32–33; Shoghi Effendi, *The World Order of Bahá'u'lláh*, p. 203.

54. Shoghi Effendi, *The Advent of Divine Justice*, ¶117.

55. Shoghi Effendi, *Citadel of Faith*, p. 36; Shoghi Effendi, *The Advent of Divine Justice*, ¶33.

56. Shoghi Effendi, *The Advent of Divine Justice*, ¶32; Shoghi Effendi, *Citadel of Faith*, p. 37.

Chapter 5: The Staggering Responsibility
of the American Bahá'ís

1. 'Abdu'l-Bahá, cited in Shoghi Effendi, *Citadel of Faith*, p. 29.

2. Shoghi Effendi, *The Advent of Divine Justice*, ¶34.

3. Ibid.

4. Shoghi Effendi, *The World Order of Bahá'u'lláh*, pp. 156, 155; Shoghi Effendi, *Citadel of Faith*, p. 56.

5. Shoghi Effendi, cited in Ruhíyyíh Rabbani, *The Priceless Pearl*, p. 355.

6. Shoghi Effendi, *Citadel of Faith*, p. 124.

7. Shoghi Effendi, *The World Order of Bahá'u'lláh*, p. 183.

8. Shoghi Effendi, *The Advent of Divine Justice*, ¶36.

9. Ibid., ¶37, 53.

10. Ibid, ¶59.

11. Ibid., ¶50; Shoghi Effendi, *Citadel of Faith*, p. 149.

12. *Century of Light*, p. 135.

13. Fritjof Capra, *The Turning Point*, p. 16.

14. Ron Miller, *New Directions in Education*, p. 2.

15. *Century of Light*, p. 136.

16. The Universal House of Justice, in *Fire and Gold*, p. 79.

17. Shoghi Effendi, *The World Order of Bahá'u'lláh*, p. 42.

18. Bahá'u'lláh, *Gleaning from the Writings of Bahá'u'lláh*, no. 27.2.

19. Ibid., no. 122.1.

20. 'Abdu'l-Bahá, *Paris Talks*, no. 44.14.

21. Shoghi Effendi, *The World Order of Bahá'u'lláh*, p. 33.

22. Shoghi Effendi, in *Compilation of Compilations*, vol. I, no. 3.3.

23. *Century of Light*, p. 90; 'Abdu'l-Bahá, Lawḥ-i-Aflakiyyih (Tablet of the Universe), anonymous provisional translation, http://bahai-library.com/provisionals/universe.html.

24. Michael Talbot, *The Holographic Universe*, p. 46.

25. 'Abdu'l-Bahá, *Selections from the Writings of 'Abdu'l-Bahá*, no. 150.1–2; 'Abdu'l-Bahá, *The Promulgation of Universal Peace*, p. 10.

26. David Bohm, quoted in Michael Talbot, *The Holographic Universe*, pp. 48, 61.

27. 'Abdu'l-Bahá, *The Promulgation of Universal Peace*, p. 48.

28. 'Abdu'l-Bahá, *The Secret of Divine Civilization*, p. 59.

29. Shoghi Effendi, *Citadel of Faith*, p. 125.

30. The Universal House of Justice, *Messages 1986–2001*, no. 183.27–28.

31. E. F. Schumacher, *Small is Beautiful*, p. 82.

32. Martin Luther King, Jr., *I Have a Dream: The Quotations of Martin Luther King, Jr.*, pp. 4–5.

33. John Medina, *Faith, Physics, and Psychology*, p. 237.

34. Thomas Paine, cited in Jack Weatherford, *Indian Givers*, p. 126.

35. Black Elk, cited in Joseph Epes Brown, *The Spiritual Legacy of the American Indian*, p. 18.

36. Chief Luther Standing Bear, cited in Kent Nerburn and Louise Mengelkoch, *Native American Wisdom*, pp. 43–44.

37. Francis Bacon, cited in Fritjof Capra, *The Turning Point*, p. 56.

38. Crane Brinton, et. al., *A History of Civilization*, p. 486.

39. Jerome Weeks, "About Doubt," *San Diego Union Tribune*, January 20, 2005, pp. E1, E4; Charles Van Doren, *A History of Knowledge*, p. 235; Thomas Jefferson, cited in Jerome Weeks, "About Doubt," *San Diego Union Tribune*, January 20, 2005, p. E1.

40. Jerome Weeks, "About Doubt," *San Diego Union Tribune*, January 20, 2005, p. E4.

41. John Adams, cited in Jerome Weeks, "About Doubt," *San Diego Union Tribune*, January 20, 2005, p. E1.

42. Richard Thomas, *Racial Unity: An Imperative For Social Progress*, p. 72.

43. Deganawidah, cited in Christopher Buck, "Native Messengers of God in Canada?," http://bahai-library.com/bsr/bsr06/66_buck_messengers.htm.

44. 'Abdu'l-Bahá, *Some Answered Questions*, p. 19; 'Abdu'l-Bahá, quoted in Shoghi Effendi, *Citadel of Faith*, p. 16.

45. Shoghi Effendi, in *Lights of Guidance*, no. 2029.

46. D'Arcy McNickle, *The Clash of Cultures*, pp. 315, 323.

47. French Jesuit missionary, cited in Gary Nash, *Red, White, and Black*, p. 20.

48. Christopher Columbus, cited in Bill Bigelow, "Discovering Columbus: Re-reading the Past," *Rethinking Columbus,* p. 7.

49. John Medina, *Faith, Physics, and Psychology,* p. 236.

50. Chief Joseph, cited in Kent Nerburn and Louise Mengelkoch, *Native American Wisdom,* p. 87.

51. International Monetary Fund, cited in Jeannine Aversa, "Global Recession Worst Since Depression, IMF Says," Associated Press, April, 2009; Jeannine Aversa, "Global Recession Worst Since Depression, IMF Says," Associated Press, April, 2009; Josette Sheeran, cited in David Stringer, "World Food Program Warns of 'Silent Tsunami' of Hunger," *San Diego Union Tribune,* 22 April, 2008; Angel Gurria, cited in Emma Vandore, "Report: Gap Grows Between Rich and Poor," *San Diego Union Tribune,* October 21, 2008.

52. The Universal House of Justice, from a letter dated October 20, 2008, addressed to the Bahá'ís of the world.

53. *Century of Light,* p. 89.

Chapter 6: Capitalism: A Barrier to America's Exalted Destiny

1. Shoghi Effendi, *Citadel of Faith,* p. 125.

2. *Century of Light,* p. 135–36.

3. Shoghi Effendi, *The Advent of Divine Justice,* ¶34; 'Abdu'l-Bahá, quoted in Shoghi Effendi, *Citadel of Faith,* p. 35.

4. Shoghi Effendi, from a letter dated 25 August 1939, as cited by Hooshmand Badí'i, *The True Foundation of All Economics,* p. 137

5. John Medina, *Faith, Physics, and Psychology,* pp. 274–75.

6. Kevin LaMastra, "Haiti: From Charity to Justice," *NEA Today,* May/June, 2010, p. 56.

7. Bahá'u'lláh, *Gleanings from the Writings of Bahá'u'lláh,* no. 118.5.

8. Carmen Gonzalez, "Beyond Eco-Imperialism: An Environmental Justice Critique of Free Trade," *Denver University Law Review,* vol. 78:4, 2001, pp. 1003–4; John Medina, *Faith, Physics, and Psychology,* p. 276; See http://www.globalissues.org; Bahá'u'lláh, *Gleanings from the Writings of Bahá'u'lláh,* no. 130.

NOTES

9. John Medina, *Faith, Physics, and Psychology,* p. 342.

10. Ibid., pp. 340–42.

11. John Medina, *Faith, Physics, and Psychology,* p. 342; The Universal House of Justice, *The Promise of World Peace,* pp. 10–11.

12. 'Abdu'l-Bahá, *The Secret of Divine Civilization,* p. 24.

13. John Medina, *Faith, Physics, and Psychology,* p. 275.

14. Bryan Bender, *The Boston Globe,* November 13, 2006.

15. John Stockwell, *The Praetorian Guard,* p. 61; James Loewen, *Lies My Teacher Told Me,* p. 118.

16. *Century of Light,* p. 88.

17. See John Stockwell, *The Praetorian Guard;* Walter LaFeber, *Inevitable Revolutions;* Noam Chomsky, *Year 501: The Conquest Continues;* Howard Zinn, *A People's History of the United States,* p. 174.

18. John Stockwell, *The Praetorian Guard,* p. 61.

19. Walter LaFeber, *Inevitable Revolutions,* pp. 8–9.

20. See http://www.washingtonpost.com/wp-srv/inatl/daily/march99, www.ppu.org.uk/genocide/g_guatemala1.html; Walter LaFeber, *Inevitable Revolutions,* pp. 8–9; Deborah Menkart, *Rethinking Columbus,* p. 60–61.

21. *Century of Light,* p. 3.

22. 'Abdu'l-Bahá, *Foundations of World Unity,* p. 43.

23. Howard Zinn, *A People's History of the United States,* p. 291.

24. John Medina, *Faith, Physics, and Psychology,* p. 283; See Noreena Hertz, *The Silent Takeover.*

25. 'Abdu'l-Bahá, *The Promulgation of Universal Peace,* p. 217; See John Medina, *Faith, Physics, and Psychology,* p. 294–95.

26. Shoghi Effendi, *The World Order of Bahá'u'lláh,* p. 204.

27. John Medina, *Faith, Physics, and Psychology,* pp. 276–78; See Joseph E. Stiglitz, *Globalization and Its Discontents;* Biplab DasGupta, *Structural Adjustment, Global Trade, and the New Political Economic Development.*

28. Michele Stoddard, "Michel Chossudovsky: The Globalization of Poverty: Impacts of IMF and World Bank Reforms," http://covertaction.org//content/view/79/75/; Dennis Brutus, "Africa 2000 in the New Global Context," http://www.namebase.org/ppost13.html.

29. See http://www.globalissues.org; Dennis Brutus, "Africa 2000 in the New Global Context," http://www.namebase.org/ppost13.html.

30. Sheraz Sadiq, "Timeline: Cochabamba Water Revolt," http://www.pbs.org/frontlineworld/stories/bolivia/timeline.html.

31. See http://www.pbs.org/frontline/stories/bolivia/didyouknow.html.

32. Oscar Olivera, cited by Sheraz Sadiq, http://www.pbs.org/frontlineworld/stories/bolivia/timeline.html.

33. Oscar Olivera, cited by Earthjustice.org, "Bechtel Surrenders in Bolivia Water Revolt Case," http://www.earthjustice.org/news/press/006/page.jsp?itemID=27533.

34. The National Labor Committee, "Where Ships and Workers Go to Die," *USW@Work* magazine, Fall 2009, Volume 4/4, p. 30–31.

35. Charles Kernaghan, Ibid.

36. Carmen Gonzalez, "Beyond Eco-Imperialism: An Environmental Justice Critique of Free Trade," *Denver University Law Review*, 2001, pp. 984–85.

37. Ibid., pp. 1,003–5.

38. Ibid., p. 986.

39. Ibid., p. 988.

40. Ibid., p. 989.

41. Ibid., p. 993.

42. Bahá'u'lláh, *Gleanings from the Writings of Bahá'u'lláh*, no. 104.2.

43. Bahá'u'lláh, *Tablets of Bahá'u'lláh*, p. 69.

44. Ron Sider as cited by Stan Guthrie in "The Evangelical Scandal," *Christianity Today*, April 13, 2005, http://www.christianitytoday.com/ct/2005/april/32.70.html.

45. See Ron Sider, *The Scandal of the Evangelical Conscience: Why Are Christians Living Just Like the Rest of the World?*

46. S. R. Shearer, http://www.antipasministries.com/html/file0000108.htm.

47. Matthew 6:19–21.

48. Matthew 19:21.

49. Luke 16:13.

50. 'Abdu'l-Bahá, quoted in Shoghi Effendi, *Citadel of Faith*, p. 16.

51. Akwesasne Notes, ed., *Basic Call to Consciousness*, pp. 77–78.

52. Shoghi Effendi, *The World Order of Bahá'u'lláh*, p. 42.

53. *Century of Light*, p. 135.

54. Theodore Roszak, cited in E. F. Schumacher, *Small is Beautiful: Economics as if People Mattered*, p. 9.

55. Bahá'u'lláh, *Gleanings from the Writings of Bahá'u'lláh*, no. 106.1.

56. 'Abdu'l-Bahá, *Paris Talks*, no. 26.5.

57. *Century of Light*, p. 136.

58. Shoghi Effendi, *The Advent of Divine Justice*, ¶34; 'Abdu'l-Bahá, quoted in Shoghi Effendi, *Citadel of Faith*, p. 35.

Chapter 7: A "Spiritually Blessed and Enviable Nation"

1. Shoghi Effendi, *The World Order of Bahá'u'lláh*, p. 203.

2. Shoghi Effendi, *The Advent of Divine Justice*, ¶34, 59.

3. Shoghi Effendi, in *Lights of Guidance*, no. 449.

4. Shoghi Effendi, *The World Order of Bahá'u'lláh*, p. 78.

5. Bahá'u'lláh, *Gleanings from the Writings of Bahá'u'lláh*, no. 153.8

6. 'Abdu'l-Bahá, quoted in Shoghi Effendi, *The Advent of Divine Justice*, ¶60; Shoghi Effendi, ibid.

7. 'Abdu'l-Bahá, quoted in ibid., ¶89.

8. Shoghi Effendi, *The World Order of Bahá'u'lláh*, p. 78.

9. Shoghi Effendi, *Citadel of Faith*, p. 131.

10. Shoghi Effendi, *The Advent of Divine Justice*, ¶117.

11. Shoghi Effendi, *Citadel of Faith*, pp. 37, 38.

12. Shoghi Effendi, *The Promised Day is Come*, p. 123.

BIBLIOGRAPHY

Works of Bahá'u'lláh

Epistle to the Son of the Wolf. New ed. Translated by Shoghi Effendi. 1st ps ed. Wilmette, IL: Bahá'í Publishing Trust, 1988.

Gleanings from the Writings of Bahá'u'lláh. Translated by Shoghi Effendi. Wilmette, IL: Bahá'í Publishing, 2005.

The Hidden Words. Translated by Shoghi Effendi. Wilmette, IL: Bahá'í Publishing, 2002.

The Kitáb-i-Aqdas: The Most Holy Book. 1st ps ed. Wilmette, IL: Bahá'í Publishing Trust, 1993.

The Kitáb-i-Íqán: The Book of Certitude. Translated by Shoghi Effendi. Wilmette, IL: Bahá'í Publishing, 2003.

The Summons of the Lord of Hosts: Tablets of Bahá'u'lláh. Wilmette, IL: Bahá'í Publishing, 2006.

Tablets of Bahá'u'lláh revealed after the Kitáb-i-Aqdas. Compiled by the Research Department of the Universal House of Justice. Translated by Habib Taherzadeh et al. Wilmette, IL: Bahá'í Publishing Trust, 1988.

Works of The Báb

Selections from the Writings of the Báb. Compiled by the Research Department of the Universal House of Justice. Translated by Habib Taherzadeh et al. Wilmette, IL: Bahá'í Publishing Trust, 2006.

Works of 'Abdu'l-Bahá

Foundations of World Unity. Wilmette, IL: Bahá'í Publishing Trust, 1972.

Lawḥ-i-Aflakiyyih (Tablet of the Universe), anonymous provisional translation, http://bahai-library.com/provisionals/universe.html.

Paris Talks: Addresses Given by 'Abdu'l-Bahá in 1911. Wilmette, IL: Bahá'í Publishing, 2006.

Promulgation of Universal Peace: Talks Delivered by 'Abdu'l-Bahá during His Visit to the United States and Canada in 1912. Compiled by Howard MacNutt. 2nd ed. Wilmette, IL: Bahá'í Publishing Trust, 2007.

Selections from the Writings of 'Abdu'l-Bahá. Compiled by the Research Department of the Universal House of Justice. Translated by a Committee at the Bahá'í World Center and Marzieh Gail. Wilmette, IL: Bahá'í Publishing, 2010.

Some Answered Questions. Compiled and translated by Laura Clifford Barney. 1st pocket-size ed. Wilmette, IL: Bahá'í Publishing Trust, 1984.

The Secret of Divine Civilization. Wilmette, IL: Bahá'í Publishing, 2007.

Works of Shoghi Effendi

Advent of Divine Justice. 1st pocket-size ed. Wilmette, IL: Bahá'í Publishing Trust, 1990.

Citadel of Faith: Messages to America, 1947–1957. Wilmette, IL: Bahá'í Publishing Trust, 1965.

God Passes By. New ed. Wilmette, IL: Bahá'í Publishing Trust, 1974.

Letters from the Guardian to Australia and New Zealand, 1923–1957. Sydney, Australia: National Spiritual Assembly of the Bahá'ís of Australia, 1970.

Messages to Canada. 2nd ed. Ontario, Canada: National Spiritual Assembly of the Bahá'ís of Canada, 1999.

The Promised Day Is Come. 1st pocket-size ed. Wilmette, IL: Bahá'í Publishing Trust, 1996.

The World Order of Bahá'u'lláh: Selected Letters. 1st pocket-size ed. Wilmette, IL: Bahá'í Publishing Trust, 1991.

Compilations of Bahá'í Writings

Badi'i, Hooshmand, compiler. *The True Foundation of All Economics: A Bahá'í Approach for the Promotion of Universal Development, Justice and Prosperity.* Rev. ed. Canada: Webcom, 1996.

Bahá'u'lláh, 'Abdu'l-Bahá, Shoghi Effendi, and Universal House of Justice. *The Compilation of Compilations: Prepared by the Universal House of Justice, 1963–1990.* 2 vols. Australia: Bahá'í Publications Australia, 1991.

Bahá'u'lláh, the Báb, and 'Abdu'l-Bahá. *Bahá'í Prayers: A Selection of Prayers Revealed by Bahá'u'lláh, the Báb, and 'Abdu'l-Bahá.* New ed. Wilmette, IL: Bahá'í Publishing Trust, 2002.

Helen Hornby, compiler. *Lights of Guidance.* New ed. New Delhi, India: Bahá'í Publishing Trust, 1994.

Khan, Peter, compiler. *Political Non-Involvement and Obedience to Government.* Ingleside: Bahá'í Publications Australia, 1979.

Kurzius, Brian. *Fire & Gold: Benefiting from Life's Tests.* Oxford: George Ronald, 1995.

Other Works

Akwesasne Notes, *A Basic Call to Consciousness.* Via Rooseveltown, NY: Mohawk Nation, 1978.

Armstrong, Karen. *Muhammad: A Biography of the Prophet.* New York: HarperOne, 1993.

Aversa, Jeannine. "Global recession worst since Depression, IMF says." *Associated Press,* April 22, 2009, http://news.yahoo.com/s/ap/20090422/ap_on_bi_ge/us_world_economy.

Babington, Charles. "Clinton: Support for Guatemala Was Wrong." *Washington Post,* March 11, 1999, A1.

Bender, Bryan. "US is top purveyor on weapons sales list: Shipments grow to unstable areas." The Boston Globe, November 13, 2006, http://www.boston.com/news/world/articles/2006/11/13/us_is_top_.

Bigelow, Bill, et al., eds., *Rethinking Columbus: Teaching about the 500ʰ Anniversary of Columbus's Arrival in America (A Special Issue of Rethinking Schools Magazine)*. Milwaukee, WI: Rethinking Schools, Ltd., 1991.

Brandt, Daniel. "Along Came the Transnationals." NameBase NewsLine, No. 14, July–September 1996, http://www.namebase.org/news14.html.

Brinton, Crane, John B. Christopher, Robert Lee Wolff, Robin W. Winks, eds. *A History of Civilization: 1715 to the Present*. Englewood Cliffs, NJ: Prentice-Hall, Inc., 1976.

Brown, Joseph E. *The Spiritual Legacy of the American Indian*. Wallingford, PN: Pendle Hill Publications, 1964.

Brutus, Dennis. "Africa 2000 in the New Global Context: A Commentary." *Africa Today*, 44,4 (1997), pages 379–84, http://www.namebase.org/ppost13.html.

Buck, Christopher. "Native Messengers of God in Canada?" http://bahai-library.com/bsr/bsr06/66_buck_messengers.htm

Capra, Fritjof. *The Turning Point: Science, Society, and the Rising Culture*. Toronto: Bantam Books, 1982.

Chatterjee, Pratap. "Bechtel's Water Wars." CorpWatch, May 1, 2003. http://www.corpwatch.org/article.php?id=6670&printsafe=1

Cherry, Conrad, editor. *God's New Israel: Religious Interpretations of American Destiny*. Englewood Cliffs: Prentice Hall, Inc., 1971.

Das Gupta, Biplab. *Structural Adjustment, Global Trade and the New Political Economic Development*. New York: St. Martin's Press, 1998.

Diamond, Jared. *Guns, Germs, and Steel: The Fates of Human Societies*. New York: W.W. Norton & Company, 1999.

Dreisbach, Daniel L. "The Bible and the Founding Fathers." Family Policy Lecture, Family Research Council, http://www.frc.org/events/the-bible-and-the-founding-fathers.

Earthjustice Press Release. "Bechtel Surrenders in Bolivia Water Revolt Case." January 19, 2006. http://www.earthjustice.org/news/press/006/page.jsp?itemID-27533...

Easterbrook, Gregg. *The Progress Paradox: How Life Gets Better While People Feel Worse*. New York: Random House, 2003.

Etter-Lewis, Gwendolyn and Richard Thomas. *Lights of the Spirit: Historical Portraits of Black Bahá'ís in North America, 1898–2000*. Wilmette, IL: Bahá'í Publishing, 2006.

Garis, M. R., *Martha Root: Lioness at the Threshold.* Wilmette, IL: Bahá'í Publishing Trust, 1983.

Gonzalez, Carmen G. "Beyond Eco-Imperialism: An Environmental Justice Critique of Free Trade." *Denver University Law Review, Vol. 78:4 2001,* http://ssrn.com/abstract=987941.

Gurian, Michael. *The Good Son: Shaping the Moral Development of our Boys and Young Men.* New York: Tarcher, 1999.

Guthrie, Stan. "The Evangelical Scandal." *Christianity Today,* May 19, 2010, http://www.christianitytoday.com/ct/article_print.html?id=34273.

Harper, Barron. *Lights of Fortitude: Glimpses into the Lives of the Hands of the Cause of God.* Oxford: George Ronald, 1997.

Hatcher, William S. and J. Douglas Martin. *The Bahá'í Faith: The Emerging Global Religion.* Wilmette, IL: Bahá'í Publishing, 2002.

Hertz, Noreena. *The Silent Takeover: Global Capitalism and the Death of Democracy.* New York: The Free Press, 2002.

The Holy Bible Containing the Old and New Testament: Authorized King James Version. World Bible Publishers, undated.

Hoskins, Lotte, compiler. *"I Have a Dream": The Quotations of Martin Luther King, Jr.* New York: Grosset & Dunlap, 1968.

Khan, Janet, and Peter Khan. *Advancement of Women: A Bahá'í Perspective.* Wilmette, IL: Bahá'í Publishing, 2002.

La Feber, Walter. *Inevitable Revolutions: The United States in Central America.* New York: W.W. Norton and Co., 1984.

LaMastra, Kevin. "Haiti: From Charity to Justice," *NEA Today,* May/June 2010.

Liptak, Adam. "U.S. prison population dwarfs that of other nations." *The New York Times,* April 23, 2008, http://www.nytimes.com/2008/04/23/world/americas/23iht-23prison.12253738.html?page.

Loewen, James W. *Lies My Teacher Told Me: Everything Your American History Textbook Got Wrong.* New York: The New Press, 1995.

Maxwell, Richard Howland. "Pilgrim and Puritan: A Delicate Distinction." Pilgrim Society Note, Series Two, March 2003, http://www.pilgrimhall.org/PSNoteNewPilgrimPuritan.htm.

May, Roy H. "Joshua and the Promised Land" excerpt, The Women's Division of the General Board of Global Ministries, United Methodist Church, Joshua Website, http://gbgm-umc.org/UMW/joshua/manifest.html.

McNickle, D'Arcy. "The Clash of Cultures," *The World of the American Indian.* Washington, D.C.: National Geographic Society: 1974.

Medina, John Fitzgerald. *Faith, Physics, and Psychology: Rethinking Society and the Human Spirit.* Wilmette, IL: Bahá'í Publishing, 2006.

Miller, Ron. *New Directions in Education.* Brandon, VT: Holistic Education Press, 1991.

Moaveni, Azadeh. *Lipstick Jihad: A Memoir of Growing Up Iranian in America and American in Iran.* Jackson, TN: Public Affairs, 2005.

Morley, Patrick. *The Man in the Mirror.* Grand Rapids, MI: Zondervan Publishing House, 1997.

Nábil-i-Aʻẓam [Muḥammad-i-Zarandí]. *The Dawn-Breakers: Nabíl's Narrative of the Early Days of the Bahá'í Revelation.* Translated and edited by Shoghi Effendi. Wilmette, IL: Bahá'í Publishing Trust, 1932.

Nash, Gary B. *Red, White, and Black: The Peoples of Early North America.* Englewood Cliffs, NJ: Prentice Hall, 1992.

National Labor Committee, "Ship Breaking in Bangladesh: Where Ships and Workers Go to Die." In *USW@Work* 4, no. 4 (Fall 2009): 30–31.

Nerburn, Kent and Louise Mengelkoch, compilers. *Native American Wisdom.* San Rafael, CA: New World Library, 1991.

Peace Pledge Union. "Talking About Genocide—Genocides: Guatemala 1982." London: Peace Pledge Union online: http://www.ppu.org.uk/genocide/g_guatemala1.html.

Public Broadcasting System. "Bolivia—Leasing the Rain." Frontline/World facts on "World Wide Water," NOW with Bill Moyers Web site, http://www.pbs.org/frontlineworld/stories/Bolivia/didyouknow.html.

Rabbani, Ruhiyyih. *The Priceless Pearl.* London: Bahá'í Publishing Trust, 1969.

Ruhi Foundation. *Teaching the Cause—Book 6.* Riviera Beach, FL: Palabra Publications, 1990.

Sadiq, Sheraz. "Timeline: Cochabamba Water Revolt." Public
Broadcasting System, Frontline/World, April 26, 2010,
http://www.pbs.org/frontlineworld/stories/bolivia/timeline.html.

Schor, Juliet B. *Born to Buy.* New York: Scribner, 2004.

Schumacher, E.F. *Small Is Beautiful: Economics As If People Mattered.*
New York: Harper and Row, 1973.

Shearer, S.R. "Apostasy,"
http://www.antipasministries.com/html/file0000040.htm.

Sider, Ronald J., *The Scandal of the Evangelical Conscience, Why Are
Christians Living Just Like the Rest of the World?* Grand Rapids, MI:
Baker Books, 2005.

Smith, Charles. "A Clash of Civilizations?" *Arizona Alumnus*, 82, no. 3,
(Spring 2005).

Stiglitz, Joseph E. *Globalization and its Discontents.* New York: W.W.
Norton and Co., 2002.

Stringer, David. "World Food Program warns of 'silent tsunami' of
hunger." *San Diego Union Tribune*, April 22, 2008,
http://wwwsignonsandiego.com/news/world/20080422-1345-
worldfoodcrisis.html.

Stockwell, John. *The Praetorian Guard: The U.S. Role in the New World
Order.* Cambridge, MA: South End Press, 1991.

Stoddard, Michele. "Chossudovsky, Michel: The Globalization of
Poverty: Impacts of IMF and World Bank Reforms." Book Review,
Covert Action, The Web Site of the Institute for Media Analysis,
Inc., April 26, 2010, http://covertaction.org//content/view/79/75/

Taherzadeh, Adib. *The Covenant of Bahá'u'lláh.* Oxford: George Ronald,
1992.

———. *The Revelation of Bahá'u'lláh, Volume 4: Mazra'ih & Bahjí
1877–92.* Oxford: George Ronald, 1987.

Talbot, Michael. *The Holographic Universe.* New York: Harper Perennial,
1991.

Thomas, Richard W. *Racial Unity: An Imperative for Social Progress.*
Ottawa: Bahá'í Studies Publications, 1993.

Universal House of Justice. *Century of Light.* Haifa: Bahá'í World
Centre, 2001.

———. Letter Dated October 20, 2008, addressed to the Bahá'ís of the World. Haifa, Israel: Bahá'í World Centre, 2008.

———. Letter dated Riḍván, 2010 to the Bahá'ís of the World. Haifa, Israel: Bahá'í World Centre, 2010.

———. *Messages from the Universal House of Justice, 1963–1986: The Third Epoch of the Formative Age.* Compiled by Geoffry Marks. Wilmette, IL: Bahá'í Publishing Trust, 1996.

———. *Messages of the Universal House of Justice, 1986–2001: The Fourth Epoch of the Formative Age.* Wilmette, IL: Bahá'í Publishing Trust, 2010.

———. *The Promise of World Peace: To the Peoples of the World.* Wilmette, IL: Bahá'í Publishing Trust, 1985.

Vandore, Emma. "Report: Gap grows between rich and poor." *San Diego Union Tribune,* October 21, 2008, http://www.signonsandiego.com/news/business/20081021-0118-eu-oecd-incomeinequality.html.

Van Doren, Charles. *A History of Knowledge: Past, Present, and Future.* New York: Ballantine Books, 1991.

Weatherford, Jack. *Indian Givers: How the Indians of the Americas Transformed the World.* New York: Fawcett Columbine, 1988.

Weeks, Jerome. "About Doubt: Many today see it as a sign of weakness, but key figures in history accepted skepticism as vital." *The San Diego Union Tribune,* January 20, 2005.

Whitehead, O. Z. *Portraits of Some Bahá'í Women.* Oxford: George Ronald, 1996.

Whitmore, Bruce W. *The Dawning Place: The Building of a Temple, the Forging of the North American Bahá'í Community.* Wilmette, IL: Bahá'í Publishing Trust, 1984.

Willis, Roy F. *World Civilizations, Volume I: From Ancient Times Through the Sixteenth Century.* 2nd ed. Lexington, MA: D.C. Heath and Co., 1986.

Zinn, Howard. *A People's History of the United States, Volume II: The Civil War to the Present.* New York: The New Press, 1997, abridged teaching edition.

INDEX

PUBLISHING
AND THE BAHÁ'Í FAITH

Bahá'í Publishing produces books based on the teachings of the Bahá'í Faith. Founded over 160 years ago, the Bahá'í Faith has spread to some 235 nations and territories and is now accepted by more than five million people. The word "Bahá'í" means "follower of Bahá'u'lláh." Bahá'u'lláh, the founder of the Bahá'í Faith, asserted that He is the Messenger of God for all of humanity in this day. The cornerstone of His teachings is the establishment of the spiritual unity of humankind, which will be achieved by personal transformation and the application of clearly identified spiritual principles. Bahá'ís also believe that there is but one religion and that all the Messengers of God—among them Abraham, Zoroaster, Moses, Krishna, Buddha, Jesus, and Muḥammad—have progressively revealed its nature. Together, the world's great religions are expressions of a single, unfolding divine plan. Human beings, not God's Messengers, are the source of religious divisions, prejudices, and hatreds.

The Bahá'í Faith is not a sect or denomination of another religion, nor is it a cult or a social movement. Rather, it is a globally recognized independent world religion founded on new books of scripture revealed by Bahá'u'lláh.

Bahá'í Publishing is an imprint of the National Spiritual Assembly of the Bahá'ís of the United States.

For more information about the Bahá'í Faith,
or to contact Bahá'ís near you,
visit http://www.bahai.us/
or call
1-800-22-unite

OTHER BOOKS AVAILABLE
FROM BAHÁ'Í PUBLISHING

FOUNDERS OF FAITH
THE PARALLEL LIVES OF GOD'S MESSENGERS
Harold Rosen
$17.00 U.S. / $19.00 CAN
Trade Paper
ISBN 978-1-931847-78-0

An exploration of the lives of Moses, Zoroaster, Krishna, Buddha, Jesus Christ, Muḥammad, and Bahá'u'lláh that examines their backgrounds, missions, teachings, and legacies, and finds the patterns that link these Founders of the world's religions.

Founders of Faith explores the lives of the Founders of the world's major religions—including Judaism, Zoroastrianism, Hinduism, Buddhism, Christianity, Islam, and the Bahá'í Faith—and reveals that they are linked by sets of striking patterns. These patterns suggest that our world's religions share universal teachings and have a common divine source. Author Harold Rosen explains how the Founders of the major religions function as the teachers of humanity; how their station differs from that of seers, visionaries, and minor prophets; and how their teachings transformed not only the civilizations that embraced them, but also humanity as a whole. *Founders of Faith* provides an examination of the rise and fall of religious civilizations, an illustrative overview of six such civilizations, as well as the background and apparent shape of the emerging global civilization.

FOUNTAIN OF WISDOM
A COLLECTION OF THE WRITINGS FROM BAHÁ'U'LLÁH
Bahá'u'lláh
$14.00 U.S. / $16.00 CAN
Trade Paper
ISBN 978-1-931847-80-3

A timeless collection of writings penned by the Prophet-Founder of the Bahá'í Faith with a universal message that all humanity is one race, destined to live in peace and harmony.

Fountain of Wisdom is a collection of the writings of Bahá'u'lláh, the Prophet-Founder of the Bahá'í Faith, in which He explains some of the "precepts and principles that lie at the very core of His Faith." Revealed during the final years of His ministry, the sixteen tablets contained in this volume cover a wide range of topics and place emphasis on principles such as the oneness and wholeness of the human race, collective security, justice, trustworthiness, and moderation in all things.

PROMISES FULFILLED
CHRISTIANITY, ISLAM, AND THE BAHÁ'Í FAITH
Nabil I. Hanna
$16.00 U.S. / $18.00 CAN
Trade Paper
978-1-931847-77-3

An examination of the promises made in both the Bible and the Qur'án concerning the coming of the Promised One.

Promises Fulfilled examines the promises made in both the Bible and the Qur'án concerning the coming of the Promised One, and sheds light on the principal objections that prevent Christians and Muslims from accepting the Bahá'í Faith. The book also discusses some of the verses in the Bible and Qur'án that are the cause of tension between Christians and Muslims. Such verses may appear to differ on the topics of Christ's crucifixion, His ascension, and the meaning of Sonship. As *Promises Fulfilled* demonstrates, however, no contradiction exists between the sacred texts. In addition, this book introduces explanations from the Bahá'í writings that can bridge misunderstandings that have arisen between Muslims and Christians, and demonstrates the shared values between the two religions. Some of the topics covered include the Word of God, the Day of Resurrection and Judgment, salvation, the meaning of life and death, miracles, parables, and the meaning of the phrase "the seal of the Prophets."

SPIRIT OF FAITH
The Oneness of God
Bahá'í Publishing
$12.00 U.S. / $14.00 CAN
Hardcover
ISBN 978-1-931847-76-6

The new Spirit of Faith *series presents a selection of uplifting prayers and writings that focus on the oneness and unity of God for spiritual seekers of all faiths.*

Spirit of Faith: The Oneness of God is a compilation of writings and prayers that offers hope for a better future—one filled with unity, understanding, and acceptance between all peoples and religions of the world. This collection of sacred scripture demonstrates that we are all part of a single, unfolding, divine creation. The *Spirit of Faith* series will explore important spiritual topics—such as the unity of humanity, the eternal covenant of God, the promise of world peace, and much more—by taking an in-depth look at how the writings of the Bahá'í Faiths view these issues. The series is designed to encourage readers of all faiths to think about spiritual issues, and to take time to pray and meditate on these important spiritual topics.

To view our complete catalog,
Please visit http://books.bahai.us